D1171324

THE
INNER LIFE
OF
WORSHIP

CHARLES M. MAGSAM, M.M.

GRAIL PUBLICATIONS
ST. MEINRAD, INDIANA

ACKNOWLEDGMENTS

Grateful acknowledgment is tendered to the following for their kind permission to quote copyrighted material: Bruce Publishing Co., Milwaukee; Benziger Brothers, Inc., New York; Hanover House, Doubleday & Co., Inc., New York; Ronald Press Co., New York; Bollingen Foundation, Pantheon Book, Inc., New York; Henry Regnery Co., Chicago; Sheed and Ward, Inc., New York; Newman Press, Westminster; P. J. Kenedy & Sons, , New York; Fides Publishers, Chicago; Doyle and Finegan, Collegeville; Columbia University Press, New York; Longmans, Green & Co., Inc., New York; Macmillan Co., New York; B. Herder Co., St. Louis; Desclee Co., Inc., New York; Sower Press, South Denis; Charles Scribner's Sons, New York; Harper & Brothers, New York; Catholic University of America Press, Washington; University of Notre Dame Press, Notre Dame; and to the periodicals: *Amen,* Chicago; *Today* Chicago; *America,* New York; *New York Times,* New York; *Renascence,* Milwaukee; *Maryknoll,* Maryknoll; *Spiritual Life,* Milwaukee; *Cross Currents,* New York; *Catholic Mind,* New York; *Catholic Digest,* St. Paul; *Woman's Home Companion,* Doubleday & Co., New York; *Lumen Vitae,* Brussels; *Orate Fratres* (now *Worship*), Collegeville; *Catholic Art Quarterly,* Newport; *Pilot,* Boston; *Liturgical Arts,* New York.

Imprimi Potest:
>JOHN W. COMBER, M.M.
>*Superior General*

Nihil Obstat:
>FREDERICK R. MCMANUS
>*Diocesan Censor Deputatus*

Imprimatur:
>✠ RICHARD J. CUSHING
>*Archbishop of Boston*

November 15, 1957

WORSHIP IS FAITH PRAYED

PREFACE

FATHER Magsam presents for our close study and edification the many beautiful facets of corporate and private prayer. It is a timely treatment of a subject vital in the life of every priest, religious and lay person and deserves a wide circulation.

While we mean primarily by worship the public homage offered God in the way officially ordained by Himself and His Church and, par excellence, the Holy Sacrifice of the Mass, it has also a wide application to all our acts directed toward Him. Included are our individual and personal exercises of piety and the popular devotions of the faithful.

Inspired by the great encyclical of Our Holy Father, "Mediator Dei," Father Magsam unfolds before us in the light of our present day attitudes the basic concepts of all worship. He shows the interdependence of official and private worship and how one strengthens and exalts the other. The reader will appreciate the well balanced and Catholic perspective given to the words, liturgical and non-liturgical. How narrow, for example, would be the religious life of one who would prefer his own private devotions to the exclusion of the grace giving liturgy of the Church. By the same token, as though there were some inner conflict or inconsistency between these two acts, how foolish would it be to look with disdain on the pious soul saying her rosary while assisting at Mass. The fundamental reason for all devotion, public or private, is the same, and the same spirit should permeate both.

Union with God through Our Lord and His Blessed Mother is the object of all worship. May we constantly deepen our understanding of the spirit and the acts associated with it. They are the noblest and most important of which man, with the help of Divine Grace, is capable.

CONTENTS

Preface v

Introduction ix

1 The Scope of Worship 1

2 The Use of Reason and Worship 25

3 Christian Being is the Basis for Worship 42

4 Worship is a Living Tradition 62

5 Worship is the Doing of What Christ Did 85

6 The Mass is the Heart of Worship 105

7 The Sacraments are the Channels of Life 128

8 Worship is Union with God 144

9 Worship is Union with Men in Christ 159

10 Worship Bears Fruit 170

11 Worship Develops Christian Personality 180

12 Worship and the Mission of the Church 202

13 Worship with Voice and Hands 221

14 Mary is the Queen of Worship 257

15 Sacramentals Prepare Us for Worship 274

16 The Father is the Leader of Family Worship 288

Index 301

INTRODUCTION

THESE pages concern, not a science nor speculation, but a practical art, i.e., the thinking of sublime thoughts, the doing of sublime actions, the making of sublime songs, gestures, things, for the glory of God and the redemption of men. Their purpose is not art for art's sake, but a practical thinking, a practical doing, and a practical making that issue in holy being.

Our thinking begins with the words and example of Our Lord, "The Father is greater than I." All reality, all worship centers in the fact that God is greater than we are, greater as an infinite Creator is above a tiny creature and greater as an all-holy God is above a sinner. The saints feel deeply this difference between the all that God is and the nothing that we are. The more we enter into sanctity, the more we are ready for worship.

Worship is faith prayed. Faith, prayer and worship embrace the entire human person and the full human destiny.

We are made to know God and man by faith and reason, to love God and man and to create in thoughts and words, in songs and music, in family duties and community needs, in actions and things. In this knowing, loving and creating, centered in the Mass, we find our joy. This is the inner life of worship that makes the Mass an act of corporate worship, a joyous celebration, an experience of belonging to a vital organism, the Mystical Body of Christ, engaged in fruitful and significant action.

Chapter One

The Scope of Worship

THERE is such a thing as being allergic to a word. Some words are antibodies, good in themselves but foreign substances to a person's mental and emotional make-up. And every time a person hears one of those antibody words he breaks out in an emotional rash.

Liturgy can be such a word. That is not to be surprised at, for the same happens to many things of importance. A word can take on what Maritain has called "a meretricious dynamism." Truth is often counterfeited just because it is so precious. An excellent means is often made into a monstrous end. A word can become an end, something that is presumed to have life and to give life of itself, a magic force that inspires or a hated goal to be smashed. Any virtue can go to excess; and the excess is a vice. When part of a truth is substituted for the whole truth, the part becomes a heresy. When a general truth is applied to a particular case it becomes as a razor's edge and a hair to either side is untruth.

The shades of difference between true and false, between means and end, between virtue and vice are not always easy to see, even at best. And, at worst, they become more difficult in proportion to the attachments and antipathies that cloud our thinking. There is the further complication of personalities who rub any normal person the wrong way. The greatest enemies of any movement are its own over-emotional extremists.

When any conviction, whether for or against, lacks a rational basis it is not virtuous at all. Yet a conviction that is ours, just because it is ours and defends our habits of thinking and living, can be erected into a golden calf that we ridiculously worship. Something relative then becomes a man-made absolute. It is possible to be very dogmatic about the fact that there should be no dogma, to be enthusiastic about the fact that we should never be enthusiastic about anything, to make an absolute of the fact that all things are relative and a certainty of the fact that we cannot be certain about anything. And the joke may not be evident.

In the same way, it is possible to proclaim very loudly and most externally that worship should be merely internal and very unobtrusive, without ritual or prayer-formula; and the joke may not be evident.But that amounts to saying that we should be a complete man when talking to men and only half a man when talking to God. It presupposes that man is very much interested in what he sees but imperfectly, i.e., his inner spiritual relationships, and that God is not at all concerned about what He sees perfectly, i.e., about maintaining His rights over the whole man and having the needs of His creatures fulfilled. But did not Christ cleanse the Temple before He preached the Sermon on the Mount? In other words, He came out for fitness in a place of worship before He proclaimed His ethics. He did not proclaim this sequence as a dogma but His example illustrates a point.

If liturgy is a word that evokes an emotional rash, then let the individual use another word. Words are only symbols; they should not be given a dynamism they do not deserve. It is the reality that matters. What St. Pius X called the primary and indispensable source of the true Christian spirit is too important for us to miss because somebody's mistakes and excesses have developed in us an emotional allergy.

"The Mass is the chief act of divine worship; it should also be the source and center of Christian piety. . . . The most pressing duty of Christians is to live the liturgical life, and increase and cherish its supernatural spirit."[1] A creatures' first duty is to worship God. A Christian's first duty is to worship in and through and with Christ to the glory of the Trinity. Worship is our all-pervading duty; it touches life at every point; it is just as essential to every part of life as it is to mystical and to eternal union with God.

Under another aspect, liturgical life can be taken as the source of Christian life or, time-wise, as a part of Christian life. It is a case of emphasis, an emphasis to satisfy a special need. In this picture-age in which everything is pictured and dramatized we have a way of life that can serve both divine and human purposes. Man's duty to worship God is dramatized in our official public worship. Doctrine and morals are integral parts of that grace-giving dramatization. The Church year is the life of Christ, His Mother, and His saints dynamically dramatized. God works through secondary causes and He may be using our legitimate love of picture and drama to prepare us for a return to a full liturgical life, i.e., a life centered in worship that flows out from the altar into every day and into every duty and joy and sorrow of the day.

[1] Pius XII, *Mediator Dei*, New York, America Press, 1948, par 201, 197.

For those with seminary training, liturgy might suggest a study of rubrics. That is a necessary part of the picture for those who have the responsibility for the carrying out of official worship; but rubrics are only instruments. Overemphasis on rubrics can either kill interest in the heart of worship or lead to a pharisaical externalism in ceremonies. Primary concern should always be with the doctrinal and inspirational aspects of worship. Where there is faith and reverence and love, then carefulness in rubrics will follow.

How much attention should be given to rubrics? As much as it is needed to perform them carefully and well or to train others to do so. They are a way of having part in divine worship, a way of giving one's whole being, body and soul, to the Father in and with and through the Son's worship. Given one's duty in the matter, our reverent participation in worship at the altar and around the altar becomes the will of God for us at the moment. For such precious moments time stops and nothing else in the world matters. Not only the service itself but practice for services, whether singing or ceremonies, calls for reverence and devoted carefulness. Since we may call upon mountains and seas, heat and cold, beasts and birds to bless the Lord,[1a] we can be sure that every human act, especially practicing for divine services, if done for love of God, is a far greater and more acceptable worship.

Happily, lay participation in worship is bringing people more and more into processions and singing and various ceremonies. Therefore, what Pius XII says about seminarians applies in its own measure also to lay people. "Readily provide the young clerical student with facilities to understand the sacred ceremonies, to appreciate their majesty and beauty and to learn the rubrics with care, just as you do when he is trained in as-

[1a] Daniel 3: 57-87.

cetics, in dogma and in canon law and pastoral theology. This should not be done merely for cultural reasons and to fit the student to perform religious rites in the future, correctly and with dignity, but especially to lead him into closest union with Christ, the Priest, so that he may become a holy minister of sanctity."[1b] Providing such explanations for the laity is declared obligatory for the new Holy Week services. "Local Ordinaries ... should take care that the faithful also during the holy season of Lent should be effectively taught properly to understand the restored Ordo of Holy Week so that they, mentally and spiritually, may take a devout part in the services."[1c]

Those who like history may wonder about the relation of Christian archeology to liturgy. The mountainous thirty-volume encyclopedia of Cabrol-LeClercq-Marrou gives great weight and great detail to such an approach.[2] In those hills lies the gold of tradition, the essential source of all our worship. The record of the past serves for the understanding and guidance of the present. It not only provides the historical roots of our worship but also shows, through the history of worship, that the Church goes back to apostolic times. It is clear from the record, finally, that all along our worship has been an instrument of the teaching authority of the Church.

Liturgy, therefore, may be considered as a continuous living development, growing organically out of the past, vitally active in the changing present and enduring gloriously into the future. In the Old Testament there is a wealth of ritual (Exodus) and prayer (Psalms, Esther, Judith, Prophets), all divinely inspired. In the New Testament live all the essential elements of modern worship. In the present there is the official wor-

[1b] *Mediator Dei,* par. 198.

[1c] Decree and Instruction of the S. Congreg. of Rites, Nov. 16. 1955.

[2] *Dictionnaire d'Archeologie Chretienne et de Liturgie,* Cabrol, Le Clerq, Marrou, Paris, Librairie Letouzey et Ane, 1950.

ship contained in the Liturgical Books and the unofficial worship that we call popular devotions. For the future there is the communication of divine life which is the beginning of heaven and the flowering of heaven's worship, the everlasting rapture.

For the legally-minded, the logical approach to worship would be through the various official Liturgical Books. These books are, of course, the essential text and guide for everyone. For surety on this point the Sacred Congregation of Rites on May 17, 1911 provided an official list.

In the first place there is the Roman Missal; and to this must now be added the new Week Ordinal. Secondly, there is the Roman Berviary. Not officially listed but very close to both of there is the *Liber Usualis* which contains officially sanctioned music for both Missal and Berviary. A third source is the Roman Ritual to which must now be added the various vernacular Rituals that are officially approved for individual portions of Christendom. Not to be neglected are the *Memoriale Rituum*, a ceremonial for smaller churches, and the Martyrology which catalogues the martyrs and saints according to their place in official worship.

Sixthly, the Roman Pontifical contains the functions reserved to bishops. This is very important in view of Christ's wise arrangement of channeling His teaching, sanctifying and governing powers to us through His hierarchy. Somewhat similar to the Pontifical is the Ceremonial of Bishops which gives general directions, ceremonial and otherwise, for special episcopal functions and activities. Some of these affairs are official worship; others are not, e.g., the formal visit of a bishop to the civil ruler of a province. The Ceremonial also contains some matters for persons who are not bishops. The eighth source of official worship is the Clementine Instruction for Forty-Hours Devotion.

And the final constantly expanding source is in the several volumes of the Decrees of the Sacred Congregation of Rites. Actually, most of the Third Book of the Code of Canon Law pertains to worship. Perhaps some day, when the presently developing reform of worship is completed, we may hope for a masterly codification of all laws, decrees and scholarly authors who provide orderly guides in masters of worship.

The various Liturgical Books organize the distilled worship-life of centuries. The prayers and forms of ritual are sufficiently generalized to serve the needs of many peoples of many nations. That gives our official worship both the strength and weakness that is found also in a good law. A law has to be general to cover many possible cases but its very generality makes it less accurately applicable to each particular case. Yet a good law embodies wisdom. And so does traditional worship. Is anything needed more than the wise ways of the ages put into our restless hands?

The very nature of man suggests that he needs to pray in words and ways that express his deepest needs, aspirations and affections of the moment. Even though such words and ways are not always the best, the Church as a true mother knows that they can serve a very personal need. Hence there is both tolerance and encouragement for many forms of devotion that are not in the official books of worship. It is essential that prayer be sincere, from the heart. That sincerity will usually take the ways that show how a person normally lives. Such ways of living and praying may be open to considerable improvement, as anything human usually is, but the improvement cannot run so far ahead of a general doctrinal and ethical formation that it turns worship into a foreign mannerism. When by other means of instruction and by frequenting the sacraments, a person's Christian formation has been brought to a certain point, then the right form and formula of worship will itself add to and speed up his formation. This is presupposed by Pius X and Pius XII in their penetrating statements about the formative value of worship.

Even when the present liturgical restoration is completed and our official worship becomes once more "A new city in which the man of our age can live and feel at ease,"[3] will there still be a place for popular devotions? Probably, for both the intellectual and the affective parts of man's nature, reflecting a diversified culture, will require it, since universal principles of worship naturally flow into particular devotions. The mind is as much inclined to apply the valid universal to the fluid particular as to conclude from the particular to the universal. Feelings not only are stimulated by the particular but are dynamic drives from within that carry a powerful impact upon the outward particular.

Even though it was true that in the early Church official worship was also the whole popular devotion of the people, there are several limitations upon establishing a parity with modern times. For one thing, even the official worship was in a very fluid state. It varied from patriarchate to patriarchate and to some extent even from bishopric to bishopric, not to speak of minor changes from priest to celebrating priest, church to church, home to home, service to service. There was, of course, a major core of uniformity. It was a case of "freedom within a given schema. . . . A close parallel can be drawn between the variegated history of oriental liturgies and that of the West; here, too, until well into the Middle Ages, there

[3] Bugnini, *The Simplification of the Rubrics,* Collegeville, Minn., Doyle and Finegan, 1955, p. 22.

were various liturgies and therefore also various forms of the Mass."[4]

Secondly, ancient worship allowed private silent prayer before the orations. And the orations themselves were improvised for the first four centuries. Besides, there was a simplicity about it, especially in the domestic services, that allowed for active participation. There were litanies; there were responsories intermingling with psalms and the frequent versicle and responsory prayers, especially the great amen and alleluia. Finally there were the charisms: prophecy, teaching, ecstatic speech, inspired affective prayer.

Thirdly, whatever the extent of the local variations, they still moved within the comparatively narrow limits of the Mediterranean world. Within that world, Hebrew, Greek and Latin peoples shaped and seasoned worship to their various needs, often mingling elements of all three cultures in one service. Other peoples of the Near East also had their own ways of worship. What of the people and cultures beyond the Mediterranean?

Man is a complex composite but people everywhere have the same driving forces. Feelings trigger energy for action and thought. Feelings have to be respected, given their proper outlet and directed to streamlined action in the service of God's glory and man's spiritual destiny. Feelings respond to and express local and contemporary ways of thinking and doing, just as much as they respond to and express the lights of reason and universal doctrine and practice.

In worship also, within its unifying reverence and dignity and spiritual nourishment, the affective life of man needs expression and satisfaction. The worship contained in official texts and rites serves this purpose to a great extent but not

[4] Jungmann, *The Mass of the Roman Rite,* New York, Benziger, 1951, vol. I, pp. 49, 44.

completely, because, being universal and used by people of
all nations, it is more restrained and less spontaneous. Man
needs to express himself as he is and feels, not at his worst but
at the best he can manage at the moment. Sincerity is the breath
of prayer-life, even though the life might not be entirely healthy.
Popular devotions, because less impersonal, more easily reflect
a person's true dispositions, aspirations and needs. He does not
have to go to them. He goes because he chooses to do so, out
of a felt need.

A part of popular devotions are the hymns. Pius XII has
told us that this religious music, though not primarily a part
of official liturgy, ". . . can exercise great and salutary force
and power on the souls of the faithful . . . these popular religious hymns are of great help to the Catholic apostolate and
should be carefully cultivated and promoted."[5]

This is not to say, of course, that all popular devotions and
hymns are of equal merit, equally satisfactory. It is only to
suggest that we make the most of the best of them. God can
accomplish great good through them in spite of their imperfections, just as He hides sanctity under real imperfections.
Gentle St. Francis de Sales said, "There are some saints I would
not care to live with."

It may be stressed at this point that the value of a devotion
depends, presupposing doctrinal correctness and the acceptance
of Church regulations, on the strength of our attraction for it.
Hence, given prudence, sound doctrine and a consistent effort
to live by what we believe, we can grow spiritually through
popular devotions. The Church is always the mother. Knowing and sanctioning the importance of the strength of attraction, she has often allowed it to determine the ranking of feasts

[5] Pius XII, *On Sacred Music*, Washington, D.C., N.C.W.C., par.
36-37.

of the saints and to some extent even the feasts of Our Lord and Our Lady.

This principle of attraction applies with equal force to popular devotions. Partly because they are in the vernacular and partly because they allow for active participation, they do often have a greater attraction than would Vespers in Latin, or a similar service. This is not to advocate a policy but only to state a fact. Happily, the restoration of official worship is dominantly in the direction of participation and the vernacular.

This point of attraction is probably one of the reasons for the specific mention of "popular customs" in the official instruction on the new Holy Week liturgy. This matter is of special importance to missionaries. The instruction says, "Since there are in various places and among various peoples, many popular customs connected with the observance of Holy Week, local Ordinaries and priests having the care of souls should seek prudently to harmonize customs of this kind which appear to contribute to solid piety with the restored Ordo of Holy Week."[6]

Perhaps another reason for this tolerance of "popular customs" is religious conservatism, which is tougher and slower to change than any kind of conservatism.[7] Associated with all-holy and unchanging divinity, religious customs and devotions seem to take on something of the permanence of divinity, at least as far as a particular generation is concerned. In any case, they become deeply embedded in the feelings of people and draw them to worship. Besides, they are in part an expression of man's deep religious instinct. As such they merit respect;

---

[6] S. Congreg. of Rites, Nov. 16, 1955, par. 23.

[7] Even when Our Lord insisted on the radical differences between the Old and New Testaments and the need for a new approach, He added the sympathetic illustration, "No man after drinking old wine immediately desires new; for he says, 'The old is better.' " Lk. 5:39.

and any proposed changes or replacements must be prepared for most carefully.

One good reason for respecting popular devotions is that some of them follow the traditional ground plan of our official worship, i.e., instruction-song-prayer.[8] A novena service or Lenten sermon, followed by Benediction of the Blessed Sacrament, embody the traditional schema in a general way.

It is also to the merit of popular devotions that many items now in official books of worship began as popular devotions. It has been computed that some twenty-nine prayers, antiphons or versicles now used in the Ordinary of the Mass originated in this way. Instance the prayers at the foot of the altar, the last blessing, the last Gospel. "Popular" here is used to embrace the private devotions of priests.

A profound reason why popular devotions merit respect is the importance of the consensus of the faithful in the tradition of the Church. Their spontaneous and primitive reasoning power is elevated by Baptism and Confirmation and illuminated by faith and the gifts of the Holy Spirit. In union with the teaching Church, the people help to form the whole Christ speaking. It is in part through the faithful that the Holy Spirit reveals the fullness of Christ. The consensus of the faithful, or the Christian sense, refers to the mind and not to religious sentimentality. It embraces both the intellectual content and its outward expression, principles put into action intuitively, almost instinctively.

Cardinal John Henry Newman tells how Father Perrone, speaking to him personally, stressed the "sensus" and "consensus fidelium," as a "compensation for whatever deficiency there might be of patristical testimony in behalf of various points of the Catholic dogma. . . ." Then Newman continues,

[8] Cf. Jungman, *Liturgical Worship*, New York, Pustet, 1941, p. 67.

"I will set down the various ways in which theologians put before us the bearing of the Consent of the faithful upon the manifestation of the tradition of the Church. Its 'consensus' is to be regarded: 1) as a testimony of the apostolic dogma; 2) as a sort of instinct deep in the bosom of the mystical body of Christ; 3) as a direction of the Holy Ghost; 4) as an answer to its prayer; 5) as a jealousy of error, which it at once feels as a scandal. . . .

"I shall set down some authorities for the two points successively, which I have to enforce, viz., that the Nicene dogma was maintained during the greater part of the fourth century: 1) not by the unswerving firmness of the Holy See, Councils, or Bishops, but 2) by the 'Consensus fidelium'. . . .

"Each constituent portion of the Church has its proper functions, and no portion can be safely neglected. Though the laity be but the reflection or echo of the clergy in matters of faith, yet there is something in the *pastorum et fidelium conspiratio,* which is not in the pastors alone. The history of the definition of the Immaculate Conception shows us this; and it will be one among the blessings which the Holy Mother, who is the subject of it, will gain for us, in repayment of the definition, that by that very definition we are all reminded of the part which the laity have had in the preliminaries of its promulgation. Pope Pius IX has given us a pattern, in his manner of defining, of the duty of considering the sentiments of the laity upon a point of tradition, in spite of whatever fullness of evidence the Bishops have already thrown upon it. In most cases when a definition is contemplated, the laity will have a testimony to give; but if ever there be an instance when they ought to be consulted, it is in the case of doctrines which bear directly upon devotional sentiment. Such is the Immaculate Conception. The faithful people have ever a special function in regard to those doctrinal truths which relate to the Objects of worship."[9]

The last word in this matter is, of course, the word of authority; and Pius XII has spoken: "There are certain exercises of piety which the Church recommends very much to clergy and religious. It is Our wish also that the faithful, as well, should take part in these practices. The chief of these are: meditation on spiritual things, diligent examination of conscience, enclosed retreats, visits to the blessed sacrament, and those special prayers in honor of the Blessed Virgin Mary among which the rosary, as all know has pride of place. . . .

"From these multiple forms of piety, the inspiration and action of the Holy Spirit cannot be absent. Their purpose, in various ways, is to attract and direct our souls to God, purifying them from their sins, encouraging them to practice virtue and, finally, stimulating them to advance along the path of sincere piety by accustoming them to meditate on the eternal truths and disposing them better to contemplate the mysteries of the human and divine natures of Christ. Moreover, by nourishing the spiritual life of the faithful, they prepare them to take part in sacred public functions with greater fruit, and they lessen the danger of liturgical prayers becoming an empty ritualism."[10]

Relating public to private prayer, Pius XII says also: "It is true that public prayers, prayers, that is, that are offered by Mother Church, because of the dignity of the Spouse of Christ, excel any other kind of prayer; but no prayer, even the most private, lacks its own dignity and power, and all prayer is immensely helpful to the Mystical Body. In that Body thanks to the Communion of Saints no good can be done, no virtue

[9] *Cross Currents,* Summer 1952, pp. 75, 81, 83.
[10] Pius XII, *Mediator Dei,* par. 173-175.

practised by individual members without its contributing something also to the salvation of all."[11]

Against every tendency to limit liturgy to rubrics, to archeology, to Gregorian Chant, to special books or to external things, it must be said that liturgy centers most of all in persons. Such a personal worship is not only divinely ordained but it also satisfies our primal instinct to consecrate to God the most precious of things, i.e., human life.

"The sacred liturgy is the public worship which our Redeemer as Head of the Church renders to the Father, as well as the worship which the community of the faithful renders to its Founder, and through Him to the heavenly Father. It is, in short, the worship rendered by the Mystical Body of Christ in the entirety of its Head and members."[12]

To include both the divineward and humanward directions, liturgy can also be defined as the corporate worship of the Mystical Christ in which He both glorifies the Trinity and brings divine life to His members.

Liturgy's formal cause includes three elements: a) worship, which is the due homage paid to God by intelligent free persons; b) corporate worship, for it is the Mystical Body of Christ in the action of prayer; c) the Church at worship, for it is the homage of all the validly baptized. This presupposes, of course, that although ". . . all the members of the Mystical Body partake of the same blessings and pursue the same objective, they do not all enjoy the same powers, nor are they all qualified to perform the same acts."[13]

Liturgy's final cause is to pay God the homage of adoration, reparation, thanksgiving and petition, and in this way to satisfy

[11] Pius XII, *Mystici Corporis*, Washington, D.C., N.C.W.C., par. 87.
[12] Pius XII, *Mediator Dei*, par. 20.
[13] *Ibid.*, par. 39.

man's obligation to worship. It aims also to produce in man
the double effect of taking away his sins and sanctifying him
for his eternal destiny.

The efficient cause of worship is more complicated. We
must say, to begin with, that Christ as God is the principal
efficient cause. His divinity gave infinite value to His atoning
death. And, as God, He also attached the giving of grace to
the matter and form of the sacraments; that is something only
God could do. What He did in His Passion and Death He continues to do daily on the altar in an unbloody manner. Having
"an everlasting priesthood... therefore he is able at all times to
save those who come to God through Him, since he lives always to make intercession for them."[14]

As man, Christ is the efficient cause meritoriously, secondarily,
instrumentally. "Christ produces the inward sacramental effect,
both as God and as man, but not in the same way. For, as
God, He works in the sacraments by authority; but, as man,
His operation conduces to the inward sacramental effects meritoriously and efficiently, but instrumentally.... Christ's Passion
which belongs to Him in respect of His human nature, is the
cause of justification, both meritoriously and efficiently, not as
the principal cause thereof, or by His own authority, but as
an instrument, insofar as His humanity is the instrument of
His Godhead."[15]

After Our Lord Himself, the most important efficient cause
of worship is the Church in its work of regulating the renewal of
Christ's Calvary Sacrifice and the ministrations of the Sacraments
He instituted. It has, moreover, the authority to institute sacramentals and to regulate everything that pertains to persons,
places, times and instruments of worship.

The sacrament of holy orders gives to priests that exclusive

[14] Hebr. 7:24-25.
[15] *Summa Theologica*, III, q. 64, a. 3.

consecrating and absolving power which makes them first the representative of Christ the Head and then of His members at worship. This makes them secondary instrumental efficient causes of worship, not by delegation of the people but by divine endowment.

The members of Christ, also, in their own way are truly secondary instrumental efficient causes of worship, for "By the waters of Baptism, as by common right, Christians are made members of the Mystical Body of Christ the Priest, and by the 'character' which is imprinted on their souls, they are appointed to give worship to God; thus they participate, according to their condition, in the priesthood of Christ."[16] They not only offer Christ in sacrifice through the hands of the celebrant but they offer themselves as co-victims with Christ; and they provide the material means for the continuation of all worship.

Among the secondary instrumental efficient causes of worship, are, of course, the sacraments themselves.

Even the material cause of worship centers in persons. Christ Himself was the one sacrificial Victim. Celebrant and people also offer themselves as co-victims with Christ. Then as instruments in the hands of persons at worship, there are the matter of the sacraments, liturgical music, the various liturgical gestures such as the imposition of hands in holy orders, the several liturgical official books, the vestments and all the other instruments of worship.

Hence, through all the complications of many varied rites and through all the pages of thousands of books about worship the central point always is that worship is a person-to-person relationship.

However much attention a person may give to external appearances, to the things that mark him as an individual in the eyes of other people, he knows and is quick to insist that others

---

[16] Pius XII, *Mediator Dei*, par. 88.

recognize that what makes him human is something inside,
something interior. The human driving forces are within a
person. Before God and man it is the mind and the will that
matter, and mind and will in their essential acts. Man is an
embodied spirit, yet a spirit that is made to govern, use and
bring the body to glorification. He is self-subsistent and self-
possessed, yet always in a relation of dependence and duty to
God. Our relation to God all-holy is what makes us sacred,
for we are privileged to be redeemed in the depths of our soul
by the influx of the indwelling Trinity; our prayers have tremendous power because they are presented to the Father by
the Son from within the Trinity; and we are destined for the
inner light of glory that will make God our heaven, for we
shall be at peace in being with Him whom we love.

On this earth, too, our worship of God begins with the inner man. As St. Thomas says, by devotion in the will man
offers himself to the service of God who is his last end,[17] and
by praying he surrenders his mind to God.[18] That is the heart
of all worship and everything else flows from these inner movements. "The internal acts of religion take precedence of the
others and belong to religion essentially."[19] Worship is the
social exercise, the corporate expression of an inner disposition,
i.e., of a virtue, a readiness to acknowledge the supreme rights
of God, to proclaim His surpassing majesty, to propitiate Him
for human infidelities, to thank Him for endless gifts and to
petition every need from Him as the absolute creator of all things.

There is no need to stress the obvious life-principles of worship. They begin with natural life which is the source of the
activity of all the faculties. And what makes for the intrinsic
worth of prayer, its assurance of acceptance in the Trinity, is

[17] *Sum. Theol.*, II-II, q. 82, a. 1, ad 1.
[18] *Ibid.*, q. 83, a. 3, ad 1.
[19] *Ibid.*, q. 81, a. 7.

the supernatural life, the divine life shared as a source of activity, the Christ-life that keeps us united in being and effectiveness and action with Christ our Head. "Sacraments and sacrifice do possess that 'objective' power to make us really and personally sharers in the divine life of Jesus Christ."[20]

The immediate implements of natural and supernatural life are the inner faculties of mind and will. Into mind and will are engrafted the theological and moral virtues and the gifts of the Holy Spirit. From the blended impulse of natural faculty, of infused and acquired virtue and of actual grace come the mental and volitional acts that make worship sincere and distinctively human. This is the antidote to formalism and hypocrisy. In worship we must mean what we say and do, conscious of the all-holy God we speak to and of our own destiny to mystic and eternal union with Him. "God cannot be honored worthily unless the mind and heart turn to Him in quest of the perfect life."[21]

For the sake of emphasis may we restate that the meritorious and exemplary cause of worship is divinely interior? "We must always live in Christ and give ourselves to Him completely, so that in Him, with Him and through Him the heavenly Father may be duly glorified."[22] The Christ of Calvary, the Christ at the right hand of the Father is one and the same sole Mediator who dwells within and operates within each person to sanctify and lift each one into the power and majesty of heaven and earth at worship. The more we meditate the interior sources of official prayer, the more tragically petty become the exterior things that may sometimes distract us from full wholehearted participation. Worship is the time for total surrender to the word, the action or the song of each moment. There time stops.

[20] Pius XII, *Mediator Dei*, par. 29.
[21] *Ibid.*, par. 25.
[22] *Ibid.*, par. 24.

By repeated deliberate acts of such total surrender the inner being is transformed into the habit of surrender that is perfection.

Finally, the effects of worship, insofar as they pertain to man, operate in the depths of his being. "The worship rendered to God by the Church in union with her divine Head is the most efficacious means of achieving sanctity."[23] But Pius XII adds, "This superior worth does not at all imply contrast or incompatibility between these two kinds of prayer. For both merge harmoniously in the single spirit which animates them, 'Christ is all and in all' (Col. 3:11). Both tend to the same objective: until Christ be formed in us."[24]

A natural transition to the external element in worship is the essential sacrifice of Christ. Jesus supplied in historical fact what man's very nature requires for honoring the Most High God. Man needs a sacrifice as a most fitting sign of his inner dependence, submission and total giving of himself to God. The sacrifice that Jesus supplied has several special points about it. For one thing, His death is the living model of His great commandment, which is to love God with one's whole heart and strength and one's neighbor as one's self. That, for every Christian, remains henceforth the fullness of spiritual maturity. For God's glory and man's good, therefore, worship is to flow outward to the edges of man's being and action. A second point: not only is this sacrifice a giving of Christ's own body and blood but He made it also man's sacrifice. Not only does man give his whole person in his offering and his victimhood but he also provides the material forms of bread and wine to clothe Calvary's unbloody renewal. Finally, Christ empowered human persons to offer the sacrifice in His name.[25]

[23] *Ibid.*, par. 26.
[24] *Ibid.*, par. 37.
[25] "Christ, coming to take up the work of creation and make all

Again, Jesus constituted His sacrifice on the cross as a covenant, everlasting and irrevocable. Essentially a free gift of God, He yet made its effectiveness require man's acceptance and fulfillment by obedience and fidelity. Man enters this covenant by Baptism; and the Eucharistic Sacrifice is the time he consciously avows his commitment by the "Amen, Amen, Amen" that echoes and re-echoes from altar to altar, from continent to continent through century after century unto the end of days.

Finally, "The sacrifice of the New Covenant is essentially constituted as a meal, so that the offerers might gather around the sacrificial table, the table of the Lord, to eat. They are in communion with Christ who had undergone His sufferings and is now exalted; they become anew one body with Him."[26]

As far as man is concerned, worship is not self-begotten. It is always a returning to God of His own natural and supernatural gifts. And like all giving, this return gift is made to stand for man himself. Love and friendship instinctively express themselves by offering gifts. The general purpose of such gifts is to establish, strengthen or re-establish a bond between two persons, whether the occasion be the need of the beloved, the desire of the lover to be loved, sheer admiration and gratitude or, after an offense or quarrel, the need to express silently one's regret and desire to make up. Giving is not complete until the offering is accepted. It will not be accepted unless it is sincere. It is not sincere unless it conveys, represents our whole self. Worship is not completely representative of our whole self unless it expresses itself also externally through

things new among men, gave them not only the power of entering into union with Him, but also the power of acting in Him, of becoming (in total dependence on Himself) true causes themselves, offering the world to God with Him and likewise with Him giving God to the world." (Journet, *The Church of the Word Incarnate*, London, Sheed and Ward, 1955, vol. I, p. 58)

[26] Jungmann, *The Mass of the Roman Rite*, vol. I, p. 191.

formulas and ceremonies. As gift-giving is the language of love, so acclamations and songs, demonstrations and processions are the language of admiration and praise. The Latins are accustomed to shout "Viva il Christo Re!" during a Corpus Christi procession. And everyone shouts "Viva il Papa!" in St. Peter's Basilica.

Moreover, man is the lord of creation. As its king he must exteriorly represent this exterior world and use exterior instruments of worship. As for his own body, it has to its shame cooperated in sin; therefore it ought to cooperate also in the worship of reparation for sin. But to the body's glory it is also the tabernacle of the Blessed Three; therefore it should act as becomes its Divine Guests; and its most worthy action is worship. Besides, for man's vagrant senses, rites and prayer-formulas are an aid to concentration and recollection.

Taking man as a social being, there is the force of custom. Worship has always been expressed through external means. And civil and social life are full of external symbols, e.g., the flag, handshake, etc. Of greater importance is the fact that nations are natural social units. Therefore some national homage should be paid to divinity. Happily, history bears out the acceptance of this obligation. Not only the perfect society of the state but also imperfect societies within the state should express their own social debt to God. This they do, for example, through occupational Masses, e.g., Labor Day, the lawyers' 'Red Mass,' the doctors' 'White Mass,' etc.

Pius XII gives us the all-important word of authority about the quality of official prayer. "The worship rendered by the Church to God must be, in its entirety, interior as well as exterior. It is exterior because the nature of man as a composite of body and soul requires it to be so; likewise, because divine Providence has disposed that 'while we recognize God visibly, we may be drawn by Him to love of things invisible' (Roman

Missal, Preface for Christmas). Every impulse of the human heart, besides, expresses itself naturally through the senses; and the worship of God, being the concern not merely of individuals but of the whole community of mankind, must therefore be social as well. This obviously cannot be unless religious activity is also organized and manifested outwardly. Exterior worship, finally, reveals and emphasizes the unity of the Mystical Body, feeds new fuel into its holy zeal, fortifies its energy, intensifies its action day by day."[27]

Pius XI stresses the teaching value of worship. "Man is composed of body and soul, and he needs these external festivities so that the sacred rites, in all their beauty and variety, may stimulate him to drink more deeply of the fountain of God's teaching, that he make it a part of himself, and use it with profit for his spiritual life."[28]

Going back to the ultimate authority, we know that God's express commands in chapters 25 to 31 of the Book of Exodus were not just a catering to primitive naïvete but the basic pattern for all mankind's worship. Our Lord instituted Eucharistic worship when "having taken bread, he gave thanks and broke, and gave it to them, saying, 'This is my body, which is given for you; do this in remembrance of me.' "[29] Jesus also instituted the sacraments and made material instruments the channels of His divine life. Moreover, He used various rites informally in working miracles: touch, words, moistened clay, etc. He used the synagogue. He redeemed us by His passion and death when an act of the will might have sufficed, if the Father had so willed it.

In conclusion, then, we may say that just as there can be

[27] Pius XII, *Mediator Dei,* par. 23.
[28] Pius XI, *Quas Primas, Social Wellsprings,* Millwaukee, Bruce, 1942, p. 39.
[29] Lk. 22:19.

no cleavage in man's being and operation so there can be no separation in the highest expression of his destiny, which is to worship His Creator in union with Christ and His members. Man's body and soul do not merely coexist in man; they mutually interpenetrate. So must the interior and exterior worship of man mutually interpenetrate. The exterior not only stimulates and sustains the interior devotion but also provides a manner of expression that is connatural to man's being and very satisfying to his needs. "My heart is glad and my soul rejoices, my body, too, abides in confidence."[30]

[30] Ps. 15:9.

Chapter Two

The Use of Reason and Worship

THERE is an absolute deadliness about questions that never get asked because everybody knows the answer—for when they do get asked, no one has an answer ready. We can only get red in the face."[1]

It is the business of philosophy to ask a lot of questions and to know things through their ultimate causes. It is the business of Christians to be apostles who are ready to answer questions about a lot of things that they themselves have always known and always taken for granted. They move among people who often understand little of Christianity, of their manner of worshipping God and of why they worship Him as they do. The time for the red face is in school days or in private preparation or in study groups and theology courses, and not when confronted by persons who need our ready convictions and our moving persuasions.

The difficulty is precisely in the "now," the more or less

[1] Sheed, *Society and Sanity,* New York, Sheed and Ward, 1953, p. 13.

protected circle, the more or less Christian environment in which we have grown up. We are both content and eager to find our security in what we have always known and accepted. It is part of us, deeply embedded in our feelings; we like it and we are reluctant to question it. One of the greatest mistakes of the human mind is to think things are as we want them to be. We concentrate and narrow our vision on the things we want. Objections, questions and obstacles only make us impatient. We do not enjoy looking at them. We look at them less and less. And we end up by not seeing them at all. We just pretend they do not exist. Only our wish, our desire is real to us. It is one of those escapes from reality.

Then there is the plain hard work of thinking. It is much easier to imagine or to feel. We would rather not think if we can help it. Aware of our personal sloth, we have compassion on everyone else. Just the labor of untangling thought from feeling and imagination is quite a thing in itself, and to keep thought disentangled until conclusions are calmly reached is a bigger thing still. We would rather not bother. We would rather keep busy with external activity at best, or at worst simply submit to an endless succession of stimulating pictures and sensations in our picture-happy and sensation-happy environment.

We are not forgetting, of course, that in practical judgments about serious matters the united conclusions of the majority of people are, in the long run, generally sound. But such important conclusions are usually reached only after much human bungling and human suffering. Real thinking is essential to that leadership which seeks to anticipate and avoid the bungling and suffering. In discussion itself the only alternative to thinking is to exchange our pictures and our feelings, that is to say, our private prejudices. But an exchange of prejudices is no more a discussion than an exchange of gunfire.

All of this is a way of saying how difficult it is to disengage

ourselves from our environment long enough for objective thinking. Yet we must do that if we are to face the obstacles to
corporate worship, even while we keep, of course, our sym-
pathy and practical understanding of human needs. Otherwise
we shall tend to walk around those hindrances and pretend
they are not there. If you try to change things without understanding them, you are likely to destroy them altogether and
harm yourself at the same time.

To some extent it is a matter of opinion and of emphasis to
talk about which are the greatest obstacles to corporate worship. But there is considerable agreement that two things have
an important bearing on the problem. One is the lack of a
sense of mystery and the other the lack of a sense of community.
These, in turn, probably come from being unaware of our dependence upon God and unaware of the meaning of sin. This
lack of a sense of sin has been authoritatively called the greatest
moral catastrophe of the age.[2]

A sense of mystery is something that is normally very deep
in man. For centuries, during the late Patristic and early Middle Ages, it even became exaggerated as a reaction against the
Arian heresy. How we have grown up without it goes back
a long way. You could start with the Renaissance and see there
the overemphasis on the human. You could take in the Protestant Revolt against Church authority, although this was coun-
teracted somewhat by the Catholic reaction to the Protestant
denial of the Real Presence. You could talk about the revolt
against the divinity of Christ and the enthronement of reason
in the age of enlightenment. And there was Darwin's attempt
to remove man's glory as a distinct creation of God by making him simply the last stage of an evolution out of mud and
monkeys. Then there was Freud's revolution to dethrone rea-

[2] "Pastoral of the American Bishops, 1947" in *Our Bishops Speak,*
Milwaukee, Bruce, 1952, p. 139.

son and make a man a victim of physical instincts. Bring the trail across our own homeland, you could include Chief Justice Holmes who took the absolute out of public law and John Dewey who took the absolute out of public education. Finally, it is a possible aspect of ultra-scientism.

In any case, the end product has been an overemphasis on material things and on the pragmatic test of usefulness, the shifting willingness always to try another experiment, and another, and another. Certain specific consequences of this materialistic and pragmatic approach are questionable, to say the least.

For one thing, there have been so many conquests of nature that nothing seems beyond the test tube and the atom smasher. Therefore, so it goes, why bother about today's mystery for it may become the field of tomorrow's discovery. And if there is nothing beyond the measurable that is worth symbolizing, why allow for feelings or intuitions or symbols?

It is tragedy, however, when on the one hand torture and drugs and surgery are used not only to destroy human bodies but even to destroy personalities. And on the other hand it is also tragedy when hedonists claim that human bodies are useful only for pleasure.

Even material things themselves suffer from a common lack of reverence. All too often, things are used merely for profit, for exploitation, for revolution. We degrade matter and treat it irreverently. And we in our turn are degraded by matter. Where we enhance material things it is often at the expense of the human. Not yet a thing of the past is the situation described by Pius XI, "Dead matter leaves the factory ennobled and transformed, where men are corrupted and degraded."[3]

But life is never simple and there are many angles to such viewpoints. There are already signs of what Dr. R. Allers calls

[3] *Social Wellsprings,* Milwaukee, Bruce, 1942, Vol. II, p. 227.

the fourth revolution: the reassertion of the dominance of spirit over matter, of the truly human over science and technology, of hope in things unseen over despair in an age of anxiety. Europe is looking to America for leadership in psychology and psychiatry. And in America many of the big men in the field now consider themselves neo-Adlerians rather than neo-Freudians; and they talk more and more about a soul. Many top scientists not only assert their belief in God but say that science is on the verge of proving beyond doubt by its own methods that God exists.

Fortunately, too, laymen's awareness of their own vocation to sanctity is bringing them to see that God's express command to subdue the earth means that they are to be sanctified by taking the works of scientism, which is material development for the sake of progress and profit, and turn those works of scientism into works of art. "Fill the earth and subdue it. Have dominion over the fish of the sea, the birds of the air, the cattle and all the animals that crawl on the earth."[4] Men are to reveal the order and the use of things, the true, the good and the beautiful in things, for the sake of God's glory and man's corporal and spiritual perfection.

It is not the will of God to let hundreds be killed by floods when we should be planting trees for watersheds and building dams. It is not the will of God to let contaminated milk spread typhoid when we should be using pasteurization and refrigeration to prevent it. It is not God's will to let polio strike down innocent children when a vaccine will stop the tragedy. God's will is rather that men subdue the forces of violence and destruction in nature.

By subjecting nature to himself, laymen subject themselves to God. The discipline of labor and research is their asceticism. It seems to be God's will that lay people are purified largely

[4] Gen. 1:28.

through material suffering while those dedicated to the celibate apostolate are purified more by spiritual suffering. Lay people give things to God without giving them up. The more they understand the true inner nature of things and the more they understand man's personal and social psychology, the more will they find God's will for things revealed in the things themselves.

Man is not merely the recipient of Providence but also its agent. What we make happen, as co-creators with God, can be just as much the will of God as what happens outside our doing. Holiness includes fashioning ourselves to be fit instruments of God in forming persons and things according to God's purposes. That is where prudence comes in. "Prudence is love discerning aright that which helps from that which hinders us in tending to God."[5] That means both a will that aims at perfect love of God and a mind that is aware of the things that can help or hinder us in reaching it. It means the choice of the right means to the right end. But man cannot direct things to God unless he is in some way in control of them.

In education, too, there is some indication of awareness of mystery in life. In 1954 Columbia University Press published a book by Gilbert Highet, "Man's Unconquerable Mind," in which the author admits the limits of the mind. He says, "The whole history of human thought is as various, as marvelous, as unexpected, and as inexplicable as other mysteries of this universe. Science, with its search for laws, always oversimplifies. But the wise scientist always makes his way through the realm of law into the region of wonder. In a few years he can master the principle of plant and animal life, reproduction and distribution—and then, forever thereafter, he remains astounded by the incalculable multiplicity of animal forms, the unthinkable subtlety of plants, knowing that when new varieties are dis-

[5] St. Augustine.

covered they may contain something as unpredictable as a new divine creation. The complexities of human language, the intricate life of micro-organisms, the invisible radiations that fill the universe, the power of mutation in living forms—all these can be faintly or crudely grasped, but never fully understood. One of the truest sayings of the medieval thinkers was *omnia exeunt in mysterium,* all things pass into mystery. We are not intended only to diagnose and calculate, but also to wonder, to admire, to expect the unexpected."

In any case, whatever our imbalance of the moment, we did not become what we are in a day and we will not change in a day. Philosophy prepares a person to ask himself how much of this tasteless and odorless atmosphere of materialism he may have absorbed. Anyone should be slow to say that he has remained entirely immune—it may be mere wishful thinking. He should rather ask himself the unasked questions and be red-faced in a mirror. What will philosophy teach him that will heighten his awareness of mystery?

Metaphysics tells of the great transcendentals that prepare a person to know the transcendental God. Cosmology teaches the make-up and meaning of the world of things and leads a person to marvel and wonder at the world's order and grandeur. Theodicy deals both with the proofs of God's existence and with many natural lights on the nature of God. Ethics explains man's natural moral way to God. In Psychology there is the study of how man is made up both in mind and body and how his feelings have an intimate part in all he does. These approaches are basic to the full formative impact and penetration of worship into man's character.

In a particular way, Logic sharpens a person's discernment by a study of fallacies. Logic also teaches the meaning and use of analogy. Analogy is basic to the understanding and the right use of symbols and to knowing the limitations even of the queen of sciences which is theology. In general, analogy is the comparing of two things that are partly similar and partly dissimilar. More specifically, there is analogy of attribution and analogy of proportion. The analogy of proportion is the process of comparing two things which have a resemblance in the same property but in a different degree, e.g., love in man is like love in God. The analogy of attribution is the process of assigning to a thing a property that it does not have by nature, e.g., a flag stands for a country by assignment and long association. The two things compared or associated are called analogues.

The analogy of attribution is metaphor and allegory. It was the basis of the allegorical symbolism which abounded in the Middle Ages, e.g., the association of each part of the present Mass with a separate step in the Passion of Our Lord. It is commonly used by everybody, e.g., a flag stands for a country, even though the flag tells you nothing about the nature of a country. Such analogues are specifically emblems and not symbols, although it is fairly common to include them under symbols in general.

The analogy of proportion is largely simile, although it may also be expressed in metaphor, and is the basis of a true symbol. Water, properly, by a certain proportion, symbolizes the internal spiritual cleansing. Light symoblizes the nature of God. As it is the very nature of light to shine, so it is the very nature of God to exist.

All our speaking about God is by analogy, either by the analogy of attribution or by the analogy of proportion. "Effects that fall short of their causes do not agree with them in name and nature. . . . The form of an effect is certainly found in some measure in a transcending cause, but according to another mode and another way. . . . That which is found in God perfectly is found in other things according to a certain diminished participation. . . . The names said of God are predicated neither univocally nor equivocally but analogically."[6] Thus we can say that God is good and man is good, but in different proportions. There is love in God and love in man, but in a different manner.

Our Lord spoke of His love and friendship. He symbolized Himself by light, by a vine, a shepherd, a way. "I am the light of the world."[7] "I am the door of the sheep . . . I am the good shepherd."[8] "I am the true vine."[9] "I am the way."[10] The Holy Spirit came under the symbol of a dove, of invisible wind, of visible tongues like fire.

We are therefore following Scriptural example in representing God by light, the Father by a hand, the Holy Spirit by a dove, the Trinity by a triangle and intertwining circles. We have simply accepted the mystery of God and the transcendence of His being above all manner of knowing or expressing Him. There are no finite images or words for expressing the infinite. There are no adequate words to tell the mystery of what Christ meant when He identified Himself with His Church: "I am Jesus, whom thou art persecuting."[11] He had ascended alive into heaven and was yet alive and active on this earth. We call it the doctrine of the Mystical Body of Christ.

In man himself there is much that is beyond our knowing. The subtle and mysterious union of body and soul, the subtle differences between men and women, the interplay of hidden natural forces, the depths of the subconscious and unconscious, the range of intuitive knowing, the delicate reflex coordinations of creative work, the shadowy but tyrannical fears that give way

[6] St. Thomas Aquinas, *Summa Contra Gentiles,* New York, Hanover House, 1955, Bk. I, ch. 29, 34, pp. 138, 139, 147.
[7] Jn. 8:12.
[8] Jn. 10:7, 11.
[9] Jn. 15:1.
[10] Jn. 14:6.
[11] Acts 9:5.

to obedient love and joy, and the unconscious influence we have on each other, all these obscurities make a world of indefinables in man that cry out for symbols which at least suggest what is unknown and unknowable.

Even nature has its own world of mystery. Science can discover many things and its horizons keep expanding. Medicine has a lot to say about a body's capacity or lack of capacity for sustaining life; but no surgeon's scalpel has ever laid bare a sense of humor. We have definitions for things that describe effects but leave the inner nature of those things in mystery. Steinmetz and Edison were the first to say that they knew nothing about the nature of electricity, even though they were wizards in manipulating its effects.

So even in the natural order, reason seeking truth cannot crash the barrier of mystery. Though reason can know God's existence and power, it is essential to admit the breadth of mystery in God and man and nature. It is not a cult of obscurantism, not obscurity for the love of obscurity, but the simplest realism to accept the fact that mystery is the heart of life. Unless we see and accept it, the wonder and beauty of life will pass us by and we shall find ourselves growing old in heart, disillusioned and dry, cynical and selfish.

Happily, we are not left to our natural confusions. We are made to seek truth, yes, but ultimately the truth that we seek is a person, the Person of Christ. In Him are combined all the mysteries of the divine and human. Reason leads us to the feet of Christ and to a whole bundle of wonderful facts about Him. But it takes faith to open our eyes. And faith seeks more than truth; it seeks life. Faith seeking life, seeks Christ and leads to desire and to love for Him, to peace in surrender to and possession of Him. While reason crashes into the barrier of mystery and is stopped dead at the barrier, faith finds Christ at that barrier and through Christ enters into life. Jesus is Himself the fullness of all divine and human mystery; and at the same time He shares with us, in and through Himself, the mysteries of the infinite and eternal world. Faith comes to rest in reverence for life; and love is totally absorbed in Christ who is everything. There is nowhere else to go. "Lord, to whom shall we go? Thou hast the words of eternal life, and we have come to believe and to know that Thou art the Christ, the Son of God."[12]

God takes priority over everything and everybody. He is the one absolute and eternal Being from whom everything comes and to whom everything returns. He is the great Unknown who seeks to be known. He cannot be ignored. All seek Him in one way or another. He is the great Unchangeable upon whom all changeable and contingent things depend. No being can be divorced from his sustaining power. He is Love, all-Love. And all lovers find their image and their destiny in Him. He is Holy, the all-Holy. And all are made to adore Him and to be like Him, holy.

However vague man's knowledge of God, however mixed man's motive for seeking God, the search goes on, feverishly or calmly, but unceasingly. There are a thousand avenues of approach but no neat pigeonholes for a transcendent God. A thousand rivers of blessing flow from Him, the Infinite God; but there is no way of packaging His gifts in syllables. He completes our bafflement by giving us His very Self, Incarnate, in the form of bread and Indwelling. We can only stutter with Jeremias, "A, a, a. O Lord, I know not what to say."[13]

But speak we must, however haltingly. We are ennobled with intelligence and the power of expression. And the deeper one's desire for God, the stronger is the impulse to expression,

12 Jn. 6:69.
13 Jer. 1:6.

excepting, of course, the silent desires in mystical and contemplative union. Aware of the seen but only dimly aware of the unseen, we take the visible and find that through the visible, God comes to us and we go to God. The visible, therefore, is not merely a possible but a necessary avenue of worship. We need these external instruments of ritual and symbol because we are persons with human bodies, with complex feelings and five senses. We need them also because we are social beings made to live and act together for our full development. The internal and external, the personal and social not only work together, they are inseparable. Without the internal, our external worship becomes idolatry and magic. Without the personal, the social becomes a herd security, an empty ritual. Thus Christian symbols and ritual blend Plato's distinction between the spiritual and the material with Aristotle's regard for the material for its own sake.

It is most of all in our relations with God that we are fully active, complex personalities, responsible to fellow human beings and aided by them. In our approach to God, we echo God's approach to us. God's supreme revelation of Himself blended in the God-man both the world of the spirit and the world of matter. The God-man showed us how to be at ease in both worlds. Jesus Himself used ritual and symbol in several recorded cures. He instituted the Eucharist as part of a ritual meal and then commanded His apostles and their successors to continue the rite. "Do this in remembrance of me."[14] In the Mass we do as He commanded. The Mass is our supreme and reponse to God, and it blends the same two worlds of spirit and matter. Through the God-man, uniting ourselves with Him in offering and in victimhood, we unite the many in the great One.

Jesus, uniting the divine and the human in His Person, has restored unity to the world. Come as the one Mediator of the

14 Lk. 22:19.

world, He blends all His divine and human mysteries in His one priesthood. Through His sacrificial death, He catches up all of us, and everything else with us, into a vital and active unity of life and love and worship. All life is redeemed. Therefore we are not meaningless atoms whirling in space; we are brothers and sisters through Christ our Elder Brother in our Father's family. "All is yours and you are Christ's, and Christ is God's."[15] So it becomes the mystery of our destiny and being to enter with Christ into His sacrificial death and final resurrection. Our vocation is to worship with and in Christ.

That brings us back to the need of symbols. Through faith we see mysteries. Through symbols we express them. And through symbols we also recognize our limits, the limits of all wise theology. For theology must know where to stop, when to kneel and adore upon the straw of all its learning. Thus symbols prepare us for contemplation, for the darkness, the dispossession, the loneliness that empties our souls for the inflooding of divine light and love. The understanding and acceptance of symbols prepare us for that surrender to sacramental worship by which God channels His life to us. Symbols also prepare us, by leading from the known to the unknown, for those changes and adjustments in worship which are needed from time to time.

The way to passive contemplation may be long for many and when attained it comes intermittently for most. It depends partly on God's plan for each individual and partly on the individual's fidelity to God's plan and grace. And the individual's response depends in part on correct theology and in part on correct psychology.

Symbols, whether material, graphic or ritual, embody man's natural theology of worship according to his natural need to evoke, to express and to stabilize his thoughts and feelings.

[15] I Cor. 3:23.

Partly alike and partly unlike, symbols typify the known and the unknown of God that is always the stuff of our approach to God. For we know Him as the great Unknown. And what we know, we know more by the intuitions of faith and the Gifts of the Holy Spirit than by brilliance of reasoning. What we normally feel is more the instinct of reverence for majesty than the elation of conquest and familiarity. St. Thomas Aquinas was not forced to discontinue his great *Summa Theologica*. He deliberately stopped writing three months before his death when God showed him in a mystical experience that all he had written was so much straw. Many a theologian comes to a time when he would rather stop writing and talking and spend the rest of his life in prayer. All the other sciences achieve their perfection in some tangible accomplishment. Theology achieves its perfection in silence, the silence of contemplation.

With this sense of God being the All and we the nothing, we prepare for the experience of intimate union with Him. Because of their inexhaustible meaning, symbols suggest both the unknowable of God and the concrete experience of Him. They both stimulate adoration and evoke affection, for the external redounds to the internal. Being sufficiently general for both obvious and mystical meanings, symbols may serve to express the most varied and manifold thoughts and feelings of anyone at any stage of spiritual development. Hence, also, the value of a true symbol over an emblem; for the more of real proportion and the less of attribution or mere association, the more directly evocative and expressive will the symbols be. There is no denying, however, the strong emotional response that long habit may occasion merely by attribution or association, as in the case of a country's flag. But the very stimulating power of an emblem only emphasizes more strongly the still greater expressiveness and stimulation of a true symbol. How potently and naturally does bread express all food, water express cleansing, light express truth, words express wisdom, and majesty lead to God-head.

Symbols also have a value as an antidote to angelism, that unrealistic ignoring of the body and its needs which tends to ensnare the intellectuals and the perfectionists in their worship and in their personal spiritual growth. All worship aims both at the glory of God and at the union of love with God. But we come to God just as we are, with our instinct of reverence made to respond to majestic divinity, but entangled in our complex associations and feelings and limited according to our capacity for reasoning and intuition. Our personal being is a closely knit unit. Whatever stimulates the eye, the ear, the taste, the touch, the smell, can suggest the spiritual and can awaken, nourish and deepen our instinct for reverent worship. The external redounds to the internal and intensifies the internal. Symbols, therefore, promote what they express.

A correct psychology of man at worship makes yet another plea for ritual and set prayers. No one can bear for long an intense, conscious attention. There is need for relaxing the attention but without losing it and without slipping into the passive routine of ritualism. Repetition of ritual and prayer, as in a Rosary or a Litany or in the many genuflections and crosses at Mass, both allows for a certain rhythm of intensity in our attention and yet sufficiently involves the senses to keep us actively participating. Moreover, given true attention, neither strained nor indifferent, the faithful repetition can even deepen a person's understanding and love of what the ritual and prayers mean. While we consciously enter into and consciously participate, there is at the same time a sustaining sense of comfort and security in moving within a familiar pattern of worship. Here we are at home with God. Habit carries us along when feeling is wanting. Common action re-enforces our wavering fervor.

All of this presupposes an equal sincerity in living by what we believe and pray, as well as a persistent looking beyond the forms of worship to God. It also points again to the need of vital symbols and away from farfetched allegory. It is not pleasure-seeking in symbols and ritual that matters but sincere prayer and action.

Thus while the senses supply what faith needs, faith in turn will lead where the senses cannot go. Even the mystic, and especially the mystic, must speak in symbols to tell of darkness and nothing, of the cloud of forgetting and the cloud of unknowing. Come to ransom everyone, God-in-human-flesh does not disdain the things He created but redeems them by incorporating them into worship.

Need it be said that the divine and the spiritual which are the heart and reason for worship give ritual and prayer and instrument all their meaning? Need it be stressed that the reception of these sensible symbols of the divine and the spiritual must be measured by the importance of what they represent? There will be no true inner transformation without taking them seriously. God will not force His grace upon anyone. And lukewarmness is to Him an abomination. There can be no indifference about worship nor about the instruments of worship. The symbols of love at worship demand the delicate sincerity and reverence of true love. As we are compelled by our human limitations to accept symbol and instrument and ritual, so we are compelled by the nature of love to be wholehearted in love.

That means a happy medium between the uncritical use that becomes superstition and the sophistication that keeps love at arm's length. We can neither understand ritual and symbol nor can we be stirred by them without surrendering to their suggestions and movements. This can be done, without symbolism becoming idolatry and without ritual becoming formalism. Since symbol and ritual are so deeply embedded in the religious life of every people, i.e., in the most unyielding part of their lives, it is highly important both to respect the true power of them and to appreciate which of the local usages are the truer symbols and therefore the more readily adaptable to Christian meanings. It is of special interest to missioners, clerical, religious or lay, to be at home in the world of sense-images that lead to God. The Church remains ever the missionary Church. Her sons and daughters go out like rivers to meet a non-Christian world, to cleanse it and to elevate the best of it to a Christian grandeur.

Chapter Three

Christian Being is the Basis for Worship

THE CHURCH today, taken as it is the world over, is a suffering Church. The Prince of Darkness is having a shadow of triumph over the Prince of Light. It is not that God has lost control of His world but rather that He is exercising His merciful judgment, His gentle wrath. Besides, the wounds of Christ must be expected in His members. The Passion of the Mystical Body of Christ is a continuous Passion because "what is lacking of the sufferings of Christ I fill up in my flesh for his body, which is the Church."[1] It must always be so. All men are called to enter into and to live the whole Christ, including the suffering Christ.

But in this tormented century we see the tragedy of a storm that man has slowly brought upon himself. And it is doubly tragic because man finds himself baffled by it and unprepared to dedicate his torment to redeeming purposes. He has forgotten the meaning of Calvary and he has forgotten his own

[1] Col. 1:24.

42

office and dignity. Not knowing himself nor his destiny, man has a power of inflicting pain upon himself which the devil could gloat over.

The immediate historical causes of our particular wave of self-imposed suffering began when man saw the fascination of ancient pagan culture and got wrapped up in himself through the secular humanism of the Renaissance. First came the revolt against Church authority in the Reformation and against all authority in the "enlightenment" and the new capitalism of the seventeenth and eighteenth centuries. Then came the enthronement of the sovereign people in the revolutions of the late eighteenth and middle nineteenth centuries.

The next step was already in the books. St. Thomas in his "Governance of Rulers" observed and predicted that "the rule of many is changed into a tyranny not less, but perhaps more, frequently than the rule of one."[2] Or as someone has put it: "Why do revolutionaries often become tyrants?" So now in the twentieth century we have the ultimate form of secular humanism, the dogmatic materialism of the totalitarian state, the "god-state." This ultimate organization of power is the inevitable result of man's assumption that he could, by his own power, create a new and more perfect society, a heaven on earth. He has given birth to a monster, not a new creature. He has not found happiness but only new fears.

There can be no creativeness apart from the Trinity. "In the beginning was the Word ... and the Word was God. ... All things were made through him, and without him was made nothing that has been made. In him was life, and the life was the light of men."[3]

Through the infinite patterns of divine wisdom appropriated

[2] St. Thomas, *Governance of Rulers,* tr. by G. B. Phelan, New York, Sheed and Ward, 1938, p. 53.
[3] Jn. 1:1-5.

to the Second Person of the Blessed Trinity, God made each person different one from the other. In the work of creating human beings God never repeats Himself. Every time a child is born there is something new under the sun. Not in any humorous sense, but in a sacred and beautiful sense, in a divinely-intended sense, there was never anyone like the individual person of the moment, and there never again will be anyone just like him or her. No two persons ever have been or ever will be just alike.

Only God is capable of such unlimited variety in multiplicity. When we start to multiply things in quantity, what do we do? We set up punch presses to punch out each piece alike or molds to mold each piece alike. Then we have an assembly line with inspectors to make sure that one refrigerator is assembled just like another. But God creates each soul as an individual part of a separate and individual human being. Each angel is a separate species. Each soul is meant for a special person. At every conception God creates a distinct soul for the uniquely new body that begins to form. So at each birth there comes into the world a unique, unmatched human personality. Only God could make each of us so truly and genuinely different one from the other. He never repeats Himself. He never exhausts Himself. "How incomprehensible are His judgments, how unsearchable are His ways!"[4]

As each person comes fresh from the creating hand of God, He says, "Make the most of yourself for you will never happen again!" Each one is a special revelation of God's power and goodness. God loves variety because in the infinitely varied goodness of each of His creatures, God puts a reflection of His own infinite goodness. The face of each flower differs from every other in the garden. And "star differs from star in glory." Person differs from person.

[4] Rom. 11:33.

God always has a reason for what He does. Being supreme-
ly intelligent, He creates a particular person for a particular
work and a particular way of life. He had something in mind
for each person when He made each one different from the
other.

What God had in mind He always keeps in mind. In spite
of millions and millions of human persons that ever have been
or ever will be, God knows each one better that he knows himself. He is more aware of each one of us than we are aware
of ourselves. When we go to sleep and cease to be aware of
ourselves God still goes on thinking about us. God never sleeps.
He never daydreams. He is never distracted. We are always
on His mind. He never forgets us. If He did forget us for a
split second we would drop back into nothingness. Always, at
every moment, He holds us in the palm of His hand.

Knowing us better than we know our own first name, God
loves us better than we love the sound of our own first names.
And God's love is not merely a misty fragrance breathed upon
all mankind in general. Love is a distinctive going-out-to the
person loved. Therefore, it is specified, made special by the
uniqueness of each person loved. God has for each of us a
special love that is as unlike the love He gives to any other
as each person is unlike any other. The uniqueness in each
one He loves with a unique love. Actually, He made each person in the first place because He loved that image of each one
which He had in His mind from all eternity. We are the outpouring of His love and diffusive goodness. His love does not
repeat itself. His love never exhausts itself.

In spite of all this, the most wonderful thing about us is
not our human gifts and appearance, however fine they may
be. A person could be the smartest and most learned, the most
beautiful, the strongest or the rightest person in the world; and
still he would be only human. What we are humanly, of course,

is every reason for being completely and sincerely ourselves and for eschewing vanity. But that is only the beginning. We were born humanly in order to be reborn divinely. We are born of our parents in order to be reborn a "new creature," a child of God. God made us to be the center and master of the universe. Then He put into us something that changes us in the heart of our being. At baptism we are reborn spiritually and totally to a new divine life, the life of God.

"If any man is in Christ, he is a new creature: the former things have passed away; behold they are made new!"[5] We are a "new creature" because God in His love freely chose to share with us His own life. Our rebirth was "not of blood, nor of the will of the flesh, nor of the will of man, but of God."[6]

The newness and uniqueness and the glory that we possess in our natural being is nothing beside the divine newness of God-life shared with us. The important thing now about our natural being is that it is the outward sign of an inward grace; it is the outward instrument of an inward power. Having been reborn into God-life, our life now, our vision, our desires are not limited to time or space, nor to a social order or to a local group. We should never underestimate ourselves. As eternity surpasses time, as heaven surpasses earth, as the infinite surpasses the finite, our inner spiritual worth is beyond any measuring by reason or science or earthly honor. As St. Thomas says, "The good of grace in each one is greater than the good of nature in the whole universe."[7] Just as naturally as birds fly through the air and as naturally as fishes swim through water, we are made to live connaturally in the infinity of God. Grace perfects nature; it does not destroy it. As we pray in

[5] II Cor. 5:17.
[6] Jn. 1:13.
[7] *Sum. Theol.*, I-II, q. 113, a. 9, ad 2.

the Offertory of each Mass, "O God, who in a wonderful manner didst create and ennoble human nature, and still more wonderfully hast renewed it; grant that by the mystery of this water
and wine, we may be made partakers of His divinity who vouch-
safed to become partaker of our humanity, Jesus Christ Thy
Son."

That is a divine beginning. But there is more. More than a
divine nature has been shared with us. Jesus said, "If anyone
love me, he will keep my word, and my Father will love him,
and we will come to him and make our abode with him. The
Father will give you another Advocate to dwell with you forever, the Spirit of truth. You shall know him, because he will
dwell with you, and be in you."[8] The three divine Persons,
Father, Son and Holy Spirit, dwell in us and make each of us
a "new creature." We are distinctively and individually fashioned as tabernacles of the Trinity. We are and will remain
forever divinely new and young with the youth and joy of heaven
itself. Spiritually we are born old with original sin and are
meant to die young with shared divine life. God is heaven
and God is in our hearts. "Grace is nothing less than the beginning of glory."[9] "Habitual grace and the Beatific Vision are
one in kind and one in nature."[10] That helps us to understand
the words of the Requiem Preface, "Life is only changed; it
is not taken away." As the oak is in the acorn, as the flower
is in the bud and as the adult is in the child, so we possess the
seed, the beginning of eternal glory in our hearts. In the change
that is death, and after the purification that is purgatory, faith
will become sight, hope will become everlasting possession and
love will become the ecstasy of the eternal embrace. All of this
means that we really do not know people at all unless we know

[8] Jn. 14:23, 16-17.
[9] *Sum. Theol.,* II-II, q. 24, a. 3.
[10] Tanquerey, *Spiritual Life,* Tournai, Desclee, 1932, p. 58.

them by faith. Only by faith do we know the most important thing about them.

There is something more still. God is a very practical Person. He gave us a life; and life is a principle, a fountain of activity. With the God-life we are made new with a whole elaborate and delicate organism of infused virtues and gifts. The infused theological and moral virtues and the gifts of the Holy Spirit are the immediate faculties, the inclinations, the impulses, the instinctive insights and instinctive sureness that help us to live in the mighty possession of the eternal Three as our guests and our glory, to be at home with divinity. We are newly equipped to live as friends of God. "You are my friends if you do the things I command you. No longer do I call you servants, because the servant does not know what his master does. But I have called you friends, because all things that I have heard from my Father I have made known to you."[11]

Another wonderful thing about the "new creature" that we are is that we are forever signed and sealed as members of the living Christ; and through membership in Christ we are adopted as sons and daughters of the Father; we are adopted into the family in the Trinity. "God sent his Son ... that we might receive the adoption of sons."[12] Because we have been adopted as brothers and sisters of Christ, we are also joint-heirs with Him of eternal life. "All things are yours; things present, or things to come—all are yours, and you are Christ's and Christ is God's."[13] Therefore Jesus said, "Father, I will that where I am, they also whom thou hast given me may be with me: that they may see my glory which thou hast given me."[14] We are one supernatural organism with Jesus as the Head and with

[11] Jn. 15:14-15.
[12] Gal. 4:5.
[13] I Cor. 3:23.
[14] Jn. 17:24.

every other member of Jesus through all ages and all over the earth.

The Father loves us precisely as members of His Son. The divine life in us is also the Christ-life. And everything we do for Him and in Him, as the outflowing of that inner Christ-life, takes on the power and merit of Christ's own words and actions and gives everything an eternal worth. That is the vital unity and power in the prayer of Jesus at the Last Supper, "Not for these only do I pray, but for those also who through their word are to believe in me, that all may be one, even as thou, Father, in me and I in Thee. And the glory that thou hast given me, I have given to them, that they may be one, even as we are one: I in them and thou in me; that they may be perfected in unity, and that the world may know that thou hast sent me, and that thou hast loved them as thou hast loved me."[15]

That is a breath-taking mystery. We could never imagine it. God had to reveal it. That is the vital power of our Christian personality. No need to be frightened by the world's evil nor discouraged by human dullness and weakness. We do not work alone, nor with merely human ability and power. We are in partnership with divinity. Jesus has taken us into a most personal intimacy. He first of all prayed for our personal holiness. "I pray for those whom thou hast given me, because they are thine; and all things that are mine are thine, and thine are mine; and I am glorified in them. I do not pray that thou take them out of the world, but that thou keep them from evil. Sanctify them in truth."[16] Jesus personally commissions us as His co-workers. "Even as thou hast sent me into the world, so I also send them into the world. And for them I sanctify myself, that they also may be sanctified in truth."[17] Jesus gives

[15] Jn. 17:20-23.   [16] Jn. 17:9-17.   [17] Jn. 17:18-19.

His power to us. "Whatever you ask in my name, that I will do."[18] If that seems strange, think of what it means to baptize a person. Because grace is a share in divine life, to change a person from a state of sin to a state of grace is a greater thing than to create heaven and earth.[19] Finally, to serve Jesus personally is our highest honor. "If anyone serves me, my Father will honor him."[20]

Therefore we should not underestimate the divine in ourselves. As the human nature of Jesus was anointed with divinity in the womb of Mary, we, each of us, have been anointed at baptism with participation in His divinity. The Christ-life in us is not meant to remain dormant and inactive. God did not become man merely to change us from human imperfection to human perfection. Our vocation is not merely to be perfect human beings. For God did not mean us to seek ethical perfection for the sake of its moral beauty nor because it is easier to defend by moral principle nor because it is a bulwark against moral disaster and disgrace. God does not want us to stop even with the human perfection of Jesus Himself, because that moral perfection was simply the effect and the instrument of His divinity. Jesus said, "Learn from me, for I am meek and humble of heart,"[21] because He wanted to lead us through His human perfection to live the divine life He shares with us, to be absorbed in God, forming our thoughts, our likes, our desires, and actions by a supernatural holiness at every level and in every walk of life. "As the Father has loved me, I also love you. Abide in my love."[22] "The human charm of Christ is meant to attract but not to arrest the gaze of the soul."[23]

---

18 Jn. 14:12-13.
19 *Summa. Theol.*, I-II, q. 113, a. 9.
20 Jn. 12:26.
21 Mt. 11:29.
22 Jn. 15:8-9.
23 Leen, *Holy Ghost*, New York, Sheed and Ward, p. 85.

The seal and the grace that now mark us as members of Christ are far more than a new exaltation of being that carries a pledge of eternal heritage. There is but one Christ who lived in visible flesh in Palestine and who now lives gloriously in heaven, sacramentally in the eucharist and mystically in His members. And there is but one Mystical Body of Christ and we become Christians only by being joined to and incorporated into that one Mystical Body. There is but one priesthood and that is the priesthood of Christ, which the members of Christ share in various and distinctive ways. And the life of the one Body of Christ lives and functions only through the one life-giving priesthood and kingship and teaching of Christ. "I am the vine, you are the branches. He who abides in me, and I in him, he bears much fruit; for without me you can do nothing."[24]

"Each of the faithful is deputed to receive, or to bestow on others, things pertaining to the worship of God. And this properly speaking, is the purpose of the sacramental character. Now the whole rite of the Christian religion is derived from Christ's priesthood. Consequently, it is clear that the sacramental character is specially the character of Christ, to Whose character the faithful are likened by reason of the sacramental characters, which are nothing else than certain participations of Christ's Priesthood, flowing from Christ Himself."[25] Baptism, confirmation and holy orders are the only sacraments that imprint a character. The others do not imprint a character because "they do not empower the Christian with any public function."[26] St. Leo, speaking to the people, said, "By baptism, according to the teaching of St. Peter (II, 5:9), the royal dignity of the priesthood is common to all of you. The anointing of the

[24] Jn. 15:5, 6.
[25] *Sum. Theol.*, III., q. 63, a. 3.
[26] Anger, *The Doctrine of the Mystical Body of Christ,* New York, Benziger, 1931, p. 87.

Holy Spirit has consecrated all of you as priests."[27] St. Jerome: "You are made priests by baptism." St. Augustine: "Just as we call all Christians because of a mystic Chrism, so we call all priests, because they are members of one Priest."[28]

Pius XII has summed up this tradition: "By the waters of baptism, as by common right, Christians are made members of the Mystical Body of Christ the Priest, and by the 'character' which is imprinted on their souls, they are appointed to give worship to God; thus they participate, according to their condition, in the priesthood of Christ."[29]

A priest is a mediator between God and man. Historically, there has been no religion or priesthood without sacrifice. The power to offer sacrifice is the very first and most basic of priestly powers. Therefore anyone who has any priestly power from Christ must have at least that power. This is a great reason to give the laity confidence and self-respect. Properly speaking, 'laity' is not a word used to distinguish between the ordained and the baptized but between the baptized and the non-baptized. It is the title given to the privileged, holy, twice anointed people of God who are set aside and appointed to worship.[30]

Power is given for a purpose. How do we exercise our share in the work of Christ as Priest and Prophet and King?

PRIEST: HOW DO WE SHARE IN CHRIST'S WORK AS PRIEST?

1. We offer Christ in the Mass with and through the celebrant at the altar in a genuine common act of sacrifice. "Pray, brethren, that my sacrifice and yours may be acceptable to God the Father Almighty."

[27] St. Leo I, *Sermo* IV.
[28] St. Augustine, *De Civitate Dei*, XX, 10.
[29] Pius XII, *Mediator Dei*, par. 88.
[30] Cf. Art. "Character, Sacramental," in Parente, *Dictionary of Dogmatic Theology*, Milwaukee, Bruce, 1951, p. 45.

2. We offer ourselves as co-victims with the Divine Victim, Christ.
3. As an expression of our offering we either sing or recite the Mass with the celebrant. We do not do this in order to participate but to express exteriorly an essential interior participation which is already there and to make it more complete and perfect.
4. In emergencies the twice anointed lay person can administer baptism and holy communion. Groom and bride are the ordinary ministers of the sacrament of matrimony.
5. Everyone can offer the sacrifice of praise. Historically, the divine office was the prayerbook of the people. "The Short Breviary of the Laity" is available for individual or common use. And there is parish Vespers or Compline. There is Benediction and every parish service.

The work of Christ's priesthood and of our share in it is the redemption and sanctification of men. To inspire a desire for Christian holiness and to guide its growth, Jesus was also Prophet and King.

PROPHET—TEACHER: HOW DO WE SHARE IN CHRIST'S WORK AS PROPHET AND TEACHER?

1. Fathers and mothers are the first and most important teachers of religion for their children. Anyone can teach catechism or tell another about the Faith.
2. Our charities, leadership and cooperation in social improvements and every kind of good example are powerful teaching.
3. Everyone can have a part in mutual formation in lay groups such as YCS and YCW sections, Legion of Mary, Christian Family Movement, Cana, discussion clubs, etc.

KING—RULER: HOW DO WE SHARE IN CHRIST'S WORK AS KING AND RULER?

1. Fathers and mothers are the prime rulers of the world when they govern their families.
2. Teachers must govern a class, doctors and nurses govern patients and do supervisory work. Choir directors govern their choirs. Scientists govern in their laboratories.
3. Businessmen run their business and foremen govern their co-workers. Flight captains govern their crews.
4. Civil officials in local or federal government exercise God's authority. "There exists no authority except from God."[31] The military command the military.
5. People exercise leadership in the lay apostolate.

All this together is some suggestion of the wonder of power that God has placed in each of us who is "in Christ a new creature." It helps us understand what St. Augustine meant when he wrote, "Men go forth to wonder at the height of mountains, the huge waves of the sea, the broad flow of rivers, the extent of the ocean, the courses of the stars, and forget to wonder at themselves."

The wonders of divine life, of divine indwelling, of incorporation into Christ, of the indelible seal, all these we know for the best possible reason and that is the word of God. We know it with the certainty of faith. We cannot pinch ourselves and feel God; we cannot look in a mirror and see God within us. But the certainty of faith is greater than any certainty of reason or science. It is the certainty that leads the saints to heroic ventures for Christ and to the folly of the cross. God has spoken and that is more than enough.

Great things can be expected because "He who is mighty has done great things for me, and holy is his name."[32] The more each one appreciates his or her own share in Christ's priesthood, the more each will appreciate the still fuller share

[31] Rom. 13:1.
[32] Lk. 1:49.

that God gives to ordained priests for the miracle of the eucharist, for absolving from sin and for being the ordinary ministers of the sacraments and sacramentals. And the more each person appreciates his or her own rightful dignity and responsibility and the solid virtue required by them, the more each will respect ordained priests and pray for them. That is indicated by the fact that where the lay apostolate is strong and young people put a higher value on things spiritual, there vocations to the ordained priesthood and to the religious life are on the increase.

What St. Leo and Pius XI have called the royal priesthood of the laity, others have called the common priesthood of the Mystical Body. But it is the one priesthood of the one total Christ reaching across the world and across the centuries. He is alive and active in every baptized person. He cannot be limited to any point in history because He is eternal and because He is always alive in each one of His members. We are His hands and feet and voice. Everything good we do is under the whispered guidance of the Holy Spirit who is the Soul of the Mystical Body of Christ. Adopted into the family of the Trinity as younger brothers and sisters of our Elder Redeemer-Brother, we share in the family secrets of the Trinity revealed by the Son. And we do the Trinity's work in a most intimate vital dependence upon one another. Nothing that we do is entirely our own.

We mortify ourselves, our mind and will and flesh, in order to free the spirit and live closer to God; and at the same time, the divine life is more operative through the whole Mystical Body. "What is lacking of the sufferings of Christ I fill up in my flesh for his body, which is the Church."[33] In any given instant of the ebb and flow of life and in the infinite pattern of its destined tides, some ought to suffer for all, some nurse

[33] Col. 1:24.

the sick for all, others teach for all, still others say the Divine Office for all, always in the name of all. For it is the one Christ-life operating through the whole Christ. As St. Augustine says, "There shall be one Christ loving Himself."[34] It is Christ, the one priest offering the holocaust of all humanity through every sharer in His priesthood. Can any friend be closer to friend and more active in friendship, than we are close and active in the friendship of Christ's priesthood?

The love of God for us and for all men is just as real and vital and powerful as it was in the first moment of creation or on Calvary. It is always reaching out to us and to all men, thirsting to be accepted and returned. That is why the priesthood of Christ shared with men is not so much a state as a magnificent moment, unchanged, undimmed, and unweakened, at once a vast promise in what it holds out to men and a glorious consummation in what it already is of God and men meeting in an act of reconciliation and love. The love of God for us shown at Nazareth, Bethlehem, Gethsemani, Calvary is forever being reconfirmed and renewed. Each confirmation and renewal does for us what a gift or an unexpected kindness or a simple warm word will do for a friend.

All our brotherhood in life and friendship in priesthood is deepened and broadened and heightened by consummation in love. As Pius XII says, "The more we become 'members one of another,' 'mutually one for another,' the closer we shall be united with God, with Christ; as on the other hand the more ardent the love that binds us to God and our divine Head, the closer we shall be united to each other in the bonds of charity."[35] Love is a going-out-to, a living oneness. God is love because His very personality is a going-out-to, a relation of

[34] St. Aug., *Hom.* X, 3 on I Jn. "I sanctify them in myself, since they also are myself." (Comm. on Jn. 17:19, 108).

[35] Pius XII, *Mystici Corporis,* par. 73.

Divine Person to Divine Person in a living oneness. Our oneness in Christ is "so inherently essential that each member's
supernatural life depends entirely upon his vital union with
the Mystical Organism."[36] That is what Christ prayed for in
all His apostles: "That they may be one, even as Thou, Father, art in me and I in Thee—that they may be one in us, that
they may be perfected in unity, in order that the world may believe that Thou hast sent me."[37] That is the consummation of
member loving member. To lay down our very lives for one
another seems no longer such a faraway thing to do, for we
know with the certainty of faith that to lose our lives for one
another is for us to find life.

As we spend and are spent in bringing Jesus to fullness in
His members through life and love communicated to each other
and to all men, we will be humbly conscious that in the action
of the whole Christ we only continue what others have begun
and we only begin what others shall finish and that all the while
we are sustained by every other member. Nor will we despair
of our inadequacies. As Father Mersch puts it, "our good works
are only pieces, by themselves incomplete and unintelligible.
Their insufficiencies and excesses are like the hollows and ex-
crescences which articulate the members: they constitute the
gears by which they engage one another. What matters it if
one becomes distracted despite all his good will, in the very
midst of the actions which he has commenced for God—if at
that moment another renews his attention and he is one with
that other? Suppose one does not succeed in offering his sufferings
to God when they become intense and overpowering, if another
then presents to God in our name all suffering and all action
here below? This is the triumph of unity; it is the communion

[36] Jurgensmeier, *The Mystical Body of Christ,* New York, Sheed and
Ward, 1954, p. 262.
[37] Jn. 17:21, 23.

of saints; it is the solidarity of members: 'that the members may have care for one another,' (I Cor. 12:25). There is no room certainly for any proud self-sufficiency. The essential thing is that each one remain in the unity of Christ. In unity all is common; and in it each one, having done only his own part, has none the less done all."[38] That is the unity and consummation of love. That is the vital power of a totally Christian personality.

That is the eternal plan of the Father for us. As St. Paul says in Ephesians, "Blessed be the God and Father of our Lord Jesus Christ, who has blessed us with every spiritual blessing on high in Christ. Even as he chose us in him before the foundation of the world, that we should be holy and without blemish in his sight in love. He predestined us to be adopted through Jesus Christ as his sons, according to the purpose of his will, unto the praise of the glory of his grace."[39]

Looking beyond the human to the divine in ourselves and in men and in the world, beyond time to eternity, beyond suffering to joy, we are not going to waste time bemoaning a lost Paradise and weeping over the havoc of the Fall and of sin. We see rather the great restoration, the vital newness of things. Regardless of what Adam lost for his posterity, we have now regained far more than was lost because we have God Incarnate who lifted the human race to union with His Divine Person, called all men to be members of His Mystical Person and makes us co-offers and co-victims with Him in the Sacrifice of the whole Christ.

We now have the religion of victory. "Take courage, I have overcome the world."[40] Christ overcomes what leads to

---

[38] Mersch, *Morality and the Mystical Body,* New York, Kenedy, 1939, p. 102 ff.
[39] Eph. 1:4.
[40] Jn. 16:33.

spiritual death in order to restore and strengthen what leads to eternal life. Christianity is always renewing the youth of the world. In Christ we are always victorious. "Thanks be to God who always leads us in triumph in Christ Jesus."[41] "Behold the Lamb of God, who *takes away the sin* of the world!"[42] That was the first and greatest victory of our Redeemer: Jesus destroyed the hideous guilt of man's devil-inspired revolt against God and made man once again a temple of God and worthy of adoption and friendship and eternal life. *Death,* too, He has conquered, for He Himself "bore our sins in his body upon the tree, that we, having died to sin, might live to justice."[43] "The hour is coming in which all who are in the tombs shall hear the voice of the Son of God. And they who have done good shall come forth unto resurrection of life."[44] And the very *devil himself* is vanquished and cringes before the all-holy Redeemer. "He fell down before him, and crying out with a loud voice said, 'What have I to do with thee, Jesus, Son of the most high God? I pray thee, do not torment me.' "[45]

Because of this threefold victory our prayer and worship is now victorious worship. Previous to His great victory we could not claim a share in the gifts of God. But now we come before God as brothers and joint-heirs with Christ, as privileged sharers in the spoils of His victory. "If you ask the Father anything in my name, he will give it to you."[46] We still must ask, yes, but we do not cry out with the cringing of outcasts but rather with the confidence of adopted, chosen children and brothers and lovers of Christ. As such we expect quite simply to be heard. All our prayers have become the prayers of the triumphant total Christ. "If you abide in me, and if my words abide in you, ask whatever you will and it shall be done

[41] II Cor. 2:14.
[42] Jn. 1:29.
[43] I Pet. 2:24.

[44] Jn. 5:28-29.
[45] Lk. 8:28.
[46] Jn. 16:23.

to you."[47] Therefore, our worship becomes more a celebration than a supplication. We enter confidently into the treasure house of God and partake freely of His spiritual banquet. We must not dishonor either God or ourselves by cringing fears. We should keep only the reverence and the freedom of the children of God.

With such a religion of victory and such a worship of victory, we can catalogue all the great evils in the world and know with sober realism that Christ's conquering and redeeming power is greater than all of them. Christian optimism is the only final realism. We are not meant to be overawed by imagination nor to be beaten by feelings of fear. We are destined and equipped to see all things in due proportion by reason and faith. Evil will have its "hour," yes, and suffering is real and hell is everlasting. But hell is God's way of insisting that we get to heaven. Suffering is our way of joining our Redeemer-Brother in saving the world. And the "hour" of evil is a passing shadow, a momentary privation of good that has meaning only as the opposite face of good.

Therefore, we cannot build pharisaical walls around ourselves and shut ourselves up in a sectarian ghetto and point fingers at reprobates. Rather we should cleanse ourselves of the world's wrong attitudes and defeatism, break the chains of selfish habits and build bridges of compassionate love to those who need our Christian confidence. The measure of Christian victory may or may not be extensive, but it can always be intensive and everlasting. The cockle will always stand among the wheat. But as quickly as the working of leaven and as surely as the tiny mustard will grow into the spreading tree that feeds the singing birds, so surely will the kingdom of God grow and spread. If men will not glorify God by obedience and love they will have to glorify His justice by suffering punishment.

[47] Jn. 15:7.

In either case a victory is won. Always we are the impact of the divine against the world, the flesh and the devil. And always every martyrdom, every canonization, every act of charity, every step of spiritual progress by anyone is a new conquest by the Holy Spirit and the exercise of God's sovereignty.

"But God, who is rich in mercy, by reason of His very great love wherewith he has loved us even when we were dead by reason of our sins, brought us to life together with Christ, and raised us up together, and seated us together in heaven in Christ Jesus, that he might show in the ages to come the overflowing riches of his grace in kindness towards us in Christ Jesus."[48]

[48] Eph. 2:4-7.

Chapter Four

Worship is a Living Tradition

IN a radio address given July 11, 1954, Pope Pius XII, speaking of Pope St. Gregory VII (11th cent.), said: "He treated ecclesiastical traditions with particular care. But he also wrote the memorable words: 'The Lord did not say: I am custom, but: I am truth.' "

Our Christian faith is sound enough to seek the truth, to know the truth, to be realistic and always hopeful. The Beatitudes that preamble the Sermon on the Mount are both realistic and hopeful. Later in another great sermon, the great sermon of parables about the establishment, development and final purification of His new spiritual organism, Jesus renewed both the warning and the optimism of the Beatitudes. In the Parable of the Sower and the Seed He indicated that perhaps only a fourth of the people hearing the good news of the Gospel would respond. In the Parable of the Wheat and the Weeds He predicted even that that one-fourth would have mixed with it a deceptive wild wheat. In other words, imperfections would hinder the spiritual growth of His Mystical Body; and those

62

aberrations can scarcely be distinguished from truth and virtue until the Final Judgment. To offset the depressing effects of these two parables, Jesus then told of the mustard seed and the all-pervading yeast-leaven. "The Kingdom of heaven is like a grain of mustard seed, which a man took and sowed in his field. This indeed is the smallest of all the seeds; but when it grows up it is larger than any herb and becomes a tree, so that the birds of the air come and dwell in its branches."[1] In a warm tropical climate, when the soil is good and the rain is plentiful, this cultivated black mustard grows to twelve or fourteen feet. And the birds came for more than shade; they came to feed upon the abundance of tiny seeds.

What is true of the whole of Christ's visible organism is true also of its parts. Doctrine has gradually clarified and has had continually to be defended against error. Church laws have grown and have had continually to be reorganized and recodified. Moral theology, philosophy and the arts have grown haltingly but irresistibly. In like manner, Christian worship has grown from the mustard seed of the Last Supper to a large spreading plant that feeds with its substance all who come to dwell in it.

Christian worship is a living tradition. What do we mean by tradition? "In a theological sense, tradition is the word of God concerning faith and morals, not written but transmitted orally from Christ to the apostles and from them to their successors down to us."[2] Worship is in part a written revelation, and not in that sense, tradition, since baptism, the eucharist, sacrifice and sacrament, confirmation, penance, holy orders and extreme unction are there in the words of the New Testament. There are three kinds of tradition: divine, divine-apostolic and divine-ecclesiastical. In part worship is divine tradition taught

[1] 13:31-32.
[2] Parente, *op. cit.*, p. 284.

orally and directly by Our Lord; for such is the sacrament of marriage. In further part it is divine-apostolic tradition, i.e., not learned from the lips of Christ directly but from the inspiration of the Holy Spirit: "The Advocate, the Holy Spirit . . . will teach you all things, and bring to your mind whatever I have said to you."[3] In final part it is divine-ecclesiastical tradition: for if it is true of popular devotions, as Pius XII says, that ". . . from these multiple forms of piety, the inspiration and action of the Holy Spirit cannot be absent,"[4] then the divine is at work also in the official worship of Christ's Church. There is scarcely any need to add that many human elements, both good and bad, have been embedded in the living tradition that is worship.

Our worship is much more than the effect of converging divine and human elements. It is also an instrument for transmitting tradition, an organ of the living teaching authority of the Church and a witness to Catholic teaching. "All Christian antiquity considers the apostolic Tradition conserved in the various Churches, particularly in the Roman Church, as the transmitting channel of the revealed word, equal to Holy Scripture. The principal instruments by means of which divine Tradition has been conserved are the professions of faith, the sacred liturgy, the writings of the Fathers, the practice of the Church, the acts of the martyrs and archeological monuments."[5]

The Church, ". . . being divine, has more in her than the Latin genius alone—or the genius of all the peoples of the world together—can seize and live."[6] In the same way, the divine in Catholic worship not only keeps it from being destroyed by the human but assimilates the human according to

---

[3] Jn. 14:26.
[4] Pius XII, *Mediator Dei,* par. 175.
[5] Parente, *op. cit.,* p. 285.
[6] Journet, *op. cit.,* vol. I, p. 42.

the greatest and the least things that man needs to pay homage to God and achieve eternal union with God. Always a living organism blending the divine and the human, the Church and its worship has been able to grow, to adjust and change, to expand and contract, and thus give an ever fresh expression to unchanging truth and unchanging needs. "Christianity has been preserved not by resistance to change but by embracing and transforming the historic process itself."[7]

Happily, a healthy realism has dominantly shaped our worship, for there has been a marked awareness of the limitations and demands imposed by man's nature and environment as well as a marked preference for the practical and concrete, the active and the explicit. As a result, the transcendent and eternal have been engrafted into the homely and intimate but without becoming cosy and petty. Self-consolation has never triumphed over self-immolation. Restraint has mastered emotion.[8]

The key problem of worship remains many-sided: how to combine the divine and the human and, on the human level, how to combine the social and the personal as well as the exterior and the interior. For worship is never a mere science, an organization of knowledge according to its ultimate causes; it is always an art, a doing. The doing must first of all be a sincere, free, and personal doing that includes the entire person and at the same time a corporate doing that requires self-discipline and cooperation with others in a joint official action. And it is not to be wondered at that the spontaneous and the patterned have seldom blended perfectly; for very seldom is there perfect cooperation of man with divine guidance in anything, let alone in the mysterious realm of paying homage to God.

Our Christmas and Easter celebrations show how the desir-

---

[7] White, *"Campion's Strategy Today,"* 95 (1956) 225-27.
[8] Cf. Underhill, *Worship,* London, Nisbet, 1951, p. 67.

able and undesirable can mingle and why there is need for doctrine to predominate over emotion. We are fortunate to combine in our Christmas the poinsettia from Mexico, the crib from Italy, the tree from Germany, the holly from England, the window candle from Ireland and carols from everywhere. But we know only too well how easily these things can be over-commercialized, how the shopping season can destroy the spirit of advent and how pre-Christmas parties become the opposite of penance. The Easter egg is a fine symbol of our resurrection to new life, the rabbit the symbol of the abundant fruitfulness of that new life and Easter clothes the symbol of the baptismal robes worn by the newly baptized from Easter to the following Sunday. But again commerce and sentiment have taken over far too much. And how difficult it becomes to relive Christ's Passion and Death, His Resurrection and our spiritual resurrection with Him. At both Christmas and Easter it becomes almost impossible to abstract ourselves from our environment or completely to resist its influence.

Understanding these obvious present problems, we can better understand how a combination of human factors has given us much that is good and also deprived us of things desirable. In general, we have no longer the same opportunities for variations and for spontaneous prayer within official worship. Happily, the new Holy Week Ordinal allows for more of both and points the way to a better future. Except for Good Friday, we miss the great common prayer of the people; but that, too, may be included in our restored worship. We have lost the offering of bread and wine for the sacrifice brought in procession, as well as the kiss of peace, but it can be disputed how appropriate it would be to restore these practices in our generation. Of more immediate urgency is the active participation in the preparation for Christ's Sacrifice through sung prayer to greet the celebrant at his entrance, to express and intensify our meditative response to the lessons, to accompany the Offertory and finally to joyously thank God for the spiritual nourishment of Christ's Body and Blood. These things that we have lost are needed for more reasons than simply an individual's active portion in worship; they are needed also to bear witness to and to express our social and corporate union in worship.

But just as it is not so much the Fall of man that matters as his surpassing Redemption, so it is not as much what we have lost that matters as the rich heritage we possess. A full exploration of that heritage would require the pages of many volumes. It cannot be put into a single chapter. Neither does our searching into it call for a scaffolding of dates and places. Of more immediate purpose is the succession of personalities and movements as well as the flow of pertinent circumstances that altogether worked the safe of things. And what gives meaning to these outer things is the actual worship of God's people in itself.

The distinctive thing about Christian worship is that it centers in persons and not in a place nor a sacred grove nor a mountaintop nor a shrine. We know that in the beginning Calvary was made present again on the family table in homes or on the martyr's tomb as well as in great basilicas. The unbloody Sacrifice has been reduced to mission simplicities in a thousand crude circumstances where the missioner's love for His crucified Lord brings the love of Christ to His people. In the Graf Zeppelin high above the English Channel, in the crowded quarters of a submarine deep in the Pacific Ocean, under a German prison blanket at midnight, in shellcraters and on ship decks, under trees and under stars, in the tense hush of disguise around a tavern table in war-riven Spain, Christ has been offered up with equal certainty and essential effect. In tiny medical capsules Jesus came as spiritual food and a great Presence to Barcelona prisoners.

Such mobility and adaptibility is surely convincing evidence
of the vitality of a worship that embodies the twin realities of
the Mystical Christ and the eucharist as His only sacrifice and
central sacrament. Through the centuries, day after day and
hour after hour around the earth, the globe of the earth becomes
the pedestal of the sacramental cross whereon Christ incarnate
and crucified is at once the living Presence and the "Desired of
nations" washing the world with His Blood, the active Mediator between God and man and between man and God.

"This supreme worship, which by a mysterious anticipation
had been the center of gravity of prior cults and the ground
of their efficacy, would one day efface them altogether, and
remain alone valid, alone legitimate, alone capable of bringing remission of sins. . . . This decisive oblation is to be passed
on from age to age until the end of all ages. . . . This Christian
cultus is no longer pure figure, nor, as yet, is it pure reality; it
is reality, but under the veil of figures. Founded by Christ, it
is continued in the Church."[9] On this point, St. Thomas says
of the Church and its worship, "The state of the New Law
is between the state of the Old Law, whose figures are fulfilled
in the New, and the state of glory, in which all truth will be
openly and perfectly revealed. Wherefore then there will be
no sacraments."[10]

So we find the ancestry of our daily worship in the divinely
revealed and figurative cult of Exodus and Leviticus. Gradually,
the sacramental aspect of Old Testament worship became clearer
to God's people, especially from Ezechiel onward. They saw
that it was meant to stand both for the holiness of God and
the sinfulness of man. Sacrifices of grateful homage and of
atonement were offered upon many altars set up in various convenient places. When the Temple was built and localized their

[9] Journet, *op. cit.,* vol. I. p. 50.
[10] *Sum. Theol.,* III, q. 61, a. 4, ad 1.

sacrifices, even the altar itself was no longer the ultimate center of their cult. For the Holy of Holies, beyond the altar, was the special place of God's Presence. Within its awesome veils the High Priest and he alone, once a year, carried the blood of the atoning victim in order to renew in Israel's name their great covenant with the unseen God.

Wrenched away from Temple and homeland and flung into exile, our spiritual ancestors started informal gatherings for prayers and for the reading and interpretation of the Law that gradually developed into their Synagogue service. This, in turn, greatly influenced our own fore-Mass. The Psalms, of course, are the greatest single carry-over from the Old Testament.

A person needs to think of this Old Testament worship and of its splendor and development in order to keep an adequate sense of worship as a living tradition. And, it is needed to appreciate the great epistle of priesthood, St. Paul to his own Hebrews, as well as the Apocalypse, especially those chapters on celestial worship: four, five, and seven. It also helps to explain why the first followers of Christ found it natural to continue "daily with one accord in the temple,"[11] as well as "breaking bread in their houses." This eucharistic "breaking bread" also grew out of the ritual Passover Supper of God's people.

Very soon, however, their "being in favor with all the people,"[12] turned into persecution both by temple and Roman authorities. This was one of the reasons why their rich background of Old Testament worship did not quickly flower into a magnificent Christian worship, as would be expected, for they had a strong sense of the resurrected Christ as the glorious fulfillment of the Old Testament; they had a vivid expectation of His triumphant final coming to judge the world, a profound awe at the living presence and action of Christ and of His Holy

[11] Acts 2:46.
[12] Acts 2:47.

Spirit in the young Church; and they felt an intense joy in acclaiming Christ their victorious Leader. On the other hand, there was also a leaning to the spiritual and to simplicity, which, can be traced to Our Lord's warning against Pharisaical ostentation.[13] Moreover, there was an early Christian aloofness towards the material, due in part perhaps to Plato, which was the dominant philosophy of the time. Finally, there was a reaction against the sense-intoxicating pageantry of pagan worship.[14]

In any case, vitally adaptive from the beginning because divinely vital, our worship made its first oblation in that first Christian church, the mother of all churches, the upper room in Jerusalem, where Christ offered the first Mass and where later He sent the Holy Spirit in the miraculous sound of wind and appearance of fire. "It was because our Lord told us to do what he had done, in memory of him, that liturgies exist."[15] All other rites have grown out of that Last Supper and have merely amplified its essentials: bread and wine prepared; the celebrant gives thanks; he takes bread, blesses it and says the words of institution; he does the same over the wine; the Sacred Bread is broken and Christ's Body and Blood are given to the people in communion. Everything else we may do is in those essentials as the oak is in the acorn, even though our way of doing it may differ as much as the towering and spreading tree differs from the little acorn.

Already in the early second century, the synagogue instruction service was added consistently to the eucharist. There were lessons read, psalms sung, a sermon, and prayers said by all stand-

13 Mt. 6:5.
14 Cf. Jungmann, *The Mass of the Roman Rite,* Vol. I, p. 26; Vol. II, p. 1.
15 Fortescue, *The Mass: a Study of the Roman Liturgy,* London, Longmans, 1926, p. 1.

ing for all kinds of people. Added also were the kiss of peace and a collection for the poor.[16]

There was some further growth of rites and prayers in the third century. But what interests us most was the combination of uniformity and fluidity about the worship of the first three centuries. The basic uniformity is due to several things. There was the constant belief of the Fathers that the essential steps of the eucharist were a tradition from Jesus and His apostles.[17] Besides, everything was said aloud and some parts were in dialogue, so there had to be enough sameness that the people would know when to respond. While many of the prayers were extemporized and therefore fluid in phrasing, they tended to uniformity because in general they asked for more or less the same things. Moreover, since the psalms and the Lord's Prayer and the eucharistic consecratory narrative set a pattern of fixed formula, it was easy to accept the trend that a prayer formula repeatedly heard in such a holy setting would come to be considered the right one.

The fluidity of detail within a more or less fixed outline was due largely to the undeveloped state both of doctrine and administration in the young Church. It was undecided at which point of the eucharistic narrative the actual transubstantiation of bread and wine into the Body and Blood of Christ really took place. That is why there was not an elevation until the end, just before the Pater Noster. Many people went to private confession only once or twice in their life.

In the eucharist itself, aside from the consecrating narrative, which invariably began with a short dialogue and closed with the Amen of the people, each celebrant combined as he thought

[16] "Union with our Lord in His glory came as strongly into the consciousness as union among themselves came visibly to the eye by means of the meal." (Jungmann, *op. cit.*, Vol. I, p. 20)

[17] Cf. Fortescue, *op. cit.*, p. 48.

best the various essential elements: praising the Father, grateful commemoration of the redemptive work of the Son, invo-
cation of the Holy Spirit upon worshippers and their oblation,
offering of the bread and wine and the breaking of the consecrated bread. The prayers of petition were extermporized
according to various needs. Even "Hippolytus (d. 235) presents his text only as a suggestion, and expressly stresses the
right freely to extemporize a text as a right which remained
long in force. . . . The free creation of a text . . . was still in
practice at Rome in 538. . . . In Spain fixed texts were the rule,
but the right to compose Mass formulas freely is still demon-
strable in the seventh century."[18]   J. Lebreton thinks that the
Liturgy of St. Hippolytus ". . . displays in more than one point
the personal impress of its author, but it was not wholly created
by him; it was a codification of a previous usage, the terminus
of a long tradition."[19]

So from the beginning of worship there was combined basic
ritual type with fluid and unstylized public prayer, the historical
with the mystical and eternal, sacramental forms with spontaneous or planned improvising, order with liberty and the
fervor of the individual with the prudence and restraint required
of a community prayer. "The 'praying Church' of the first centuries demanded from all her members and not from her ministers alone a personal life entirely ruled by the spirit of worship."[20]

Then very early began the missionary expansion of the Church.
Moving out from the great centers of Jerusalem, Antioch, Alexandria and Rome, apostles and missioners made new converts
and celebrated the holy mysteries according to forms they had

[18] Jungmann, *The Mass of the Roman Rite,* Vol. I, p. 30.
[19] Lebreton-Zeiller, *History of the Primitive Church,* New York, Macmillan, 1949, Vol. I, p. 466.
[20] Underhill, *op. cit.,* p. 242.

heard in their mother-church. This intense loyalty made for patterns of unity, though it allowed for freedom in details. Tending to uniformity also were the forces of travel, continual communication between all churches, the great reputation of certain famous bishops who were disciples of the apostles and, finally, the strong sense of unity between the churches. This missionary work and loyalty to mother-churches gave rise to the various Oriental rites.

While we follow worship as a living tradition, instinctively and rationally resourceful yet tenaciously conservative, we need not resort to the dialectic materialism of Hegel and Marx nor even depend on Toynbee's philosophy of stimulus and reaction as the meaning of history. Rather, we are much nearer the truth when we trace the running battle between the Prince of Light and the Prince of Darkness. Right from the start, the living organism that is the Mystical Christ has been guided by the Holy Spirit both to unmask the evil that threatened from natural and preternatural sources and to adjust for further growth. When persecution started in 44 A.D. the Christians broke away from the synagogue to hold their own exclusive services. Against the Gnostics and Manichaeans, St. Ephrem composed poems and hymns to instill the true Christian teaching. And against them God was acclaimed in the Creed as the Creator not only of the invisible but also of the visible, the material things. Because of the Arian denial of Christ's divinity, of His equality with the Father, "Glory be to the Father through the Son" became "Glory be to the Father and to the Son." Because of the Macedonians' denial of the divinity of the Holy Spirit, He is given full acclamation in the third section of the Creed.

Father Bugnini in his commentary on the "Simplification of the Rubrics"[21] lists further adjustments in worship. "The necessity of defending the divinity of Christ in the anti-Arian strug-

[21] Bugnini, *op. cit.,* p. 11.

gles of the fourth and fifth centuries increased the Christological elements in the liturgy: *Deum verum de Deo vero, Qui tecum vivit et regnat;* against the Pelagians: *Deus in adjutorium, Credo . . . remissionem omnium peccatorum;* against the Manichaeans: *sanctum sacrificium, immaculatam hostiam;* against Nestorius: *sancta Dei Genitrix;* against the Adoptionists: the *Credo;* against Berengarius and the Protestants of the following centuries: the whole grand development of the worship of the most holy Eucharist with the related formulas."

It is not our purpose to give a full history of worship, but only to stress its adaptive character as part of the growth of a living organism. Unfortunately, not all the adaptation was healthy growth; part of it was regression; and part of the true progress had undesirable features in it.

During the fifth and sixth centuries our worship came to a considerable maturity and was especially laudable for the extent of the active participation of the people. The language of worship was for the most part the language of the people. But already in the East fewer people completed their part in the Holy Sacrifice by receiving holy communion. This had begun in the fourth century because of the insistence upon our Lord as the majestic Judge to be served in fear and trembling. That insistence was meant to be a remedy against the Arian denial of Christ's divinity. For the same reason, ceremonies took on greater splendor and altar-railings rose between altar and people. It seems that there was also some decline in the general fervor of the people.

Moving west to Rome, we find ourselves in the dark about how the fluid Greek eucharist of Hippolytus developed into the late fourth century Latin Canon. Somehow, through all the disasters of the Empire breakdown and the invasions from the north during the fifth and sixth centuries, official worship did continue to develop. Then at the turn of the seventh century,

Pope St. Gregory the Great is credited with shaping our present Mass by making adaptations of the Gelasian Sacramentary. During the seventh century the papal stational services were stabilized by usage and finally set down in writing.

In the meantime the northern kingdoms beyond the Alps were stabilizing. In the mid-eighth century King Pepin of France decreed the acceptance of the Roman Liturgy and a few decades later Charlemagne wished it to be uniform throughout his kingdom. St. Boniface's missionary work took the Roman rite into Germany in the early eighth century. St. Augustine's apostolic work, begun in England at the turn of the seventh, flowered at the mid-eighth century into adoption of the Roman rite.[22]

As Jungmann says, "Thus the Roman liturgy acquired a new home, a hothouse for a further growth that would be determined for more than two hundred years essentially on Franco-German soil."[23] The transfer over the Alps seems to have depended largely on books. And the Roman Sacramentary dealt only with the elaborate papal stational services. We can only guess about the simplifications in the smaller churches of Rome and in the country towns. In any case, adaptations in the north were inevitable. But so great was their regard for the Roman texts that it was not for two hundred years that they dared to set down a conscious revision and expansion of the Roman liturgy.

[22] The Creed took a different route to receive adoption in the Mass by Charlemagne, with the consent of Pope Leo III. In the sixth century when the Creed was "admitted into the Mass in the Orient, it appears also in a similar employ in Spain, a portion of whose coastline was under Byzantine domination.... Various indications point to the theory that the custom came to the Irish from the Spaniards, and was by them carried to the Anglo-Saxons and so, through Alcuin, the custom reached Acchen." (Jungman, *op. cit.*, Vol. I, p. 469)

[23] *Ibid.*, Vol. I, p. 75.

The Gallican adaptations showed more the influence of the Orient than of Rome. Quite evident was the increase of the dramatic. To the one incensation at the entrance of the celebrant were added others at the beginning of the fore-Mass and at the Gospel. There were introduced the Gospel procession and the reading of the Gospel at the top of the ambo. There appeared also the poetic and later the dramatized sequences that began as fillers for the extended alleluia melodies and developed to the point where they had to be moved out into the church square and became the mystery and miracle plays. Already in the tenth century the embellishments of the Easter and Christmas Introits developed into Latin dramas.

Equally obvious was the multiplication of prayers and blessings. The private prayers of the celebrant, said in a low voice, were increased. In these the "I" and the singular dominate; and the hands are folded. At the same time confessions of guilt and unworthiness grew and grew, and then later, shrank again to our present Confiteor.

Other changes in worship reflected changes in doctrinal emphasis. The Arian denial of Christ's divinity brought the defensive stressing of His equality with the Father, prayers addressed to Him directly and more prayers addressed to the Trinity. Less was made of Christ as Mediator and of the community of the redeemed united in Christ as one Mystical Body. Instead of Mass being the memorial thanksgiving of the Mystical Christ offered up to the Father, it became in current thinking rather the great gift of God, the mystery of God descending to us at the climactic consecration. Less thought was given to the relation between the death of Christ and the sacrament and to the sacramental Body as the essential nourishment of the Mystical Body. Communions decreased. Unleavened bread came in and the offertory procession lost its meaning. At communion, instead of being placed in the hand of the person receiving, the consecrated particle was placed on the tongue. They gradually came to kneel while receiving and this brought the communion-rail. The true meaning of the Mass was often obscured by assigning allegorical meanings to everything.

A critical change was the acceptance of worship in a language that was no longer the people's native tongue. For one thing, neither the Romance languages nor the German dialects had developed into a literary language which alone would be considered fit for worship. For the same reason there was no thought of translating the Scriptures into the vernacular. "And because even amongst the laity the leaders were so impressed by things Roman that they recognized and acknowledged therein the highest culture, there was therefore no wish or demand for the use of their own language."[24] But how could they enact their part in the Mass? Among the Slavs, Scripture and liturgy were in Slavic.

Whatever else may be said of this period, the great creativeness is evidence of an intense spiritual vitality. And there was a deliberate effort to encourage active participation in worship. To the period's merit also must be gratefully cited the creation of our finest chant melodies, even though they ceased for the most part to be the songs of the people. In any case, of the Gallican additions that remain in our Roman liturgy, Fortescue for one feels that they are very welcome. "The few non-Roman elements in our Mass take nothing from its dignity and yet give it enough variety and reticent emotion to make it most beautiful."[25]

As the first unification of worship was achieved externally by polictical power under Pepin and Charlemagne, so the second unification was directly or indirectly fostered by the power of the Romano-German empire. In this second case the influ-

---

[24] *Ibid.,* Vol. I, p. 81.
[25] Fortescue, *op. cit.,* p. 184.

ence went from north, where vitality and creativeness were
intense, to south, where Rome was going through a period
of collapse. Northern liturgical books replaced those in local
southern use. But the uniformity was still only relative. "We
find throughout the later Middle Ages a great variation in all
those parts of the Mass-liturgy which were not fixed as a heritage
of the ancient sacramentaries—variation not only from country
to country but from church to church, in fact from Mass book
to Mass book."[26]

Finding too much diversity, the Franciscans adopted a new
type of Roman Mass book that included both a sanctoral cycle
and an effort at simplification. They kept the right to make
changes but carried the complete missal all over the world.
With the coming of printing, it was used throughout the whole
Latin Church and prepared the way for the reforms of Trent.
Other orders, especially the Benedictines, had their own important
part in unification.

But back in the ninth century private Masses had already
begun to multiply. The most decisive influences were the increased demand for Votive and Requiem Masses on the part
of the people and the compacts between various monasteries
to offer a definite number of Masses for deceased members.
Partly responsible also was the theological insistence that each
Mass has a special propitiatory effect. The custom of offering
Mass for a definite intention and accepting a stipend worked a
like effect. So did the private devotion of the priests themselves. The increase of clergy in the thirteenth century brought
a new increase in daily Masses. Altogether, this tendency resulted in a multiplication of Low Masses and less attention on
the feasts and mysteries of the Church Year. Altars and missals were greatly increased. And confusion in Mass practices
grew, especially about the opening and closing parts. Over-

[26] Jungmann, *op. cit.,* vol. I, p. 97.

emphasis on the effects of merely attending Mass and on the results of successive numbers of Masses within a given period verged on superstition. And there was ground for the accusations of avarice and irreverence.

The Protestant Revolt stressed these weaknesses and went to the extreme of denying that the Mass was a Sacrifice. This heresy heightened the previous emphasis on the Real Presence and greatly increased the veneration of Christ in the Blessed Sacrament.

Long before Trent, adaptations and simplifications were recommended and attempted. The Council of Trent itself legislated only against the most obvious abuses and tried to eliminate any avarice, superstition or irreverence. It left Missal and Breviary reform to the Pope. The commission of Pius V then decreed a uniform Missal for the whole Latin Rite. It was a great improvement in order and simplicity and there was again a proper doctrinal emphasis on the Mass as a Sacrifice and on receiving communion at each Mass. That more was not done must be attributed partly to the limits of historical research at the time and partly to the fact that the people were not prepared spiritually for a stronger union with the celebrating priest.

Besides denying that the Mass is a Sacrifice, the religious revolt took three other directions that brought unfortunate reactions. Just when the Romance languages were maturing into suitability for worship and when printing came into power, the "reformers" refused to accept any special priesthood and, to replace the Mass, made their religion center in vernacular Bible reading and in the use of the vernacular for prayers and hymns. The smear of association with heresy clung for a long time to the lay priesthood, bible reading and the vernacular. As an antidote, it was the Sacrifice of Christ that was proclaimed, more than the part of the Church in offering His Sacrifice; and the faithful were merely to view the veiled mystery of the Mass and to have no active part in it. There was little Scripture reading, which is so important for being at home in worship. Caution against the vernacular was at first so strong that Pope Alexander VII in 1661 condemned a translation of the Roman Missal into French and forbade any further translations under pain of excommunication.

But early in the seventeenth century the great Cardinal Berulle re-emphasized the mediatorship of Christ, linked private prayer with public and made participation in worship the basis of piety. His ideas carried on in the religious communities he founded, like the Incarnate Word; but his thinking and practices were ahead of their time and never became popular.

The seeds were sown, however, and by the end of the seventeenth century there was a mounting desire for participation. Songs and prayers in the vernacular, including the Rosary, accompanied the Mass. Finally, prayerbooks and hand missals for the faithful began to appear. The German Sung-Mass helped to increase a sense of community. Holy communion was received more frequently.

Unfortunately, too many of these attempts at improvement were smeared by association with the Enlightenment and its excessive rationalism and naturalism. They were, in fact, without full official sanction and sometimes the motives of leaders were questionable. There was inevitably a clash between the tendency to more frequent communion and the common attitude towards Mass as the great veiled mystery and the eucharist as the awesome Presence. Jansenism was one extreme resolution of the clash and the other was the unauthorized methods of participation in worship. In any case, an excessive traditionalism ruled the day. Liturgy was to be considered a finished work of art, wrought by the Holy Spirit and untouchable.

Even though Gueranger broke from some of the excesses of

"traditionalism," he still viewed the Mass too much as the veiled mystery and was little interested in lay participation. But what he did do was invaluable and we are very greatly indebted to him. The work he initiated flowered in the first mighty steps of restoration that were initiated by St. Pius X and which are now being vigorously resumed by Pius XII.

As we come out of the forests of history we realize how blessed we are to be living in this age. Jesus compared His light burden and easy yoke to what had gone before and said, "Blessed are the eyes that see what you see! For I say to you, many prophets and kings have desired to see what you see, and they have not seen it; and to hear what you hear, and they have not heard it."[27] We are blessed. But we must be wise. We have the facts of history and must take them and sit them on the knee of wisdom and make them teach us to be prudent as well as hopeful. Our worship has come to us as a living tradition born of a living Church. "All peoples, each with their special aptitudes, are her children and all bring their gifts into the sanctuary. . . . It is a great, supranational tidal wave of faith in God and love of Christ, nourished and supported by the special powers of every individual nation and of every individual man, purified and inspired by the divine spirit of truth and love."[28]

At once unchangeably divine and changeably human, our worship remains perennially vital. Seeing changes such as have not been seen for four hundred years, we must not become over-eager nor impatient. Father Bugnini records a warning on this point: "The attempt of Cardinal Quinonez (first half of the sixteenth century) to free the Church's prayer of its superstructures and give it a practical meaning and one more adapted to

[27] Lk. 10:23-24.
[28] Adam, *Spirit of Catholicism,* New York, Macmillan, 1940, p. 168.

the pastoral life, had the fault of movements in the vanguard of breaking too sharply and suddenly with tradition."[29]

Speaking of how the new criterions used in recent changes touch all sectors of worship and bring a new breath of life into them, Father Bugnini says, "We are concerned with 'restoring' —the term is exact—a city which has grown up, little by little, in nineteen centuries, with diverse elements and styles, which now needs to be freed from redundant superstructures and restored to the original harmonious, simple lines."[30] The way many people are likely to react and are in fact reacting is described by Dr. Thomas Caulfield, practicing Boston psychiatrist, in writing about the new Holy Week adaptations: "The effects of these changes in time and content of the ceremonies of Holy Week will be gradual and they will meet with resistance. The anxieties of this age are great enough so that resistance to any change is at a high level. It took courage, as well as foresight to make these restorations now. The person with the injured limb greets the removal of his cast with mixed emotions. Psychiatrists well know how vigorously most people oppose the unfamiliar, even if it means a greater potential fulfillment. All of us may pray that the goals, which the Holy Father seeks, be attained and that the living vital Church, speaking to us through the medium of its liturgical observances, move us toward a more perfect worship of God."[31]

Besides, the naturalism of our age leaves us open to several special mistakes. We could easily make too much of external changes, expect them to work like superstitious magic and forget that changing the inside of us is still our job. Emotions fix on particulars, exaggerate them and end up by substituting the particular for the whole thing. Piety becomes mathematical

[29] Bugnini, *op. cit.*, p. 14.
[30] *Ibid.*, p. 21.
[31] Caulfield, *The Pilot*, Boston, March 3, 1956.

magic and numbers of days, repetitions, etc., substitute for the designs of the eternal Father, the mediation of His Son and our personal dispositions.

Another possible outgrowth of naturalism in this age of self-analysis is that we might substitute psychological experience, an emotional elation, for a true religious experience, the mystical experience that begins with active recollection and grows into passive recollection. Understanding and active participation in worship have a helpful part in promoting true spiritual growth.

Happily, many solid improvements in Catholic life give us hope for general acceptance of what Rome is doing so ably. There is in this country an increasing number who are better informed about their faith because of an expanding school system and an expanding lay apostolate. There is increased reading of Scripture and of other spiritual books. There is a better understanding also of worship and a growing active participation. There is such vitality as to produce lay missioners working in foreign fields.

But there is yet much to be done. We are given a mighty challenge. Are we capable of forming and carrying out and passing on to future generations a worship that will not be as much criticized by them as we have criticized what has been given us? We have to build "... a new city in which the man of our age can live and feel at ease. The liturgical restoration must take place in such a way that the Church's prayer remains the prayer of the ages, holds itself above the contingencies of time and of earthly things, and speaks to the souls of today and tomorrow with the spiritual vibrancy and immediacy with which it spoke to the Christian generations that created these rites."[32] We have therefore the great responsibility of being objective and of not embodying our weaknesses in worship and thus inflicting them on future generations.

[32] Bugnini, *op. cit.*, p. 22.

In particular, we have a special obligation in loyalty to a living Church that has mothered us through the centuries. We have to make the most of what she puts into our restless hands at the moment. Taking our present forms of worship, we have to further active participation prudently until the restoration is complete. Care should be taken that Mass does not become a dialogue between the lay leader and the people instead of celebrant and the people. It is also better to use part of the Mass prayers comfortably than all of them hurriedly. We should use the vernacular wherever possible. We should cultivate devotion to the Holy Spirit to prepare for a broadening expression of His true part in worship, as Christ intended it to be.

Our concern is not a complete return to the more primitive and still undeveloped worship of the first four centuries, in spite of its simplicity and many desirable features. The present program seems to aim rather at taking the more mature worship of the fifth and sixth centuries, cleansing away "the disfiguring accumulations of the years ... saving the desirable additions of the Church's marvelous perennial fruitfulness,"[33] and building a new city of worship for our times.

Gertrude von Le Fort summarizes majestically the vitality of the Church's prayer. "Your prayers are bolder than all the mountains of thought. You build them like bridges over shoreless waters, you fly them like eagles to measureless heights. You send them out as ships into unknown seas, like great frigates into a wilderness of fog. The world shudders at your folded hands and trembles at the ardour of your kneeling."[34]

[33] St. Pius X, *Abhinc Duos Annos.*
[34] Le Fort, *Hymns to the Church,* New York, Sheed and Ward, 1942, p. 26.

Chapter Five

Worship is the Doing of What Christ Did

ALL Christian religion rests on revelation. And in our Christian worship, well over half the time we are praying the Old Testament. To this, of course, must be added the essential New Testament Sacrifice and New Testament readings. So the regulation of worship by the Mystical Christ, the Church, is simply a continuation of the detailed regulation of worship which God made for His first chosen people in Exodus, chapters 25 to 31.

But in prescribing the Mosaic ritual God worked with material that He had previously put into this world. For there was a still earlier worship which we know from Genesis, which is illuminated by St. Paul in Hebrews and which has been confirmed by modern archeological research. That was the religion which sprang from the covenant of God with Noe. It can be called a religion of nature, in the sense that God took the people just as they were in their primitive condition and revealed Himself through nature. By that covenant God bound Himself to

85

observe the laws of the seasons, to send rain and dry weather at the proper times. Thus His people would know God's personal care of them by His fidelity in giving His gifts. The sign of this covenant of nature was the rainbow.[1]

St. Paul showed that this was a beginning that grew into the ultimate Christian revelation, and not a religious fossil in the dead past. He said as much to the pagans at Lystra who were so overwhelmed by Paul and Barnabas that "the priest of the Jupiter that stood at the entrance to the city brought oxen and garlands to the gateways, and with the people would have offered sacrifice. But on hearing of this, the apostles Barnabas and Paul rushed into the crowd, tearing their clothes, and shouting, 'Men, why are you doing this? We are also mortals, human beings like you, bringing to you the good news that you should turn from these vain things to the living God who made heaven and earth and the sea and all things that are in them. In the generations that are past he let all the nations follow their own ways; and yet he did not leave himself without testimony, bestowing blessings, giving rains from heaven and fruitful seasons, filling your hearts with food and gladness.' "[2]

It was to pagans also that Paul referred when he wrote to the Romans, "Since the creation of the world his invisible attributes are clearly seen—his everlasting power also and divinity—being understood through the things that are made."[3]

But that primitive religion was corrupted into all sorts of idolatry. "They have changed the glory of the incorruptible God for an image made like to corruptible man and to birds and four-footed beasts and creeping things."[4]

But there was at least one who kept that primitive religion

[1] Gen. 9:8-12.
[2] Acts 14:12-16.
[3] Rom. 1:20.
[4] Rom. 1:23.

unspoiled. It was the priest-king of ancient Canaan, Melchisedech, who presented the offerings of the Canaanite religion as
a welcome to Abram when he arrived in the land of promise.
"Then Melchisedech, the king of Salem, brought out bread and
wine; for he was a priest of the Most High God. He blessed
Abram and said, 'Blessed be Abram by the Most High God,
creator of heaven and earth. Blessed be the Most High God,
who has delivered your enemies into your hand.' Then Abram
gave him a tenth of everything."[5]

Melchisedech lived in a primitive time when the function
of priest was exercised by the head of the family or tribe. There
was as yet no specialized priesthood as such. But Melchisedech
prefigured Christ as the sanctifying Head of His Mystical Body.
And it is part of the continuity of God's personal dealing with
men, that in our time there is a new recognition of the family
as a little Mystical Body, and of the father as the spiritual head
of the family who takes the place of Christ.

Man is the priest of all the physical world and offers worship
in its name. In this sense, Melchisedech's priesthood offered the
sacrifice of all mankind. His sacrifice could be offered anywhere.

Melchisedech was a true precursor, ready to "rejoice when
he hears the bridegroom's voice." He, the priest of the religion of nature, met and welcomed Abram, the father of a new
covenant religion. Melchisedech had the heroic virtue of a
master of the old who could yet become a disciple of the new.
He did it with a blessing upon Abram, the new agent of God.
Even Abram thus bowed to ancient greatness. "That which is less
is blessed by the superior."[6]

Then, among Abraham's great-grandsons, priesthood would
be limited to a particular tribe, the tribe of Levi. Worship was
to become more and more localized in a single place. The an-

---

[5] Gen. 14:18-20; cf. Hebr. 7:1-3.
[6] Hebr. 1:7.

cient cults of Canaan and Melchisedech were forbidden. "Destroy without fail every place on the high mountains, on the hills, and under every leafy tree where the nations you are to dispossess worship their gods."[7]

These necessary demolitions of former expressions of worship were not a substitution of something totally new for something that ceased totally to exist. It was rather a succession, a new order which fulfilled and included the old. God carried His action forward to a new stage.

Four hundred and fifty years after Abram had been blessed by Melchisedech, the Israelites came back out of Egypt to Canaan. Already in the desert Christ as God, the Word-to-be-Incarnated, was with them, sending manna that He was to use as the great figure of His own eucharistic feeding.[8] As they took over Canaan for their homeland, God directed them to borrow certain elements from ancient forms of worship and to substitute their new covenant religion for the former worship itself.

Once there had been child sacrifice. But when God sent an angel to interrupt Abraham when he was at the point of sacrificing Isaac, that was a warning that such things were to be no more. The first-born lamb was to be substituted for the first-born of the family. And ultimately the first-born lamb would prefigure the Lamb of God to be slain for the redemption of the world. The cursing of the serpent in the story of the fall was a warning against adoration of the serpent. (Only later would it become a sign of Christ lifted up on the cross.) Thus, purification of worship went on and on as a preparation first for the prescribed Tabernacle worship set down under Moses and then for the Sacrifice of Christ that would give efficacy to

[7] Deut. 12:2.
[8] Cf. I Cor. 10:1-5.

all the sacrifices offered all the way back to Adam.[9]

Although psychologically we think of past, present and future as moving backwards and forwards from ourselves at this moment, there is another and broader view, the doctrinal view of the world, the viewpoint of God looking upon human history. God's viewpoint divides human history into three parts: 1) The time of preparation for the coming of the Redeemer; 2) The great day of Salvation that began with the coming of Christ and will continue to the Final Judgment; 3) The eternity beyond time.

Once God stepped into human history He did not give man much rest. He kept man longing and looking and seeking for something beyond his immediate grasp. God would not let man settle down. He uprooted Abraham from his native land of Ur of the Chaldeans, promised him both a future homeland and a future Savior of the world and projected him forward into our own time so that we can say in the Mass, after the Consecration, "our Patriarch Abraham." God promised His people a home but He sent them down into Egypt for four hundred years and led them wandering back through the desert for more than a whole generation before He brought them into Palestine.

Even in their new home, life was a shifting battle for existence. Sometimes they won, sometimes they lost. For a long while they were away in the captivity of Babylon. And the Prophets from Moses on always kept them conscious of their utter dependence upon God and always looking forward to the future Messias. In the desert, when the Israelites complained and wanted to go back to the flesh-pots and security of Egypt, God would not let them; He insisted that they keep moving. Saul wanted to find his security in preserving the finest spoils

[9] Cf. Callan, *Epistles of St. Paul,* New York, Wagner, 1931, Vol. II, p. 416.

of his conquered enemies (Amalec); and God rejected Saul.[10]
Solomon wanted to be content with his many wives and God
rejected Solomon.[11] Psalms 33, 41, 62, 131 express this thirst
and yearning of the people for God and their coming Savior.

Then through an immaculate Virgin the Savior came into
this world. Ever since God became man all Christian worship
is Christ worshipping in and through us, His members. For all
worship involves three things:

1. A memory of the past, including all that God did to prepare for Christ's coming, and all that Christ Himself did
   to redeem us and all that He has continued to do through
   His Church.

2. Action in the present, for it is the present possession of
   Christ, God and man; it is the sacrifice of Christ and
   the giving of Himself in holy communion; and it is the
   increasingly active union with Him as God.

3. Hope in the future, for it is a journey forward to a double
   fulfillment: Christ's final day of judgment and victory
   and our final entering into everlasting glory with Him.

The *present* aspect of our Christian life can never explain
itself. It can be explained only by including also, and more im-
portantly, the past and the future. Christian life is a supernatural vitality that coalesces past, present and future into one.
Our life now is an effect of the past and an anticipation of the
future. This is true because it is the one Christ-life that we
all live. We cannot think of Christ without remembering the
wounds in His hands nor without looking forward to His
glorious second coming. Even at Christmas when there is
very great concentration on His humanity, it is still true to
say that it is not only the birth of Christ that we celebrate but

[10] I Kgs. 15.
[11] III Kgs.

also Christ Himself, the whole Christ. And we look beyond Christmas to His second coming.

And Christ came not to destroy but to fulfill: He did not destroy the covenants of Moses and Abraham any more than Abraham destroyed the covenant of Noe. Christ was another and final moving forward of God's action in redeeming the world. The influence of Christ's doctrine and personality and way of life were so great that His manner of praying and serving the Father became the basis and the ideal of Christian prayer and worship. What then was His practice of prayer? What was His teaching concerning prayer? To what extent can we do what He did?

To begin with, Jesus frequently withdrew into solitude to pray, especially before great events like the Sermon on the Mount. That was natural, because a person should normally seek the surroundings which enable him to pray most easily. Jesus was too well known to find any peace and solitude for prayer. In the shadows of Gethsemani He was perforce alone when He poured out into agonized words the inner shuddering of His human body at the morrow's devastation.

Speaking of prayer, Jesus insisted on genuine, honest prayer modestly said, a prayer that reaches out from the innermost depths of man's being and takes hold of the entire man. "When you pray, you shall not be like the hypocrites, who love to pray standing in the synagogues and at the street corners, in order that they may be seen by men. Amen I say to you, they have had their reward. But when thou prayest, go into thy room, and closing thy door, pray to thy Father in secret; and thy Father, who sees in secret, will reward thee. But in praying, do not multiply words, as the Gentiles do; for they think that by saying a great deal, they will be heard. So do not be like them; for your Father knows what you need before you ask him."[12]

[12] Mt. 6:5-8.

As for content, all His prayers begin with the word "Father." This is one reason why most of the prayers of our liturgy are addressed to the Father, through the Son.

The thoughts of His praying embrace the normal range: praise, thanksgiving, resignation, petition.

PETITIONS:

a) General: that the kingdom of God might come, that the will of the Father might be done.

b) Specific: Faith for Peter. "I have prayed for thee, that thy faith may not fail; and do thou, when once thou hast turned again, (i.e. when thou are repentant after thy fall) strengthen thy brethren."[13]

c) Glory of Father and Son: "Glorify thy Son, that thy Son may glorify thee."[14]

d) Holiness and salvation of His disciples: "Not for the world do I pray, but for those whom thou hast given me, because they are thine; and all things that are mine are thine, and thine are mine. I do not pray that thou take them out of the world, but that thou keep them from evil. Sanctify them in the truth, thy word is truth."[15]

e) Unity: "Holy Father, keep in thy name those whom thou hast given me, that they may be one even as we are. I pray . . . that all may be one, even as thou, Father, in me and I in thee; that they also may be one in us."[16]

Accepted prayer forumlae were a normal part of Our Lord's prayer. In fact, the psalms were like a missal in which the great high priest of the new covenant could read the liturgy of His passion and glorification. The way in which Christ corrected contemporary interpretation of the Psalms regarding Himself;

---

[13] Lk. 22:32.
[14] Jn. 17:1.
[15] Jn. 17:9, 10, 15, 17.
[16] Jn. 17:11, 21-22.

the way in which the devil tried to tempt Him by stressing certain passages, never doubting that Jesus applied them to Himself; and finally, the fact that Jesus chose the psalms to express His supreme sorrow, "My God, My God, why hast Thou forsaken Me?"[17] and to express His complete resignation, "Into Thy hands I commend My spirit"—[18]all these evidences show clearly enough that the psalms were, during the days of His life, Christ's own habitual prayer.

Moreover, Jesus habitually used spontaneous ritual gestures:

a) Working miracles, e.g., curing deaf-mute "And looking up to heaven, he sighed (in prayer) and said to him, 'Be thou opened.' "[19]

b) Gethsemani: He fell upon His face—admonished disciples—repeatedly returned to prayer.

c) Last Supper: Washed the disciples' feet. Institution of the eucharist: "Jesus took bread, and blessed and broke, and gave it to his disciples. And taking the cup, he gave thanks and gave it to them."[20]

There are several recorded instances of the *public personal* prayer of Jesus:

a) Cure of deaf-mute: "And looking up to heaven, he sighed (in prayer)."[21]

b) Return of the seventy-two disciples: "I praise thee, Father, Lord of heaven and earth, that thou didst hide these things from the wise and prudent, and didst reveal them to little ones."[22]

c) Raising of Lazarus: "Jesus, raising his eyes, said, 'Father, I give thee thanks that thou hast heard me. Yet

---

[17] Ps. 21.
[18] Ps. 31.
[19] Mk. 7:34.

[20] Mt. 26:26, 27.
[21] Mk. 7:34.
[22] Lk. 10:21.

I know that thou always hearest me; but because of the people who stand around, I spoke, that they may believe that thou hast sent me."[23]

d) Philip and Andrew present the Greeks: "If anyone serve me, my Father will honor him. Now my soul is troubled And what shall I say? Father, save me from this hour! No, this is why I came to this hour. Father, glorify thy name!"[24]

e) Sacerdotal prayer at Last Supper in chapter 17 of John.

In regard to *public common* prayer:

a) Jesus gave a common prayer formula in answer to a request, even though He meant it primarily as a "manner" of praying: "Our Father ... Give us ... our bread ... forgive us ... lead us."[25]

b) He encouraged public common prayer: "Where two or three are gathered together for my sake, there am I in the midst of them."[26] "If two of you shall agree on earth about anything at all for which they ask, it shall be done for them by my Father in heaven."[27]

c) At the Last Supper He participated in public common prayer: "After reciting a hymn, they went out."[28]

Jesus sent His Holy Spirit to be the Soul of the Mystical Body at prayer.

a) The Holy Spirit operates in and through the liturgy when the liturgy conserves, transmits and testifies to Christian doctrine: "When the Advocate has come, whom I will send from the Father, the Spirit of Truth who proceeds

23 Jn. 11:41.
24 Jn. 12:26-28.
25 Mt. 6:9-13.

26 Mt. 18:20.
27 Mt. 18:19.
28 Mk. 14:26.

from the Father, he will bear witness concerning me."[29]
"He will teach you all truth."[30]

b) The sacraments are to be administered in the name of
the Trinity: "Baptizing them in the name of the Father,
and of the Son, and of the Holy Spirit."[31] "Receive the
Holy Spirit; whose sins you shall forgive, they are forgiven."[32]

This prayer-aspect of Christ's life could be elaborated much
further, but it is more to our purpose to make the practical application. What Jesus did as the God-man is the central point
of all history and of all worship. His action in the Old Testament as pre-existing God, the Word-to-be-incarnated, is the one
timeless divine action that functioned also through a true human
nature in the Incarnation and that continues to function in the
present through Christ's Mystical Body.

When Jesus rendezvoused with His Apostles on that mountain
in Galilee and solemnly missioned them to convert men of all
nations to be His followers, He also assured them, "And behold, I am with you all days, even unto the consummation of
the world."[33] So the real self of the Church is Christ Himself.
The real action of the Church is always the action of Christ.
The Church is the earthly veil of divine truth and life at work
over the world. Christ is in the Church and in His members as
in His fullness; and the Church and His members are in Christ
as in their source of life. Christ is all, and we enter into life
and into power by entering into Him.

Jesus is therefore no longer limited in His apostolate by roads
or boats or the number of hours in a day. Through His Holy

[29] Jn. 15:26.
[30] Jn. 16:13.
[31] Mt. 28:19.

[32] Jn. 20:22,23.
[33] Mt. 28:20.

Spirit divinely poured out, Jesus is equally present and effective everywhere at once, across oceans and continents and across centuries. "All Christ's actions and sufferings operate instrumentally in virtue of His Godhead for the salvation of men."[34] "Just as all other things which Christ did and endured in His humanity are profitable to our salvation through the power of the Godhead, so also is Christ's Resurrection the efficient cause of ours, through the Divine power whose office it is to quicken the dead; and this power by its presence is in touch with all places and times; and such virtual contact suffices for its efficiency."[35]

That is why it is important to think of Christ's prayer-life. Everything that He did, insofar as it works to our salvation, merits for us the grace to do the same thing.

Christ's unique death did not interrupt His personal existence. Always, at every moment and in every place, He is a Person at work, a Person who loves and wants to be loved, not for His own security but for the glory of the Father and the glorification of each person who dares really to love Him in return. Every moment is touched by His eternity, every place is filled by His omnipresence and every myriad gift blends into His simplicity. As a martyr blazes like a meteor in the sudden brilliance of his burning out and in that holy brilliance reveals the long-lived heroism that preceded it, so each moment, place and gift reveals the everlasting and all-pervading glory of Christ.

That is why we can love the Church and be loyal and obedient to it with no least trace of ignoble servility. Rather, with the noble spirit of faith, we can see through its sometimes imperfect veils to the Christ who is always there as absolute truth, absolute justice and absolute goodness. It is Jesus Himself whom we see and love and obey in His Church. Our choice is the free choice of love. Our obedience is a deeply religious act, an act

---

[34] *Sum. Theol.*, III, q. 48, a. 6.
[35] *Ibid.*, q. 56, a. 1, ad 3.

of faith involving our will that prepares us for contemplation. And with divine nobility, God respects our freedom and individual gifts, works in them and through them at their connatural best and thus brings each person to his or her highest individual development and maturity. Free citizens of God's eternal city, free children in God's family, we find that in the Church our personal religious life is carefully protected against intrusion both in matters of conscience and in the multiple solid forms of piety that express our personal experience of Christ.

Moreover, by the offices of His Holy Spirit, Jesus opens our being to the influx of His being, so that His divine life and truth and grace flow directly into our souls. Hence the Christian thought: "It is Christ who evangelizes, Christ who baptizes." Jesus is the principal cause, the final source and the efficacy of everything the Church does. Men and things are only instruments. Perhaps it was to minimize human error and imperfection that Jesus took impersonal and sometimes inanimate things and made them the channels of grace in the sacraments. Jesus did not leave Himself in pictures to be gazed upon but in sacraments where we find Him by faith. In any case, this personal action of Jesus is what gives the sacraments their immediate power through the performance of the sign. When matter and form conjoin according to what Jesus instituted and intends, then its valid accomplishment causes the sacramental grace. In baptism when the water is poured upon the head of the child in the name of the Father, Son and Holy Spirit, divine life replaces sin. The Father says, "This is my beloved child." The Son says, "This is my brother. This is my sister." The Holy Spirit says, "This is my temple." That child belongs to the Trinity; it is ready for the courts of the Trinity.

Our worship, therefore, is the earthly, temporal expression of the eternal relation between Father and Son brought into the realm of time and man by the Incarnation. It is the doing,

the enacting of Christ's great work. As Christ was sent to do
the Trinity's work of redeeming men for the glory of the Trinity, so Christ sends His Mystical Body, alive with His Holy
Spirit, to continue the Trinity's work. As Christ actively con-
sented, affirmed and carried out the Trinity's will, so every
Christian must actively consent to, affirm and carry out Christ's
work, especially in worship.

Christian worship is the bringing forward of all mankind's
worship to the present moment and the enacting of what must
continue to the end of days. In instituting the eucharist under
the appearance of bread and wine, Jesus showed its continuity
with the covenant of Noe and Melchisedech. And the institution during a Passover meal showed its continuity also with the
covenant of Moses. Thus carrying out the Old Testament worship and giving reality to what had been only signs, Jesus
gathered all sacrifices into His own one Sacrifice and expressed
the longing of all worship in every religion, at all times and
places. This is important for the missionary nature of the
Church. The longing of all peoples for an adequate mediator
is fulfilled in Christ and in Him alone. And in bringing them
Christian worship we are answering their unspoken desires.

Our Lord's mission was and is, first of all, to be a priest, a
mediator to atone and plead and sanctify. When He said, "Do
this in remembrance of me,"[36] He at once initiated Christian
worship and ordained His first priests for carrying it on. "For
as often as you shall eat this bread and drink the cup, you proclaim the death of the Lord, until he comes."[37] He commanded
us to do what He had just done, i.e., to re-enact in an unbloody
manner the sacrifice of the cross. "In obedience, therefore, to
her Founder's behest, the Church prolongs the priestly mission
of Jesus Christ mainly by means of the sacred liturgy. She does

[36] Lk. 22:19.
[37] I Cor. 11:26.

this in the first place at the altar, where constantly the sacrifice of the cross is represented and, with a single difference in the manner of its offering, renewed. She does it next by means of the sacraments, those special channels through which men are made partakers in the supernatural life. She does it, finally by offering to God, all Good and Great, the daily tribute of her prayer of praise."[38]

"The Church is from the Apostles, the Apostles from Christ, Christ from God."[39] Knowing each Mass to be a coming and a passage of the Lord in His great act of mediatorship, we plead again and again in prayer after prayer of the Mass, "Through Christ our Lord." For "He, because he continues forever, has an everlasting priesthood. Therefore he is able at all times to save those who come to God through him, since he lives always to make intercession for them."[40] In each Mass we offer, in each sacrament we administer, we are doing what Christ did because He commanded us and because we so much need this worship that is the joint doing of Head and members.

As the Consecration is the climax of the Canon, so the Gospel is the climactic coming of the Lord speaking to us. "The Lord is in heaven, but He is Truth and is here with us. Listen to the Lord."[41] The Gospel is never a mere recall but always a proclamation of a present mystery, the mystery of a glorified Redeemer present and active. It is Christ the Prophet speaking and inspiring through His human agent. It is the ideal of every reader and preacher to be like John the Baptist. "The two disciples heard him speak, and they followed Jesus."[42] It is their embarrassment to be complimented for any human qual-

[38] Pius XII, *Mediator Dei,* par. 3.
[39] Tertullian, *De praescriptione,* 37.
[40] Hebr. 7:24-25.
[41] St. Augustine, *Tract. in Joan.*
[42] Jn. 1:37.

ity that attracts attention to itself and thus defeats its own purpose.

This holy presence of Christ speaking is the reason for the solemn Gospel procession of candles and incense, the standing at attention, the kissing of the book, the special melody; it is a tribute to a living Person who not only speaks through His shared priesthood but at the same time gives to well-disposed hearts the grace to receive His living word. It is like Our Lord calling and forming His Apostles. At the moment that He said, "Come and see. Follow me," He was also putting grace into the hearts of those Apostles. As Bugnini says, "The priest is only the instrument by means of which grace, that is, Christ, operates in souls."[43]

The Ordinary of the Mass embodies all the great mysteries of Christ's life and invokes their sanctifying power in the context of the climax of Calvary. The Proper of the Mass takes each mystery in particular and makes each one an instrument of Christ at work in souls. "While the sacred liturgy calls to mind the mysteries of Jesus Christ, it strives to make all believers take their part in them so that the divine Head of the Mystical Body may live in all the members with the fulness of His holiness. Let the souls of Christians be like altars on each one of which a different phase of the sacrifice, offered by the High Priest, comes to life again, as it were: pains and sorrows which wipe away and expiate sin; supplication to God which pierces heaven; dedication and even immolation of oneself made promptly, generously and earnestly; and, finally, that intimate union by which we commit ourselves and all we have to God."[44]

This is possible because we are dynamically united with Jesus and with one another in the very heart of our being. Baptism

---

[43] Bugnini, *op. cit.,* p. 23.
[44] Pius XII, *Mediator Dei,* par. 152.

at once engrafts our natural being into the divine source of activity and engrafts divine life into our natural being as divinity's instrument. This double movement both elevates us to a divine level by participation and brings Christ closer to us in human brotherhood.

What began in baptism continues in the eucharist as sacrifice and sacrament. Jesus did not leave Himself with us in a static memorial that was to be considered only for quiet adoration. Such an attitude was largely a reaction against a heresy that denied the Real Presence. Unleavened bread, in itself a thing apart from normal consumption, was also partly responsible. Jesus is to be adored in the Sacred Host. But the important prayer of the celebrant that concludes our Benediction song insists on the eucharist as a memorial of Christ's world-redeeming Passion.

Jesus promised Himself as the bread of life, meant to be the great food of life on the natural level of form and to suggest the communicate life on the supernatural level of substance. Again and again, each time with added force, Jesus said, "Eats my flesh and drinks my blood."[45] He instituted the eucharist as: "take and eat . . . take and drink . . . blood poured out." So He gave Himself to us as the broken, sacrificed, crucified Victim who in seeming defeat marvelously redeems the world, even though He is also mysteriously alive in the eucharist, as He is alive and always making intercession for us at the right hand of the Father. Happily, this dynamic aspect of the eucharist is emphasized on Good Friday by singing the Passion Psalm, Psalm 21, during the distribution of holy communion. There is no forgetting the price of divinity in wafer-form that rests so gently on the tongue. This is not to suggest that holy communion or benediction be a time of imagining the bloody horrors of Calvary. It is rather to say that we should beg for deeper

[45] Jn. 6.

faith both in the bloody cost of such convenient fragility and in the power of divinity always-in-act that it silently enfolds.

This point has been emphasized because of the human tendency to be scandalized at the cross. But there is no escaping the fact that the cross is central in everything that Christ did and in everything He continues to do through worship. "Christianity is a sacrificial religion. . . . Christian worship is unintelligible if we eliminate the tension which is inherent in it, and the unconditioned self-offering by which it is crowned."[46]

So Christ is first and last an active Leader in worship who requires our own active participation. "There is no eucharist except by means of the Word of God in Christ as it came to its fullest expression on the eve of Good Friday; the Word of God in Christ achieves the perfect sacrifice and gives us the heavenly food for divine life only because in Christ Himself, this Word finds its echo in the perfect thanksgiving of men."[47] He is a King who demands our loyal co-action. At every level of worship He exercises His leadership through His representatives. The Bishop is Christ in pontifical worship. The priest is Christ in parish and community worship. The father is Christ in family worship. The teacher is Christ in classroom worship. This adds at once to the dignity and impartiality of leaders in worship. Their human accidents and appearances are unimportant.

What matters is that Christ is actively alive and at work and that we do His work when we worship. Born out of Christ's side on the cross, the Church herself came into existence at the very focal point of Christ's redeeming crucifixion. So "the liturgy in its unity and in its perfection is to be seen as the meeting

[46] Underhill, *op. cit.*, p. 72.
[47] Bouyer, *Liturgical Piety,* Notre Dame, University of Notre Dame Press, 1955, p. 139.

of God's people called together in convocation by God's Word through the apostolic ministry, in order that the People, consciously united together, may hear God's Word itself in Christ, may adhere to that Word by means of prayer and praise amid which the Word is proclaimed, and so seal by the eucharistic sacrifice the Covenant which is accomplished by that same Word."[48]

In and through Christ, therefore, His Mystical Self, His Church perpetuates and fulfills His mission of prophet, priest and king: it teaches the end, the means, the nature and reward of His kingdom; principally, it sanctifies and gives spiritual life; it rules, unites and directs the teaching and sanctifying.

All these missions of Christ and His Church come from the Father and their fulfillment is directed to the Father. Therefore, the prayers of Christ and for the most part the prayers of His Church are addressed to the Father. Christ was the *Father's Prophet*: "The words that thou hast given me I have given to them. And they have received them, and have known of a truth that I came forth from thee, and they have believed that thou didst send me."[49] Christ was the *Father's Priest* on earth: "Thou art a priest forever according to the order of Melchisedech."[50] His sacrificial death: Christ "Humbled Himself, becoming obedient to death, even to death on a cross. Therefore God also has exalted him and has bestowed upon him the name that is above every name."[51] Christ was the *Father's ruling King* on earth: His power, "That Father dwelling in me, it is he who does the works";[52] His glory, "The glory that thou hast give me, I have given to them, that they may be one, even as we are one: I in them and thou in me";[53] the *Judge,*

---

[48] *Ibid.*, p. 29.
[49] Jn. 17:8.
[50] Ps. 109:4.

[51] Phil. 2:8-9.
[52] Jn. 14:10.
[53] Jn. 17:22-23.

"For neither does the Father judge any man, but all judgment he has given to the Son."[54]

This is the thinking and willing and doing that Christ did. This is what we continue to do at worship. It is entering into the thinking and willing and doing of the Blessed Three in a way that not even the angels of heaven can accomplish. For the Son of God did not become an angel but a human being like to ourselves. It is not angels but human beings that He made His members and empowered to do His work.

[54] Jn. 5:22.

Chapter Six

The Mass is the Heart of Worship

H E made our nature His own, that He might offer it for us and thus redeem us through what is ours. For this was the one reason of the incarnation: that the flesh which has sinned might be redeemed by itself."[1] Because it was the Trinity's will, Christ chose to redeem us by offering Himself for destruction in the crucifixion. Tortured and broken, in utter disgrace, His blood drained out upon the ground, crucified as a criminal among criminals, Christ the God-man offered the one complete and perfect sacrifice for sin. His immolation gave meaning and force and acceptability to all the sacrifices for sin offered by men of every nation. The universal sense of guilt before God need not be any longer a devastating frustration; it can become a healing sorrow for sin, because Christ by His death merited for everyone the grace to believe in Himself as the world's Redeemer and to be sorry for the right reasons.

What Jesus accomplished on Calvary in a bloody manner is continued on the altar in an unbloody manner, for the same

[1] St. Ambrose, *De Incarn.,* c. 6, no. 56.

reasons. Man's sorrow for sin and therefore his need for an atoning sacrifice is all the greater because he should have given God nothing but worship in the first place, worship expressed in sacrifice, dedication, consecration of the best within him and of the best in his possession. God put in man a deep instinct of reverence and religious worship to prompt man's reason and will and body to be faithful to the duty of sacrifice. But man has often failed in this prime duty to adore, to petition God for every need and to thank Him for gifts daily received. Christ as the one Mediator and Head of all humanity offers the one adequate sacrifice of adoration, atonement, thanksgiving and petition.

Within the framework of the Old Testament Passover meal, Christ at the Last Supper with His own Twelve, His new priestly hierarchy, instituted the continuation of His bloody sacrifice in an unbloody manner. This unbloody sacrifice became at once the central worship of His New Testament, His new covenant between God and men. In His bloody sacrifice Christ was the sole Priest and Victim. In His unbloody Sacrifice, offered first at the Last Supper and continued in every Mass, He offers Himself through the hands of men and associates men with Himself also as voluntary co-victims. All the baptized members of Christ offer the divine Victim and themselves as victims with Him. Only the ordained priests are chosen and consecrated as instruments of the miracle of transubstantiation that makes Christ present in the state of victimhood under the separated forms of bread and wine.

So the Mystical Body of Christ offers to the Father the natural Body of Christ in substance as a seal, a pledge, a witness of the offering of itself. On Calvary that was not possible, for all humanity was dead in sin, excepting those like His Mother to whom by anticipation the merits of Calvary had already been applied. Then "Christ also died once for sins, the Just for the unjust, that he might bring us to God."[2] Now, regenerated and sealed and made alive by baptism, the living portion of humanity, make one Body with Christ and offer with Him the one sacrifice for all the world of men, past, present, and future. Baptism incorporates into the one Christ and gives a share in His one priesthood; it empowers and delegates each member to a certain share in His life, His work, His dignity. At Mass the baptized exercise their inner life and power.

At the baptismal font, in the confessional and at the altar the sadness of sin is washed away. Lonely in weakness and sin, we are homesick for heaven. We crave for new life and strength, for spiritual rebirth and renewal that bring happiness. Then reborn, living for the eternal youth of heaven, we already feel something of heaven's joy. In this spirit of hope we come to the altar of God. "God giveth joy to my youth." At the foot of the altar we are about to go unto the "holy hill" of God where Calvary is made alive and rivers of life open up to flow out and cleanse and enliven the world. At every moment, somewhere in the world a priest is climbing up the altar steps to renew and proclaim again "the death of the Lord, until he comes."[3] We can go with him and enter with him into the perfect worship of the Mass. It is no longer the case, as in the Old Testament, of the High Priest going alone into the Holy of Holies to offer the blood of atonement. Not the priest alone, but all the members of Christ are invited every day to offer His one sacrifice and to partake of the one sacrificial meal.

Confident of receiving joy and new life from our protecting and sanctifying God, we can face ourselves as we are before God and men and admit what sin has done to turn this world upside down and to breed tragic disunity, sensuality and inner turmoil. All of these things we bring to the altar of God. In

[2] I Pet. 3:18.
[3] I Cor. 11:26.

the confiteor, priest to people and people to priest accuse themselves before the whole court of heaven and the jury of earth.
We are not pointing fingers. We are talking about ourselves.[4]
We need pardon from God and pardon from one another. Our
sins are seldom strictly private. They usually are an offense or
a bad example to others. They divide and antagonize. Only
through pardon and reunion with one another can we be re-
united with Christ our Victim-Head in offering Him to the
Father and in receiving Him as the one Bread of the world.

Taken alone, each of us is hopeless and helpless and useless
to attain grace or heaven. We therefore beg pardon and grace
through our Brother Christ, through our Mother Mary and
through all the saints and members of Christ. He is our new
covenant, established and confirmed anew upon the altar. At
Mass earth and heaven are united in worship and prayer. Hearing this powerful prayer, God lets His mercy shine like the sun
to warm us with forgiveness. "If your sins be as scarlet, they
shall be made as white as snow; and if they be red as crimson,
they shall be white as wool."[5] That is the song of white hope,
the "Asperges" with which we open the sung Mass on Sunday.

Having fulfilled our part of self-accusation and sorrow for
infidelity, we are sure that God will uphold His covenant with
us. "Thou wilt turn, O God, and bring us to life. And Thy
people shall rejoice in Thee." We conclude our public confession with the formal oration, "Take away from us our
iniquities," which looks back to our sins and forward to the
holy of holies into which we now enter. The altar is the holy
place on which the Body and Blood of Christ will rest and it
stands for Christ Himself. Hence the celebrant, after reunion

---

[4] Historically, of course, the prayers at the foot of the altar began as
the private prayers of the priest, and at a chanted Mass the people do
not hear the prayers at all.

[5] Is. 1:18.

through forgiveness, goes up and kisses with reverence this holy place and thus shows also the affectionate union of all of us with Christ in His sacrifice.

The Introit serves a threefold purpose. It is a song or prayer that intones the instruction service and suggests the theme of the Feast. But it also is a processional chant, a hymn to the dignity of Christ who comes to sacrifice Himself through the ministry of the celebrant. Finally, sung by a special choir, it is a hymn to the dignity of the worshipping community who join with Christ in His great oblation.

The Kyrie, although in Greek, is not a remnant of the time when the Roman Liturgy was in Greek, for that ended about the middle of the third century. Rather it was part of a litany taken over in the fifth century from the Greek liturgy. Originally it was addressed to Christ and was the song of the people, the deacon leading and the people responding. The plain litany-quality of the old Kyrie chants can still be seen in the Kyrie of the Requiem Mass. For us, it is first of all a recognition of the Persons of the Trinity as the source and sovereign of all that is. Secondly, it embodies two of the great purposes of the Mass, reparation and petition, for it is a courteous plea for forgiveness by praising the Trinity's mercy. Finally, as a litany remnant, it is also a people's prelude to the prayer of the celebrant that will sum up, in the collect, the prayer of the whole Christ.

The Gloria, like other ancient hymns, begins with a biblical phrase as a theme. It reminds us of the French proverb: the gods give the first line and the rest is up to the poet. The Gloria in the first part sings the remaining two great purposes of worship, i.e., adoration of God in His sovereign lordship and lyrical thanksgiving. It embodies the perfect love-song of every lover, for we may say with deep reverence: Thank you just for being you, O God. But the Gloria is also missionary, for it proclaims, not so much the work already completed as the plan and purpose of what is yet to be done: "May God be given glory and may men in Him find peace." Christ has done His part: "I have glorified thee on earth; I have accomplished the work that thou hast given me to do."[6] And at every Mass that consummation of His work is achieved again, for glory is given to God and to God's people, grace and peace. In the second part of the Gloria, Christ is praised for His own sake and invoked that His work may continue. Pleading for God's people, the Gloria is meant to be the song of the people.

Drawn out of ourselves by the selfless Gloria, we are summoned to the prayer of petition first by the prayer-greeting, "The Lord be with you." That summons alerts us throughout worship to an important action that is to follow. It recalls also the living presence of God in action. Having again kissed the altar in reverence and affectionate reunion with Christ, the celebrant turns with outstretched hands to pray the active presence of God upon each worshipper, to unite himself with them in Christ and to draw them together into the following prayer of the whole Christ. Their response, "And with thy spirit," is a grateful return blessing, a prayer for the celebrant's union with Christ, a prayer that in his heart he desires; it is ratified by their "Amen" at the end of the oration.

"Let us pray" is the second specific summons to official prayer. The point of the call is to invite everyone first to make their own silent petitions. Then the celebrant collects their prayers in Christ's and his own. He prays with hands upraised as a modest reverent appeal and as an image of Christ crucified. In the name of the people he addresses himself generally to the Father, with regard to His majesty as the transcendent God, but sometimes, just as respectfully, to the Son. Then he states our petition. And it is taken for granted that we are really with

6 Jn. 17:4.

him, that we really do have a petition. Otherwise there would be less force to our ratifying "Amen."

The conclusion to our formal prayer is a critical point. We pray through Christ, the Father's own Son and our Elder Brother, the one appointed Mediator between God and man. It is not merely that all created gifts, including grace, come to us through Him. And it is not merely what He is and what He did, His lovableness and merits. Our special concern is what He presently is doing, His actual mediation. "He, because he continues forever, has an everlasting priesthood. Therefore he is able at all times to save those who come to God through him, since he lives always to make intercession for them."[7] So when we say, "Through Christ," our direct approach is to Christ who stands in the Father's presence, who lives and reigns there and speaks to the Father in our name. Besides, we are united to Christ through the Holy Spirit. Through such divine bonds we are, at Mass, the whole Mystical Body of Christ at prayer; we are the whole Christ praying and we are bound to be heard. "If you ask the Father anything in my name, he will give it to you . . . ask, and you shall receive, that your joy may be full."[8]

Those present respond in the name of the whole people of God, "Amen. Let it be so." This ratification, completing the entrance rite, should include, both the general petition and the specific intentions of individuals. And this wondrous intercession is going on every hour. Around the clock somewhere in the world a priest is at the altar now inviting us, as borther and sisters of Christ, to join Him in prayer. Praying with one another and for one another, excluding no one, we have the all-embracing love, the right disposition for opening our minds and hearts to the instruction that is to follow and for entering with Christ into His sacrificial death.

[7] Hebr. 7:24-25.
[8] Jn. 16:23-24.

The Holy Spirit, Soul of Christ's Mystical Body, illumines the world through the inspired Scriptures. He gives us readings from the Old Testament because they prophesy and illustrate the New Testament. He gives us New Testament readings, not merely as primitive accounts that witness past deeds and sayings, but especially as present graces, present messages of God.[9] They are the living voice of Christ recalling us to the spiritual world we must live in and to our destiny for a heavenly home. They urge us to seek a Christian solution to our present problems, to judge all things in the light of God's revealed word. Naturally, therefore, we receive the Gospel standing, i.e., in the position of alert and reverent attention. We sign ourselves upon the forehead, lips and heart to signify that we stand ready to defend Christ's Gospel with an open mind, to speak of it with courage and, above all, to guard it with the loyalty of love. Our, "Praise be to Thee, O Christ," at the end of the reading is in part gratitude but it is also and primarily our spoken acceptance and affirmation of what we have heard —like an answer to a summons.

In between the Scripture readings are verses of affective prayer that provide a pleasing rhythm and variation in our worship. The Gradual is a lyrical meditative rejoicing over the word of God that has touched our hearts; it should be a reflection upon the thought of the Epistle in relation to the Feast of the day. The Alleluia and its verse are rather a preparation for the Gospel, an anticipation of its thought. Such an interpretation of the verse is not difficult in view of the essentially Christward direction of the psalms.

The doorway that leads from the service of instruction into the heart of worship is the Creed. This is in the singular because originally it was a profession of faith before baptism.

---

[9] Hence the procession of royal honor, with candlebearers and incense, that accompanies the singing of the Gospel in a Solemn High Mass.

And at this point of the Mass it is a healthy recall to our baptism which alone makes possible our capacity to offer the Mass through the celebrant and to take part in the love-feast. Therefore, by God's grace, we proclaim our loyal belief in the Father under the aspect of Creator, in the Son as our Redeemer-Brother and in the Holy Spirit as the Soul of Christ's Mystical Body. Throughout this profession of faith the stress is on unity, as if in answer to St. Paul's summons, "...careful to preserve the unity of the Spirit in the bond of peace: one body and one Spirit, even as you were called in one hope of your calling; one Lord, one faith, one Baptism; one God and Father of all, who is above all, and throughout all, and in us all."[10]

The Offertory begins when the celebrant turns and says, "The Lord be with you." That greeting and blessing again alerts everyone to another important step in the great action of sacrifice. When he says, "Let us pray," he is not referring immediately to the gifts to be prepared for the sacrifice but is inviting everyone to bring their needs and hopes, their joys and trials, their family and friends and enemies to be offered with the divine Victim. For the Mass is more than prayers and readings from Scripture, more than a time for Communion. Above all else it is a sacrifice, Christ offered and acceptable to God the Father.

Anything so awesome demands gradual preparation, both as a delicate courtesy to God and as a needed stimulation to better human dispositions. So the celebrant calls everyone present to offer with him and through him the host on the paten, and the wine in the chalice, the host and wine which are to become Christ our Savior. Wheat has been worked into bread, worked and stamped with man's life and personality. Many grains form one host. Grapes have been worked into wine. Many grapes form one chaliceful. Many members of Christ

10 Eph. 4:3-6.

form one Christ. All of us together offer the one sacrifice in the name of all the members of Christ, living and dead. The Mass, therefore, is the parish and community family sacrificing and praying for all.

The Offertory prayers are not so much an anticipation of the Canon as a suggestion of its main thought and action. They are a sort of pre-dedication, a provisional offering of material gifts, with an emphasis on the sacrificial gift, Christ's Body and Blood, that will issue from the heart of the Mass. The host is called "spotless" because at the consecration it will become the Body of Christ, the perfect atonement for "all faithful Christians living and dead." The commingling prayer suggests that the wine poured into the chalice stands for divinity and the water for humanity, the divine and the human that are united hypostatically in Christ and the divine that is given to our humanity by participation. Those few drops of water are so absorbed by the wine that they share the qualities of the wine. So we, in a wonderful manner created and ennobled, are still more wonderfully renewed by sharing in divinity. But our union with God is more dynamic than the placid union of wine and water. We are joined to God by being made "partakers of His divinity." Participating in God's own life, we are children of God, adopted sons and daughters, incorporated into Christ's Mystical Body and become joint-heirs with Him of eternal life. "Exult in the hope of the glory of the sons of God."[11]

Another point: the water of the Offertory represents us, not as isolated individuals, but as persons who are perfected in union with God by perfecting our union with other members of Christ. The more perfectly we unite with one another through love, the more perfectly shall we be united with our Lord. And we unite with one another both in offering Him in sacrifice and in living a sacrificial life for love of Him. That is the

[11] Rom. 5:2.

only way to "our own salvation and that of the whole world."

And these prayers of blessing upon the chalice go yet deeper and become still more precise and penetrating. They mean also this: only what we offer to God of ourselves can be transformed and made new in this sacrifice of Christ that renews the world. Only total surrender to His will is good enough, with no holding back, no unrepented sins, no sinful habits, no occasions of sin clung to, no grudges nor rebellions. What cannot be given to God must go out of our life. That is the "spirit of humility and contrite heart" that alone will make our offering sincere. That is the first step to mystical union which is meant to deepen with each Mass.

All Christian living naturally suggests the delicate operations of the Holy Spirit. So we beg Him above all to come and bless this redeeming and transforming sacrifice. "The Spirit himself gives testimony to our spirit that we are sons of God. But if we are sons, we are heirs also ... joint heirs with Christ, provided however we suffer with Him."[12]

In our time we feel as much need for repeated purification as people did in the ages when the Arian denial of Christ's divinity brought a great emphasis on the awesome majesty and holiness of Christ and on human sinfulness in His sight. Today we feel a need for cleansing for a different reason. With us it is rather due to the confusion and anxiety that have resulted from an attempt to ignore the guilt of sin and to ignore God's right to obedience and to a sacrificial worship. So the ritual washing of hands and Psalm 25 that goes with it fit our thinking very well. From the beginning, the symbolic cleansing has always been the primary meaning of the washing. The holy water font suggests the same symbolic cleansing for the people. At one time there was also a certain practical need to wash after handling the gifts of bread and wine that were brought in an

[12] Rom. 8:16-17.

Offertory procession for the sacrifice. Now the most solemn part of the Mass is about to begin and we want to cleanse ourselves for entering into the heart of worship. "Present your bodies as a sacrifice, living, holy, pleasing to God. . . . And be not conformed to this world, but transformed in newness of mind."[13]

As the former entrance procession concluded with the Collect and the Communion procession concluded with the Postcommunion prayer, so the Offertory procession concluded with the Secret. The Secret was once the only Offertory prayer and was spoken softly (hence the name, Secret) by the celebrant. Now it is preceded immediately by the prayer to the Trinity and by the invitation, "Brethren, pray" (this last is really a substitute for, "The Lord be with you" and "Let us pray"). The Secret prayer aims both to sum up the prayers of the people for various intentions and to explain the material gifts just offered. These gifts are transformed into the language of prayer. The sacrifice of the gifts is to merge into the sacrifice of Christ and the gifts stand for the mystical exchange between God and men which is to be consummated in the Canon and Communion.

The conclusion of the Secret, spoken aloud, indicates that the introductory dialogue of the Preface simply continues the preparation of the sacrificial gifts and thus forms the entrance into the great action, the great eucharistic prayer. "The Lord be with you" continues and renews the invitation to bring our offering forward to the solemn climax of transubstantiation. "Lift up your hearts" to union with Christ (suggested by lifting the hands) brings the joyous confirmation in our response, "We lift them up unto the Lord." The union with Christ at the right hand of God and our joy in such union flows naturally into gratitude, "Give thanks to the Lord our God." Gratitude predominates over adoration and petition in the Preface; and

13 Rom. 12:1-2.

this is the proper introduction to the heart of the Mass. While it is our basic religious instinct to adore and praise our Creator and Lord, it is also our special Christian vocation to recall Christ's redeeming death. "Do this in remembrance of me."[14] Such a recall must properly center in gratitude for redemption, gratitude expressed in worship before God. For the Mass is a sacrifice only as an unbloody memorial renewal of a sacrifice already consummated. So our gratitude expresses our faith in redemption. Naturally, therefore, the Preface varies with the liturgical year so as to recall the different mysteries of Christ's redeeming life.

Our thanksgiving song breaks into a song of praise for the all-holy God. The "Holy, Holy, Holy" of Isaias (6:3) and Daniel (7:10) expands to embrace the Incarnate God who at once joins heaven and earth and pours out His light and His Spirit upon all the peoples of the earth.

Thanksgiving and offering are closely linked in Christian thought. It is a thanksgiving that centers in the self-offering and self-sacrifice of Christ. Therefore, the opening prayer of the Canon proper is a plea for acceptance that resumes the thought of the Preface in a specific reference to the sacrificial gifts, "bless" being a plea for transubstantiation. And the benefits we plead for in and through Christ's sacrifice concern first of all Christ's whole Mystical Body. It is truly a "catholic" and missionary prayer that seeks stability through unity and peace in the one family of God ("adunare") under the guidance of the Holy Spirit ("regere").

As the sacrifice of the whole Christian society, the Mass is a social prayer. It gives a certain doctrinal basis for social welfare work and at the same time makes us look beyond it. We need one another, in practically everything. God made us to live and work together, to love one another and to pray for

[14] Lk. 22:19.

one another. In the Mass we pray best for each other because we pray together as members of Christ and in union with Him as our Victim-Head. The Father accepts our prayers as part of the great sacrificial mediation of His Son. "If you ask the Father anything in my name, he will give it to you."[15]

Quite naturally, then, almost from the beginning of Christianity there has been a constant desire to bring those to be remembered into the heart of the sacrifice. In the solemn moments before the Consecration, the celebrant pauses to remember the living. This is the place in which formerly a whole list of intentions were read out loud. The celebrant, therefore, has sound reason for pausing briefly at this moment. And people are slow to resent such a delay, for it is an important personal moment for them. But no sooner are personal intentions mentioned than our prayer-thoughts at once expand to embrace the needs of everyone present and their family and friends.

To sanctify our oblation still further and to make it still more acceptable, we join ourselves with the saints of heaven and beg their protection. This communion with the saints is our way of pleading with the Father and that we who offer this sacrifice are a "chosen race, a royal priesthood, a holy nation, a purchased people,"[16] whose outstanding members are already before the throne of the Father.

But very quickly in the prayer, "This oblation," we return to awareness of our sins. And we go back to the dawn of sacred history for a gesture that indicates how Jesus our Savior "bore our sins in his body upon the tree."[17] God commanded Moses, "Let Aaron (the high priest) lay both his hands upon the head of the live goat, and confess over him all the iniquities of the

---

[15] Jn. 16:23.
[16] I Pet. 2:9.
[17] I Pet. 2:24.

children of Israel."[18] We literally make the God-man our scape-goat, for He became "the propitiation for our sins: and not for ours only, but also for those of the whole world."[19] Calvary is our only hope. The Mass is the great sacrifice of atonement. Through the priest at the altar we dare, as if in desperation, to reach out our hands and put our sins upon Christ and offer Him to the Father in our place. Only Christ who was God and man could make adequate atonement for our sins; so all our sins are put upon Him. His sacrifice is our only hope of forgiveness and of reaching heaven. We accept, of course, our personal responsibility for our guilt and pledge ourselves to do all we can to atone by personal prayer and penance.

As "a purchased people," we are still "a chosen race, a royal priesthood, a holy nation." And gratitude is a mark of nobility. To bless a gift is to thank the giver. To thank is thus to offer, to sacrifice. The Mass is for us the great action of our noble estate as God's adopted sons and daughters. Through the Mass we tender God a thanksgiving worship that is absolutely unlike any other, for two reasons. First of all, only in this thanksgiving offering is there the Person of the God-man who offers Himself and is offered through His one priesthood, shared and exercised variously by the ordained and baptized. Secondly, this thanksgiving of the Mass is a divinely instituted worship of God, to be continued at His command. So our thanksgiving worship expresses also our obedience, our creaturely dependence upon God. The unique tragedy of our thanksgiving is the double tragedy of our sins put upon the all-holy Son of God and His sacrificing His life in a shameful death to atone for our sins.

In its ancient meaning, the prayer, "Which oblation," was a plea in Roman legal language that our offering be divinely exalted and spiritualized, made right for transubstantiation. For

[18] Lev. 26:21.
[19] I Jn. 2:2.

centuries we have made it simply a plea for consecration, for the miraculous change into the Body and Blood of our desperately needed Savior.

With the Consecration narrative, we approach that miracle, we enter into the heart of the sacrifice. "Giving thanks, he blessed, broke, gave. This is my Body. This is the cup of my Blood." The words of Christ at the Last Supper effect what they tell; they achieve what they say; they come to life in the telling. The Mass puts on the altar the broken Christ of Calvary, Christ in the act of sacrificing Himself to the Father. This sacramental act and state of victim is represented by His Body and Blood being apparently, though not really, separated under the differing forms of bread and wine. Yet He is there alive after the Consecration. And the only life His human body has now is glorified life. That is the mystery, a grace-giving mystery to be expounded but not solved.

Only divine power could accomplish such a wondrous thing. But God's word is enough. The Mass is a sacrament-sacrifice. A sacrament does what it signifies because God made it so to function. The sacraments are thus an entirely new world, a world of mystery that is beyond reason and that can be entered only by faith. The Mass through the separate consecration of bread and wine signifies the death of Christ, the separation of body and blood. "He is immolated, because the Calvary immolation is represented so truly, and is applied so directly, through the eucharistic Body and Blood."[20]

So the Mass is Christ actively present in sacramental immolation. We adore Him in His immolation for the sins of the world. This is Calvary made present, Calvary represented and applied, even though not in the bloody manner that brought the mockery of His enemies and ended in darkness and earth-

[20] Vonier, *Collected Works,* Westminster, Md., Newman, 1952, Vol. II, p 289.

quake. It is the same Victim and the same Offerer exercising His one priesthood through human lips and hands. But the manner is worlds part from the manner of Calvary; it is unbloody, sacramental, known by faith and very real. It is still the death of Christ which our sins have caused. It is the broken Christ adoring, loving, pleading with the Father for all of us and sealing with His Blood the New Covenant that both opens heaven for us and pledges the means to enter it.

Our Savior, therefore, instituted precisely that kind of sacrifice which is also the sacrifice of His Mystical Body. Head and members are to be united most of all in His sacramental death. He prescribed the manner of the daily immolation, commanded that it be done and empowered men with a share in His one priesthood for its consummation. So our part is far more profound than preparing the earthly gifts that become the heavenly gift of Christ's own Body and Blood. The celebrant at the altar not only consecrates in Christ's name the whole Church and especially in the name of those who are present and who offer Christ to the Father and themselves with Him through the hands of the celebrant.

Besides, just as Christ by a free act of obedience sealed the New Covenant with His Blood and became Himself our New Covenant, so we His members by our voluntary offering of ourselves as victims with Him must signify our full compliance with that Covenant, and, by our total immersion in Christ, become a part of that Covenant. God will not save us without our free cooperation. We are dedicated and sealed for the same road that our Lord traveled to resurrection and glory. "Every sacrament serves to develop in us the image of Christ according to a specified pattern which the sacramental sign indicates. Here the pattern is shown in the double formation of the eucharist; we are to be drawn into the sacrifice of our Lord on the Cross. We are to take part in His dying, and through

His dying are to merit a share in His life. . . . The sacrifice of Christ is renewed sacramentally not only in His Church but upon the Church, and is renewed daily because it is daily demanded of her (Luke 9:23). The Mass-sacrifice . . . is an epitome of Christian life and conduct."[21]

The offering prayers before the Consecration are balanced by offering prayers after the Consecration. The first of them, "Wherefore, O Lord," takes up Our Lord's command, "Do this in remembrance of me."[22] Our memorial oblation recalls especially the three central acts of our redemption: Christ's passion, resurrection and ascension. Of all God's gifts, He is the divinely supreme and summary gift who has been given to us that we might offer Him back to the Father as our own Victim-Gift. Such an all-holy gift we are unworthy to offer. So we ask in the next prayer, "Upon which vouchsafe," for a favorable acceptance. To compensate for our own unworthiness we associate ourselves with the glory of three Old Testament greats, Abel, Abraham and Melchisedech, whose sacrifices were pleasing to God. We repeat our offering by a final plea for acceptance in the prayer, "We most humbly beseech Thee." This time angels are the messengers of our worship. We have already joined with them in the Sanctus. The angels are messengers of God in the Christian order of salvation and, by patristic tradition, take part in the sacrifice that redeems us. "There was given to (the angel) much incense, that he might offer it with the prayers of all the saints upon the golden altar which is before the throne."[23] So we pray the angel to deposit our sacrifice upon the golden altar of heaven. Hence there is good reason to think of angels around each altar during Mass. In the second part of this prayer we beg the Father to intervene

[21] Jungmann, *The Mass of the Roman Rite,* Vol. I, p. 192.
[22] Lk. 22:19.
[23] Apoc. 8:3.

again and to complete the sacrifice by giving His Son as the bread of life and the outpouring of all blessings and graces. We who made the oblation have been invited from the beginning to partake of the sacrificial meal. Our hope becomes a humble petition which we put both into words and into the kissing of the altar and the sign of the cross. We then conclude our offering with an appeal to our one Mediator, "Through Christ our Lord."

The desire to have all intentions brought within the heart of the sacrifice is doubly strong in regard to the deceased, for that desire is born of the twin consciousness of their helplessness to help themselves and of their dependence upon our intercession. Besides, "The eucharist is the sacrament of the unity of the whole Church: and therefore in this sacrament, more than in the others, mention ought to be made of all that belongs to the salvation of the entire Church."[24] So our beloved departed come first in our post-Consecration intercessions. We plead the faith of those we have known and loved but we include "all that rest in Christ."

Next we bring in ourselves, once again for the sinners that we are but sinners who beg for fellowship with martyrs, apostles and all God's saints. Such daring is at once a hymn of confidence in the mercy of God who pardons our outrageous sins without any merit on our part and a glory to the powerful mediatorship of Christ our Lord.

The wording of the concluding prayers of the Canon suggests that Christ's mediatorship brings down from heaven a shower of gifts and blessings and that through Him all creation sends back to God all the honor and glory of the ages. But this beautiful hymn of praise and thanksgiving is more than a fitting conclusion to the holy sacrifice. There is a further meaning to these brief prayers. "There was formerly here a

[24] *Sum. Theol.,* III, q. 83, a. 4, ad 3.

mention of the fruits of the earth, with an enumeration of the various kinds—wheat, wine, oil, etc."[25] Hence, bearing within ourselves the perfection of the mineral, vegetable and animal kingdoms and raised to the dignity and power of being and acting in vital oneness with Christ, our Head and High Priest, we proclaim through Christ the marvelous exchange in which the Trinity gives to us all we have and in which we give back to the Trinity all we have. In this thanksgiving praise, Christ, our Head, does not stand alone before the Father, for all His redeemed are with Him in the living oneness of His life and work and prayer. Our strong and resounding, "Amen. Let it be so!" should proclaim our affirmation of this noble closing of the Canon.

The "Our Father" is meant to be a preparation for the communion rite. The first part echoes many of the thoughts of the Canon. The second part disposes us for the bread of life. Our very unworthiness even to pray such a great prayer as the "Our Father" is expressed in an introduction. But we take it up as "our" prayer because our Lord gave it to us and commanded us to pray in just such a manner. Precisely because it is a preparation for holy communion, in many places it was once normally recited by the people. Already in the Good Friday communion rite it has been restored to the people. The closing phrase, "Lead us not into temptation," expands into a longer petition for protection against all the things that might hinder our disposition for the heavenly bread ("Deliver us").

The more immediate preparation for the sacred banquet begins with the breaking of the Host. It used to be the exclusive privilege and dignity of the father of the family to break the large loaf of bread into smaller pieces and distribute them to his family and guests. It was the sign that family and guests were happily united under the father in a spirit of warmth and

[25] Duchesne, *Christian Worship*, London, SPCK, 1948, p. 182.

friendship. That could still hold wherever bread is the center of the meal. But where meat is the core of the meal it is the father who carves the bird or the roast. The idea is the same unity and love under one proper head.

In breaking the Host at Mass, the celebrant prepares the Body of Christ to be given as food at the communion banquet to which all are called. Exercising the one priesthood of Christ, he wants to unite all of us in Him. This will be done most of all through the eating of the one Bread. But we need to be prepared for it. The right preparation is unity and peace with one another in and through Christ our Head. Hence the prayer for unity and peace, "May the peace of the Lord be with you." To be at peace is to possess in security what we love. Christ is love. We possess Him indwelling in our hearts whenever we are in the state of grace. We receive Him as the bread of life to nourish and increase our sharing in His divine life. Then the celebrant drops the broken particle of the Host into the chalice. This commingling symbolizes the unifying force of the Eucharist because at one time the Pope symbolized unity through the eucharist by breaking particles of his own consecrated bread and sending them to parish priests of Rome for mingling in the chalice in their own Masses.

For the centuries during which leavened bread was consecrated for communion, there was a song to Christ as the Lamb of God which accompanied the long process of breaking the bread into particles. The song clearly addresses Christ present in the eucharist precisely as a sacrificial offering.[26] Before giving our Lord to us in Communion, the priest again holds Him up and says, "Behold the Lamb of God." The word "host" originally meant "victim." The sacred Host, containing Christ our divine Victim, is placed upon our tongue with a little sign of the

[26] Cf Jungmann, *The Mass of the Roman Rite*, Vol. II, p. 335.

cross in order to remind us of the cost of God becoming our
spiritual food.

Communion completes the sacrifice in the Christian order of
salvation, for it is a celebration of the family of God at which
we are His table guests. It is a "Partaking of the table of the
Lord."[27] To make it clear that it is His death (through separation of body and blood) that takes away the sins of the world
and gives spiritual life, Jesus said, "Unless you eat the flesh of
the Son of Man, and drink his blood, you shall not have life
in you."[28] So it is the victim Christ, Christ in the state of victimhood, mystically sacrificed and broken, whom we receive. "For
as often as you shall eat this bread and drink the cup, you proclaim the death of the Lord."[29] The mystery deepens when we
know Christ to be present in the substance of His glorified flesh.

Of the three final prayer before Communion the first is a
prayer for peace and unity. The other two beg an inner cleansing that will make us ready for the inner transformation which
Christ wants to accomplish in us. In part He wants to deepen
the quality of divine life in us. In part He wants to unite us
more deeply to one another. We receive Jesus as the victim
Savior of all men and through Him and in Him we are united
with all His members. The only soul-life we have in the one
Christ-life we all share. "Because the bread is one, we though
many, are one body, all of us who partake of the one bread."[30]

The prayers after Communion plead for the completion of
the inner unifying transformation, for the carrying out of our
Lord's command, "As I have loved you, you also love one another."[31] The invitation-blessing, "The Lord be with you,"
calls us again to unite with Christ, with His minister and with

---

[27] I Cor. 10:21.
[28] Jn. 6:54.
[29] I Cor. 11:26.

[30] I Cor. 10:17.
[31] Jn. 13:34.

one another in the action of corporate prayer. All our petitions to be inwardly changed, to be true to our love for one another and true to every duty are summed up in the official post-communion prayer. It is good to make that specific by thinking of the particular fault that most hinders the full effect of grace in us.

Finally, after another alerting of everyone with the affectionate, "The Lord be with you," and a brief petition for a further blessing, Christ imparts through His minister the blessing of Father, Son, and Holy Spirit. The Mass ends with the beautiful opening of St. John's Gospel that sums up God's whole plan of redemption. "In him was life, and the life was the light of men. . . .We saw his glory, the glory as of the only-begotten of the Father."

Chapter Seven

The Sacraments are the Channels of Life

O NE of the most heartening results of missionary work in the Orient is the faith of the Christians in the hills behind Nagasaki. When Japan was closed to the outside world those Christians kept their faith for two hundred and fifty years without ordained priests and therefore without the Mass. Thirty thousand of them welcomed the missioners when Japan was again opened to the world. Their persistent faith through generation after generation tells the power of the Sacraments, for they could baptize. They also had the sacramentals.

In the same way we are very much aware of the goodness of many Protestant people and of what Protestants have accomplished in a constructive way, even though we are equally aware of their limitations. The moral stature and achievement of their leaders is being dramatized "through various channels." The Westminster Atlas of the Bible and Dictionary of the Bible are outstanding works of useful scholarship. We pay tribute to their missionary work and to their missionary giants like Dr. Albert

Schweitzer in Africa. We are deeply indebted to the great histories of missionary work by Professor Kenneth Scott Latourette of Yale University, especially his seven volume history of the Expansion of Christianity. We can admire the very effective school system of the Lutherans and the vernacular chant of the Episcopalians. All these works are not acidents. They retained the sacrament of baptism and a large part of the Christian heritage. Among some of the Eastern Orthodox and among the Jansenists and Old Catholics there is valid ordination and therefore a valid eucharist. Besides, as Karl Adam says, "Since Christ appeared on earth and founded His Kingdom of God, there is no longer any purely natural morality, however much such a natural morality may be possible in itself. Wherever conscience is astir, wherever men are alive to God and His Holy Will, there and at the same time the grace of Christ cooperates and lays in the soul the seeds of the new supernatural life."[1]

There is also another approach to the sacramental nature of Christianity which is important in an age when we are too much inclined to judge everything by weights and measures, test tubes and atomic reactors. At present men are already finding their own frightening inadequacy precisely in trying to control a world of technology. This suggests the inadequacy of all human instruments, including the poverty of language and signs that serve for human communication. Cardinal Newman anticipated the existentialists by emphasizing the primacy of the concrete and of personal experience and by noting the imperfect, partial transposition of reality given by abstract concepts and their expression in words. Professor F. Van Steenberghen of Louvain speaks of how all knowledge is essentially personal and to that extent incommunicable. This is not an attempt to justify either nominalism nor phenomenology but only a suggestion that the

[1] Adam, *op. cit.*, p. 193.

sacraments are at once up-to-date and yet bear a similar, though vastly greater, burden of standing for the inexpressible.

It seems that from the beginning of creation God willed to enter into and sanctify the material world. He united the corporal and the spiritual in man in the closest possible union, a bond so close that man's body must have part in the supernatural elevation and sanctity of his soul. The inner beauty of grace that makes the body a holy temple remains hidden this side of heaven. If it were manifested it would be like a transfiguration, for, as St. Augustine says, "Grace is to be esteemed above all the glories of heaven and earth." In grace the body has the seed of its own future glorification and is the temple of a mystery that we can know only by faith.

That mystery deepens when we think that the divine is not only in the visible and material but actually comes to us through it. In Adam and Eve before the Fall grace was meant to be transmitted also with the natural begetting of new human beings. "God wished to treat grace as a good of the race as such, to link His supernatural fruitfulness with man's natural fruitfulness."[2] Thus in that primal state of innocence the whole universe was to be united in a most intimate and mutual dependence. It is a sign that the use of material instruments for communicating divine life had previously a higher dignity than to heal man's weakness.

But when the God-Man assumed a visible body to His divine Person and made it the instrument of His divine power He gave a whole new meaning to the material world and initiated the whole sacramental structure of Christianity. Once again, the divine was not merely to be present in the material but visible things were to be the channels for communicating divine life. Christ Himself became the first and all-embracing sacrament,

---

[2] Scheeben, *Mysteries of Christianity,* St. Louis, Herder, 1946, p. 564.

for His humanity became the instrument of sharing His divine life.

The Second Person of the Trinity revealed Himself to the visible world to an extent that no one could have imagined and at the same time entered into a union with men and the created world that was so intimate and mysterious that it had to be prepared for through many centuries and had to be revealed when it came. The Incarnation brought all men and all things into vital contact with divine holiness as the source of all consecration and holiness and life. Jesus was the visible form taken by divine love and divine life shared with men. Elements of the earth, already a corporal food, became instruments of spiritual food. Human flesh is wonderfully exalted and transfigured. In Adam it was only God's conductor of God's grace. In Christ, anointed with divinity, human flesh becomes the direct instrument of His divine Person in His supernatural, sanctifying activity.

So all that Christ was, all that He did and all that He endured have a sanctifying, divinizing effect upon men. "Since Christ's humanity is the instrument of the Godhead, therefore all Christ's actions and sufferings operate instrumentally in virtue of His Godhead for the salvation of men."[3] The central action of Christ's life was His act of dying. That action changed the world. And that action continues its power to sanctify in all the sacraments but especially in the sacrament of His death, the eucharist.[4] Christ present in His sacrament of dying, is likewise present and active in all the sacraments. His priesthood did not cease with His death. Even the Pope is not His substitute but only His vicar. And priests and faithful are His ministers.

The visible Church is the continuation of Christ's humanity and, like Him and in Him, it is also a sacrament. The Church

[3] *Sum. Theol.,* III, q. 48, a. 6.
[4] *Ibid.,* q. 73, a. 5, ad 2.

is the divine in the human, and visible form of grace. In its doctrine and morals, in its worship and in the inspiring example of its people, the Church brings Christ and His sanctifying power into action. He gives His Mystical Body a certain freedom in adopting the co-instruments of grace which we call matter and form and in specifying the conditions and dispositions for receiving these special channels of grace. And only through obedience to the Church do priests and people keep their indispensable bond with Christ and thus only are they sure that Christ acts through them.

Hence also the great reason for reverence in ceremonies that make Christ present and active in us and through us, and for the humility and holiness of life needed to celebrate the sacraments with some worthiness and dignity. It is Christ who baptizes and consecrates and forgives and heals. This is likewise the reason for the confident assurance of the prayers used in the sacraments, even those expressing human weakness and forgiveness. It is Christ speaking and acting with authority, for He knows that He will infallibly be heard. And it is the Mystical Body of Christ, the body of holiness and grace, fully actuated and making present the actions of Christ the living Sanctifier and who, therefore, will be heard.

It is a basic fact and principle that like produces like, that an agent produces an effect similar to itself. Christ acting in and through His Mystical Body produces other Christs, i.e., Christians, or preserves, restores or promotes their growth. Since the Mystical Christ is a living organism, an organism of grace, our union with it must be a living, inner union of grace forged in the depths of the soul where grace is a resplendent divine quality.

Yet the first and immediate effect of the sacraments is not grace but a prerequisite for grace which is a seal, a character. Christ does not give His merits and graces to a person unless that person has the proper right and title. The sacramental character is that title; it is an exigent of grace. In that sense, grace springs from the character. "It is only through the character that we have grace as a good to which we are fully entitled, a good that is due to us as members of Christ."[5] Grace itself, of course, ever remains more important in the order of dignity, for grace is a sharing in divine life, an entering into adopted divine sonship, an ennobling of our nature and a transformation of its activity. But in the logical order of becoming, grace is second and its production is not the essential effect. Some sacraments can be received validly even though some unworthiness in the recipient excludes grace. Christ's priesthood is not blocked nor undone because of human obstinacy and neither "are the sacramental characters, which are nothing else than certain participations of Christ's priesthood, flowing from Christ Himself."[6]

The sacramental character is an inner spiritual quality, a Christ-seal that gives a person a definite position and function in the Mystical Body and brings him into contact and union with the Redeemer who is the source of all holiness and grace. "Each of the faithful is deputed to receive, or to bestow on others, things pertaining to the worship of God. And this, properly speaking, is the purpose of the sacramental chaacter."[7]

Entering into Christ and His Church is in no sense a restriction of freedom nor a crippling of man's finest human powers. Either through a person's sponsor or directly, a person freely seeks union with Christ and, through sharing His priesthood, also freely seeks deputation to worship and to the sanctification of himself and others. And a person receives grace, the final effect of a sacrament, only by freely cooperating with all the

[5] Scheeben, *op. cit.*, p. 584.
[6] *Sum. Theol.*, III, q. 63, a. 3.
[7] *Ibid.*

required conditions of grace. Jesus, too, acts freely in each sacrament, since the grace needed for man's free cooperation is given
freely and gratuitously. In that sense, each sacrament in its full
effect is a sublime exchange of divine and human dignities.

Therefore, to enter into Christ and His Church is to expand
and develop human freedoms and powers to their fullest by a
sharing in the dignity and powers of Christ Himself. The Father is then pleased with us because He sees us as members of
His Son, somehow worthy to share in the honor paid to the
Son of God and somehow commissioned to discharge high and
sacred functions in His name. As an assurance of the special
benevolence of the Father, the sacramental character is also a
safeguard of grace. Sealed with the character of the divine Son,
we are so loved by the Father that He remains ready to give
grace back to us even when we have trifled it away. The "character is a title to grace and an exigency for grace. . . . As soon
as the obstacle is removed, grace will flow in virtue of the sacrament, without the necessity of a new rite, through the inter-
mediary of the position in the Church to which the soul has been
admitted."[8] In this revivifying, the sacramental character is an
effective instrumental cause of grace.[9]

Man perfects his faculties by exercising them; they must act
or atrophy. In the natural order God gave man the life source
of his own activity and the freedom to determine his own actions. He does the same thing in the supernatural order, through
the sacraments. The Second Person of the Trinity took humanity to Himself in order to make it His living and free instrument.
As His redeeming work began so it continues to be, an assumption and exaltation of human energy by divine power. By uniting
us to Our Lord, the sacraments engage us in His continuing

[8] Mersch, *Theology of the Mystical Body*, St. Louis, Herder, 1951,
p. 555.
[9] Cf. Parente, *op. cit.*, p. 46.

action, an action that originates in God but employs human powers for its completion. Thus the sacraments are dependent, instrumental causes of sanctifying grace. "As members of the divine-human Head we are ipso facto called to share in the activities to which He is called in His theandric character. This summons brings with it a fitness or authorization for participation in those activities, and an obligation to take part in them."[10]

The sacraments are the perfect and typical actions of Christ in His Church; and they are the model and incentive of all Christian activity. They perpetually actuate the Father's will to divinize men in Jesus and His Church. They convey the reserves of spiritual energy for work and sacrifice. But their final effect, sanctification, must still be each person's free and laborious assimilation. Each person must realize his highest personal capacities by acting and suffering with the help of the grace that God gives through the sacraments.

The Persons of the Trinity choose to glorify their own divinity and to glorify men by the corporate life of men in Christ and by the corporate action of men as Christ's members. Even the intimacies of mystical and contemplative union must rest on this social charity. Baptism is the initiation into the Christian organism, the Mystical Christ. For fallen sons and daughters of Adam it means both a death and a new life. As the waters of the Deluge and of the Red Sea destroyed some and gave new life to others, for the preservation and perpetuation of God's people, so the waters of baptism signify and effect both destruction and generation. Destroyed are the bond with Satan and his kingdom, and all attachment to his works, i.e., sins, and to his pomps, i.e., worldly and pagan allurements of every kind. The multiple exorcisms are the weapons of this battle. Every baptism is a defeat for the prince of darkness and for the evil purposes spawned by his angel's intelligence across the restless world.

[10] Scheeben, *op. cit.,* p. 585.

The most important church in the world, the favorite pilgrim church for each Christian, must be the church where he or she is baptized.

Washed in the name of the Trinity and signed upon the forehead with the sign of Christ's Cross, we are consecrated and sealed in our souls as members of Christ the Prince of Light, made alive with His divine life and, through membership in Him, made adopted sons and daughters of the Trinity. Henceforth, under the leadership of the divine Son, we are empowered and obligated to give supernatural glory to His heavenly Father. The Beatitudes indicate clearly that it will be a warfare to keep white the garments of innocence placed upon us in baptism. And we will have to guard most cautiously the light of faith, symbolized by the lighted candle, in order to keep it burning and ready to meet Christ at His judgment coming. Sharing divine life and love, we must share divine ways, season action with the salt of wisdom, and open our mouths to speak courageously, as becomes our divinely noble estate.

Besides, we have received princely anointment and share initially Christ's essential powers of teaching, governing and sanctifying. "The character of baptism is a true participation, although only initial, of the Priesthood of Christ insofar as it confers the three prerogatives of all priesthood: (1) sacerdotal being, because the character is an ontological consecration; (2) sacredotal power, because, although it is prinicpally a receptive faculty, it is also secondarily an active faculty both in the line of ascending mediation, insofar as it renders all the faithful capable of offering mediately (through the priest) the eucharistic sacrifice, and in the line of descending mediation, as it renders simple Christians suitable to administer the sacrament of matrimony; (3) the congruous exercise of the priestly power, because it demands, amplifies and defends grace."[11]

[11] Parente, *op. cit.*, p. 30.

The initial share in Christ's priesthood and in His divine life is further developed in confirmation through the imposition of hands, the anointing and the administering words. It is our own personal Pentecost. For confirmation is the sacrament of Christian maturity and fruitful activity. It is a new anointing that strengthens and deepens our membership in Christ. The character of confirmation enlarges the activity of the baptized by deputizing them to begin their apostolate of expressing, spreading and safeguarding Christian belief, worship and morals, under the direction of their legitimate pastors. This official active sharing in the Church's teaching office is the precise and distinctive effect of confirmation. Particularly, the confirmation character empowers and delegates for difficult aspects of the apostolate. Moreover, this call to sacrifice in defense of things Christian is an official introduction into the public life of the Church. Quite naturally, then, such a more dignified character demands also greater grace.[12]

This greater fullness of grace given in confirmation makes the faithful more like Christ in the fullness of His grace and thus brings to a virile and perfect maturity the supernatural organism of the inner Christ-life. Besides, the numerous meritorious works enliven and extend the inner life of the Mystical Body by enriching the treasury of the Church. And the apostolic work of the confirmed increases the number and spiritual depth of Christ's members.

The highest consecration given to men, the fullest and most perfect sharing in Christ's Priesthood and work, is given in holy orders. For this dignity, high personal competence or generous volunteering are not enough. Christ chooses His own. And the closer they come to Him in friendship and holiness, the more totally unworthy they feel of any share in Christ's Priesthood. But they are not called for their own sake. In a sense they are

---

[12] Cf. *ibid.*, pp. 57-58.

intermediaries between God and men but not because they sanctify others out of any holiness of their own, for it is Christ the one High Priest who is the one Mediator and sanctifier. And the ordained priest sanctifies, governs and teaches always in dependence upon his bishop and through the bishop upon Christ. He does not stand alone. Moreover, his priesthood reaches back to the initial baptismal character as its necessary foundation; and he remains ever both the leader and the delegated servant of the baptized people, exercising Christ's priesthood in their service when they offer the crucified Christ through his hands. And through him they receive grace. His special primary grace is self-forgetfulness. If he is not Christ he is nothing.

Holy orders is essential to worship. Its prime purpose is to provide ministers of worship. The character of holy orders is the most perfect participation in the priesthood of Christ because it confers immediate power over the body and blood of Christ, making Him present and offering Him to the Father. Having made present the physical body of Christ, the ordained priest also has direct power to teach, sanctify and govern the Mystical Body of Christ. For this highest dignity and office, the sacramental character also gives the greatest right to grace, the sanctifying grace and the many actual graces he needs to make himself into the perfect minister of Christ and co-victim.

As Christ became man to obtain salvation for us by rendering to the Father due homage and atonement for sin, so He makes Himself present in the sacrament of the eucharist to apply to us the work of redemption. This He does by renewing the sacrifice of the cross and by distributing grace through holy communion. His Body in its physical extension is and can be in one place only and that place now is heaven. In the eucharist He is present body and soul, in His divine and human natures, in a way that is so utterly unique that it must be thought of only as sacramental and nothing else. Substance is not localized and therefore the living substance of Christ's body can be in every consecrated host in the world. And since His entire substance is present in every host, He gives Himself completely to each communicant as if there were no one else in the world.

Neither bodily eyes nor any other natural way of knowing, angelic or human, can see Christ in the eucharist, for a substance cannot be seen. He is therefore essentially and necessarily invisible and unimaginable. It is no use trying to imagine the physical dimensions of His body as it was before His death or as it is now glorified in heaven. It is equally useless to reason about Him as if He were pure spirit. Present in the substance of His body, leaving the accidents of bread and wine to be sustained by divine omnipotence, Christ is in the eucharist sacramentally. He can be known there only by faith, and known with increasing intimacy only by the various means that increase faith.

But Christ is not there in a static and motionless rest. He is in the eucharist to continue the work of redemption. "As often as you shall eat this bread and drink this cup, you proclaim the death of the Lord, until he comes."[13] As His Mystical Body is always acquiring new members through baptism, so Christ is at work continually renewing and proclaiming His redeeming sacrifice, and continually feeding His members with the spiritual food of His body and blood. They need it repeatedly because temptations repeatedly threaten them "until he comes." And He does more than feed them individually; by His very feeding them He also unites them more closely in the organism of His Mystical Body. "We, though many, are one body, all of us who partake of the one bread."[14]

There is another unity created by Christ in His Church. It is the dynamic blending of two personalities in a sacramental

[13] I Cor. 11:26.
[14] I Cor. 11:17.

contract. Marriage takes the model of its unity and indissolubility from the Trinity of three Persons in one God, from the union of Creator and creature, from the hypostatic union of the divine and human natures in Christ and especially from the union of Christ and His Church. Dying upon the cross, Christ gave life to and united Himself forever to His one bride, the Church, and made her spiritually fruitful for the completion of His Mystical Body. So groom and bride by their own free will make an indissoluble contract (indissoluble by its very nature, not by any Church blessing or law) of mutual and exclusive surrender and possession, the words of the contract being the outward sign of the sacramental grace.

Marriage is a consecrated union that receives its holiness first from Christ who made it a sacrament and gives grace through it, partly from the sacramental characters in groom and bride, partly from the sanctifying and sacramental graces that groom and bride minister to one another and partly from the supernatural ends of increasing God's children and helping one another to live Christian lives for the Father's and their own eternal glory. Since the sacrament of marriage begins an enduring state of marriage, groom and bride continue from that moment to be ministers of the graces that are given them from moment to moment to live their obligations. They alone freely make the contract. And they alone can minister the sacramental graces of marriage to one another. Such a high calling demands a deep faith, mature character and most careful preparation. Husband and wife become leaders of worship, teachers, rulers and sanctifiers in the little Mystical Body that is their family.

Even the holiest of functions are embodied in sons and daughters of Adam who live out a running battle with the world, the flesh and the devil. Sometimes they lose. Yet "Jesus Christ gave himself for us that he might redeem us from all iniquity and cleanse for himself an acceptable people."[15] Both in promise and in institution Jesus closely related His Church and the sacrament of penance. From the Pope on down, Christians are uniquely blessed to have this sacrament that assures their forgiveness and restoration to God's friendship, and their deepening of that friendship. It is our glory to be the community of forgiven sinners who have been washed in the blood of the Lamb. As Christ's members, we share in His satisfactions, merits and graces. Cut off from Christ's Mystical Body, we cannot be healed by the sacrament. So the priest by the authority of Christ first absolves us from all excommunication (or interdict which does not cut off but excludes from certain sacraments) and only then from our sins.

Penance is the holiness of God mercifully active in the soul of the sinner, first giving him the grace of sorrow and honest amendment and then with confession and absolution, cleansing him from sin by the infusion of divine life. It is not a mere external agreement but an inner transformation. Even though often the change is sensibly felt, still the transformation is so great, so far beyond reason or emotion, that we must believe it. So we say in the Creed, "I believe in the remission of sins." The holiness and power of God still respects human freedom and insists that man come to absolution with true sorrow and honest resolution to change. Without that, not even the Pope can absolve a sinner. Given the valid sacrament, the penitent receives not only sanctifying grace but also sacramental and actual graces that move him to abiding sorow, to habitual self-denial, to confidence in God and unwillingness to judge anyone except himself.

As the sacramental characters have led Christ's member through life and entitled him to grace upon grace, even to restoration to grace, so those Christ-seals apply the death of Christ to

[15] Tit. 2:14.

the dangers of approaching death in each disposed member. Dying also is a Christian state, for the member dies in vital union with Christ, conformed to the dying Christ; and, united with the death of Christ, each death becomes a redeeming act. Hence Christian death is both sanctified and sanctifying. What was begun in baptism and continued through the other sacraments, especially penance, is completed in extreme unction. Where there is adequate sorrow for sin extreme unction is even an anointing for immediate entry into glory. For when the Christian receives it with all the necessary dispositions, "nothing remains in him that can prevent the soul from receiving glory at its departure from the body."[16]

With a proper Christian appreciation of the body as the God-created instrument of the soul and as the tabernacle of the Trinity, we should think of extreme unction also as an anointing of the sick and a sacrament for the healing of the body. When it is profitable for the soul God sometimes restores health to the body through this sacrament, at times with dramatic suddenness. In part it is therefore true to say that the state of serious illness is a Christian state, a state of conformity to the suffering Christ and a sanctifying state that, by the grace of the sacrament helps growth in charity, fortitude and patience. In any case, it should be administered as early and as often as real danger is present, without waiting for the last few breaths when approaching coma makes it so difficult, if not impossible, to make that perfect contrition which is so necessary for the full effects of extreme unction.

In particular, this sacrament strengthens the soul at a time when bodily weakness might weaken its defenses against the devil and morbid fears. It removes the remnants of sin, breaks attachment to the world, engenders a strong desire for union with Christ in His sufferings, death and final glory, and thus

[16] *Summa Contra Gentiles,* IV, 73.

strengthens hope and confidence. When confession is impossible, as in coma, extreme unction also forgives sins for which there is true sorrow. The complements of the sacrament are holy viaticum and the prayers for the dying; these bring heaven and earth to the bedside to safeguard and usher into eternity a consecrated member of Christ.

The theology of the sacraments is summed up in the antiphon from the Office of Corpus Christi which is used also when a priest distributes Communion outside of Mass: "O sacred banquet, wherein Christ is received, the memory of His passion is recalled, the soul is filled with grace, and there is given to us a pledge of future glory." For all the sacraments are a memory and an application of Christ's Passion and death; they are signs that effect grace in the present; and they foretell our future by giving the grace that is the pledge of our glorification.

Obviously, therefore, there is so much beyond what appears that we can know the sacraments only by faith. They are thus a good training in our approach to God. But they are also a great incentive to hope, for they constantly make present and operative the action of Christ that is the reason for all hope. Moreover, since they recall and make actively present Christ sacrificing His life for us and therefore also make present His love, they are above all a call to love God. Lastly, they empower and delegate us to love men in the practical ways of individual, family and social charity.

Hence the sacraments not only are instruments of the sanctifying, sacramental and actual graces that are the life and safeguard of our soul but they are also a school of training in the theological virtues that prepare us for the mystical and contemplative life.

Chapter Eight

Worship is Union With God

SO far the emphasis has been on the corporate nature of the official prayer of the Church, on the social exercise of that worship and on the unity and charity which must flow from its exercise.

It is time to consider the individual person in his or her direct and personal relation with God. Christianity has insisted very clearly on the importance and the particular vocation of the individual. And individual saints are the fruit and glory of Christian teaching, Christian worship, Christian life.

Everyone is destined for sanctity. It is merely a question of which degree of sanctity God has in mind for a particular person. But, as Pius XII says, "These members are alive, endowed and equipped with an intelligence and will of their own. It follows that they are strictly required to put their own lips to the fountain, imbibe and absorb for themselves the life-giving water, and rid themselves personally of anything that might hinder its nutritive effect in their souls. Emphatically, therefore, the work of redemption, which in itself is independent of our

144

will, requires a serious interior effort on our part if we are to achieve eternal salvation."[1] That is the breakdown of what St. Paul says, "But let a man first prove himself; and then let him eat of this bread and drink of the chalice."[2]

As for the means to attain sanctity, Pius XII insists further, "No conflict exists between public prayer and prayers in private, between morality and contemplation, between the ascetical life and devotion to the liturgy."[3] This is true because Christian spirituality finds in religion both the means to render God due worship and the means to perfection in love. Liturgical worship brings into magnificent exercise the theological virtues of faith, hope and charity. But to limit prayer to official corporate worship, however lofty and essential it is as a means of paying our debt to God, would be to limit all prayer to the virtue of religion. Actually, the moral virtue of religion is subordinated to the theological virtues and is a means to attain them. "No conflict exists . . . between morality and contemplation." It is through the theological virtues that we enter into mystical and contemplative union with God. It remains true, of course, that acts of liturgical worship are acts of the supernatural virtue of religion.

God put into man a deep basic need for prayer when He made man a complex creature of mind and will, imagination and feeling. The reality of man's whole being needs to accept and cooperate with all of reality: God, men and all created things. As for the devil and his kingdom, they are excluded from cooperation but not from awareness.

The almighty beginning and meaning of all things is God. Since man depends upon God, owes Him total obedience and is perfected by a heaven-bent union with God, it is a perversion

[1] *Mediator Dei,* par. 31.
[2] I Cor. 11:28.
[3] *Mediator Dei,* par. 36.

of man's natural being to try to trim God down to the size of man's own imagined security and satisfaction or to try to manipulate God into serving man's false ego-ideal or a false perfectionism. God refuses to be anybody's sentimental "Honey" or anybody's petty accountant.

Union with God is always on God's terms and on the terms that God has put into man's very nature. Therefore what man has done by sin that, by God's help, man must undo by asceticism and worship. That is where liturgy and meditation first meet: on the grounds where they prepare for one another.

Meditation leads us to see the need of subjecting the flesh to the spirit, since God has made the spirit to be man's master; and it is in the spirit that God comes and dwells. Through the spirit the flesh becomes the tabernacle of the Trinity. Through meditation we become aware of spiritual dangers and awaken the desire of self-discipline and virtue. Meditations issue in definite resolutions: there must be self-denial; and such a practice will be its shape today. Through the self-mastery gained by self-denial, the spirit is purified and set free and prepared to sweep man's whole being into the glory of worship.

Liturgy in turn increases the profit from meditation by providing a certain asceticism in the very activity of worship. Liturgy exercises us, trains us, in subjecting the flesh to the spirit and the spirit to God. Corporately, together as the Mystical Christ in the sublime activity of mediation, we must say and do certain specified things at certain specified times in certain specified ways, regardless of our personal inclinations at the moment. Often we must kneel or stand, sometimes prostrate, and always corporately submit to others and cooperate with others. We must speak, sing or keep silent as the service requires. We must sing as directed by the text and melody, and with the perfection of timing, rhythm and dynamics called for by the director who exercises Christ's authority over music's direct part in worship.

The posture and gesture of ritual train the body to speak the soul's conformity to its Maker.

Through and through, our corporate worship is an exercise in supernaturalism, in seeing things God's way and in doing things God's way. It is the antidote to naturalism, to doing things according to natural likes and dislikes. But it should not be looked upon as an ascetic discipline, to be endured resignedly. It is dominantly a joyous celebration of all that has already been accomplished for the redemption of man and a glorious expectation of Christ's final victory and of our entering into eternal peace. It is the "good news" of the Father's love for us.

But in its own way the asceticism involved in worship can serve as a model for all mortification, for it is never morbidly introspective nor morbidly motivated. The discipline of the body is always secondary, taken in stride quite naturally as the normal accompaniment of duty. There is the proper motivation of sorrow for sin which runs through the liturgy. And all the while full attention is on seeking union with God, on seeking His glory and on entering into glory with Him.

Going a step farther into the relation of liturgy and mental prayer, it can be said that in practice they intermingle. Where if not in worship would there be thoughts of God, affections and resolutions? When the Pater or Credo are said silently, when Scripture passages are read, when parts of the sung Mass or verses in the psalms are alternated, during these times silent mental prayer alternates with recited or chanted prayer.

By the monastic rule of St. Benedict, the psalms were to be recited slowly in order to allow silent prayer to accompany them. That is one reason why he set aside no special time for mental prayer. The other reason is that he meant the "lectio divina" to be meditative reading. The current tendency to efficiency, always praiseworthy in its own measure, by concentrated attention to scheduled and particularized activities seems to require special times for mental prayer even in monastic communities.

Since the ways, or methods, of mental prayer normally vary with spiritual progress, they need to be considered step by step in relation to worship. They are found to be present in, and not antagonistic to, the liturgy. Let it be taken for granted that the steps are seldom if ever clearly marked off and that elements of one stage may appear in another stage.

Accepting traditional terminology and pleading for latitude in the use of the word, "traditional," we naturally begin with discursive prayer. Its usual divisions are: preliminary dispositions, body and application. Clearly, the invitatory, the introit, the versicles and responses, while having other purposes also, do serve to alert us to the presence of God and to the action or prayer at hand. The confiteor, the hymns, the "come to our assistance" surely aim to dispose the faculties for prayer. As for the body of the meditation, the homilies of Mass and office and the Scripture passages provide ample considerations. The psalms and versicles are dominantly affective prayer, very well suited to stimulate spontaneous colloquy or, in times of dryness, to provide almost the only kind of colloquy that is possible. The homilies of Mass and office as well as the orations contain particular applications and flow easily into still more personalized needs. For thanksgiving there are the noble "We praise Thee, O God," "Glory to God in the highest," and "Glory be to the Father, etc."

With spiritual growth there is an increased thinking of what is beyond our immediate personal sorrows and joys. The sufferings of Christ Himself and of His members, the sadness and boredom of sinners, the spiritual emptiness and distress of those who know Him not become more and more our personal concern. The glory of Christ victorious in His own resurrected

body and victorious in each baptized and faithful member becomes our personal joy.

Bringing this enlarged vision and widened sensibilities to a
vital, active participation in worship, we find the psalms a ready
expression of our Christ-centered affections. And they in turn
deepen and sustain those affections for persons who are approaching a facility in affective prayer or are already at home in it.
Hymns, chants, ritual and beauty of vestments and lights and
decorations, tastefully done, help in the same direction. An
abiding sorrow for sin also finds its outlet and deepening.

Thus every need of affective prayer is touched to expression
even within each service. And as the year of worship unfolds
there is special emphasis on one or the other particular affection.
Advent emphasizes a feeling of happy expectancy both for the
relived first coming of the Savior and for His final triumphant
coming at the world's end. Christmas is a joyous resting in
the possession of a Redeemer and the anticipation of eternal
possession of Him. Epiphany awakens the desire to manifest
Him to the world, the pagan world abroad and the immediate
world of friends, neighborhood and community. Lent stresses
loyalty to Christ in His warfare against Satan and sorrow for
our disloyalty. Passiontide takes us into the depths of compassion
for our suffering Savior. Easter brings us to the heights of Resurrection joy and hope and peace. Pentecost urges apostolic desire
and action.

Within each service and through the range of affections
touched and stirred by the year's worship there is a variety of
prayers to express a variety of affections. There are hymns,
doxologies, acclamations, versicles, responses, and antiphons.
And the psalms embrace the full range of affections.

Then as affective prayer grows, it tends to simplify and, according to God's design and gifts of grace, to be generally content with one or the other particular affection. If and when that

happens a person is more likely to be satisfied with one or other psalm verse, hymn verse, antiphon, thought from a lesson, a brief responsory, versicle, perhaps an alleluia. Such brief texts are enough to sustain a person in the affective state.

Before there is any thought given to the next step, which is progress into contemplative prayer and the harmonizing of liturgy and contemplation, it would be well to think of how liturgy and mental prayer nourish and guide one another.

From mental prayer that flows into action comes the wealth of thought, the increasing fervor and the practical resolutions that can make for a more perfect participation in worship. Mental prayer promotes an increasing reverence towards all things sacred as well as a growing thought of God at all times. Mental prayer examines the motives of worship, its interior quality, its sincerity, its fruit in our lives. Thus it is a check against mere external performance of ceremony and prayer and song which is really a kind of materialism in action, a practical nominalism.

On the other hand, worship feeds mental prayer with an abundance of dramatized doctrine. The celebration of each mystery of Jesus, of His Mother and of the saints, with the Scripture readings centering the instruction service, brings into prayer-action the Old and New Testaments. This prayer-action is an exercise in and therefore a facilitating of thoughts and attitudes, affections and resolutions about our relations with God. Thus our desires for union with God and our zeal to implant Him in the minds and hearts of everyone become stirred and intensified. And our sense of union with all men is deepened, for they are one with us either in physical presence and cooperation or by the love and desire that bring them into our petitions. And need we say that any petitions we may have in mental prayer are more certain of a hearing when they are brought into worship and made one with our God-Man Victim?

Worship, therefore, helps to keep mental prayer—its considerations, affections and resolutions—within the safeguards of God's revealed word and the tradition of His Church. Thus steeped in Scripture and tradition, mental prayer is less likely to go off on sentimental tangents. It is not an accident that authors who live the liturgy write spiritual books that are safe and consistent. Fed upon such books, a person's spiritual life is more solidly consistent and unified. The essential cross will be carried in union with the mediating Christ.

Since we have put down so many ways in which liturgy and mental prayer blend, it might be in place to introject some of the ways in which they differ. Mental prayer can take place anywhere, even though normally we seek the corporal Presence of Christ in the eucharist as most conductive to union with Him. Besides, mental prayer is an inner activity of the soul; it is momentary in the sense of occupying itself with frequently changing material for thoughts, affections and resolutions; it is necessarily individual and personalized (within the bounds of reason and faith, of course) in its thoughts, affections, desires and resolutions.

By contrast, worship, being corporate and shared, is internal in origin but external in expression. It speaks in set prayers, attitudes, gestures, ceremonies. It is normally within special designated places. Its thoughts, affections, resolutions are common to all. It is permanent: hallowed and sanctioned by long and holy use. It is governed by the laws of the Church which are administered by the bishop.

To resume now the delicate, mysterious and unpredictable ways of progress into contemplative prayer, we may begin by saying that the succession of psalms, lessons, prayers, and rites are not meant to be hindrances to contemplation. They would be hindrances only for those who forget that they are prayer and either plough through them regretfully as ascetic exercises

or rest in their exterior beauty. But no art or poetry or ceremonies can ever satisfy the desire for union with God. The
elements of worship are not meant to be a mere succession of
thoughts and pictures and petitions, like discursive prayer. They
are most of all instruments for the worship of God and mediation for men. And when that worship and mediation become, by the gift of God, an inner experience of God, then
are blended the double celebration of the world-wide redemptive mystery and of a personal mystery. The mysteries of
Christ's life are then more than doctrine that is beyond understanding; they are the power of Christ that cannot be limited
to time or space and reach inexhaustibly across the centuries
from the historical moment of each event to the moment of
each person's experience of His power and presence and Person.
In that experience the succession of prayers and readings and
rites sustain a person in the various states of union which color,
dominate, and integrate everything else.

If there be any doubt about the normal blending of worship
and contemplative experience, surely it must vanish in acceptance
of the fact that the psalms were the prayerbook of Our Lord
and of Our Lady. Mary's profound experience of the Incarnation burst into the blended psalm and Old Testament thoughts
that make her "Magnificat." Christ on the cross, in the moment
of most intense human desolation, found the psalms His natural
expression.

In the prayer of recollection, or active contemplation, the
prayers of the liturgy are an excellent way of sustaining the soul
in a unified attention, a simple regard upon some thought or
affection that becomes the experience of God in this threshold
state.

In the prayer of quiet, or passive contemplation, one simple
verse of a psalm, a mere fragment or phrase, a single word can
be God's instrument for infusing intimate rest in Him. Psalmody

and song become a clear and steady refreshment for the soul in its quietude.

When the prayer of union is the soul's spiritual estate, God's revealed word in the liturgy strikes deeply and powerfully into the very substance of the soul. Consciousness of the Holy Spirit at work, already noticeable in active contemplation, becomes so intensified that the saint feels himself or herself to be at once the very voice of the Holy Spirit stirring Christ's Mystical Body and the voice of the whole Christ loving and praising the Father. As St. Teresa of Avila indicates in her "Conceptions of Divine Love," the mystics emerge from these experiences with deepened insights into the meaning of the texts of the liturgy. Others speak of the resulting intensified love for God and men. It is this experience also which has had such a violent impact upon the physical side of the saints. St. Ignatius and St. Joseph Cupertino were embarassed by the mystical phenomena that came upon them while saying the divine office. St. Philip Neri often found it difficult to finish a Mass and sometimes prolonged it for several hours. St. John of the Cross was once so beside himself as to leave the altar immediately after Holy Communion. St. Teresa of Avila had ecstasies during Mass.

The transforming union, or spiritual marriage, finds the liturgy a loving and untroubled conversation of bride and bridegroom. Now more permanently and more intimately than before, the voices of Christ and of the Church and of the soul in its mystical marriage blend in perfect harmony.

During the dark night of the senses that precedes the prayer of quiet and during the dark night of the spirit that precedes the transforming union the words of the liturgy often bring moments of respite to those in the fires of purification. In the night of the spirit they become gleams of light that pierce a terrible darkness and stir deep desire, joy and peace. No other prayer seems to have such power to plunge the saints into the depths of divine union. It should perhaps be added that the mystical phenomena such as ecstacy, visions, suspension of the senses, etc., are largely limited to one of the higher states of union and even there they are variable, intermittent and accidental. For mysticism is essentially an intuitive, immediate experience of God and therefore in its essence independent of the senses. By contrast, worship uses material instruments of grace: sacrifice, sacrament and sacramental. These require the activity of the senses, for through them the soul itself is touched and transformed by grace. But once sufficiently stirred to activity, the mind and will may continue their union with God, unmindful of the senses, and thus mystical experience is framed in liturgy.

In spite of the sound reasons for such a blending, some persons still find it difficult to harmonize the two ways of praying. In part it may be a matter of temperament. A person may be naturally reflective and retiring, with delicate sensitive perceptions and reactions, perhaps even a little timid. For such persons, sociability and group effort of any sort do not come easily. Then there is the individualism that is all too common a plague on fallen man and may be aggravated by a particular environment. Both these things can be unconsciously transferred to prayer and cause a reluctance towards corporate, external worship.

A further complication may come when a person grows spiritually to the point where there is an increased desire for silence and solitude. With that desire, God often gives great peace and makes silent prayer easy. Just because God seems so much closer than ever before and can be found so easily in silence and solitude, there is the danger that a person may want to rest in such a state, so that the good becomes the enemy of the better. Again the result is an understandable reluctance to surrender oneself to what God may wish to say or do through the liturgy. Such participation in externals may even seem like a neglect

of special graces, or perhaps at most a specialty for certain people but not something for just everybody. And when a retiring
temperament is combined with such a desire for silence and
solitude, the block set up in the mind against seeking God in
corporate worship may require some very persuasive spiritual
direction.

For such people, especially, it should be suggested that it is
neither necessary nor desirable to follow all the individual prayers
of the Mass. Thoughts are often repeated throughout many
different prayers. One of the offertory prayers, one of the intercessions of the canon, one of the offering prayers of the canon
can embrace the rest and occupy anyone profitably.

But it should be said, also, that anyone can be deceived by
that self-favoritism which wants to follow natural impulse and
inclination. Anyone can be deceived by the devil appearing as
an angel of light. As an antidote to deception it is most helpful
to keep in touch with truth and reality through union with the
worshipping Christ, with fellow worshippers and with one's
whole person, by entering, body and soul, into full active participation in worship. In that full truth and active reality God will
speak in His own time and measure.

Without doubt, the liturgy is the primary and indispensable
source of grace and therefore remains the root of all union with
God. The liturgy is Christ-centered, Christ actively mediating,
instructing, cleansing and sanctifying. To neglect the primary
and ordinary means of union with God is hardly the way to
court the intimacies of His friendship. The saints of God as a
matter of fact have shown an essential understanding and love
of corporate worship. The saintly Fathers of the Church thought
of liturgy and contemplation as spontaneously blending, both
expressing man's basic need for God and at the same time helping to fill that need. St. Teresa of Avila wrote: "I knew quite
well that in matters of faith no one would ever find me trans-

gressing even the smallest ceremony of the Church, and that for the Church or for any truth of Holy Scripture I would undertake to die a thousand deaths."[4] And Venerable Ana de Jesus said of her: "She (Saint Teresa) wanted us to participate always in the celebration of the Mass and sought out ways by which we could do this every day, even if it were in the same tone in which we recited the Hours. . . . And if now and then this was impossible it grieved her that we were deprived of that good. Moreover, when the Mass was sung, nothing prevented her from taking part, even though she had just received Holy Communion or was deeply recollected."[5]

The solicitude of St. Teresa of Avila may well have been prompted by a proper understanding of the way official worship functions. Given God's promise and the sacrifice and command of His Son, God has obliged Himself to answer the official mediation of His Church and to infuse grace into properly disposed hearts. It is His Son speaking and He cannot, as it were, say no. The powers of Christ exercised in official worship are in that sense irresistible. The divine life is channeled to open hearts according to the will of God's worshipping Church. To be united with such confident power is well worth the thousand deaths of a saint.

The mystical experience of God, on the other hand, is always God's free gift. The Holy Spirit breathes freely when and where He wills, independently of any act or condition on the part of God's Church. Nothing obliges the action of God.

But liturgy is not less a love feast because it is God's commitment to hear our prayer. The ardor of the mystic finds full and repeated expression in the texts of worship and, in turn, is deeply moved by them. When St. Teresa of Avila wrote of the Latin text of the "Canticle of Canticles" she certainly was speaking

[4] *Autobiography of St. Teresa,* ed Peers, 33:226, I.
[5] Ribera, *Vida de santa Teresa de Jesus,* Barcelona, 1908, p. 633.

of a liturgical reading or prayer. "The Lord, for some years now, has given me a great grace each time that I heard or read a few words of the Song of Solomon, so that without understanding clearly what the Latin words mean in Spanish, this recollects and moves my soul much more than the most devout books that I understand, and this happens very often."[6]

In worship we do more than celebrate the love of God shown to us through the long preparation for the redeeming Christ, through the Incarnation, life, death and resurrection of Christ and through all He has done through the ages in the Mystical Christ. In fact, so blessedly childlike, so gravely naïve is our worship at heart, that we celebrate also our anticipation of nothing less than an inexhaustible communication of divine life and gifts until the crowning of all comes in Christ's final triumph and our entry with Him into eternal peace. In other words, we celebrate not only love but also boundless faith and unshakeable hope, the faith, hope and love that are indispensable to mystical and contemplative union with God.

Worshipper and mystic alike share this restless urge to progress towards the better and higher. Love cannot rest until it rests in total possession of the divine Beloved. An immediate expression of this drive is the need of purification. That need of worshipper and aspirant to sanctity finds an instrument in exorcisms, confiteors, many washings and countless prayers of the liturgy. The Secret of the second Sunday of Advent is a summary expression: "May these holy Mysteries, O Lord, cleanse us by their powerful efficacy, and enable us to come with greater purity to Him who is their foundation." Thus the liturgy both motivates and channels grace for that active interior and exterior mortification which prepares, God willing, for the passive states of union and for passive purifications.

---

[6] *Autobiography, Peers, I.*

"While the sacred liturgy calls to mind the mysteries of Jesus Christ, it strives to make all believers take their part in them so that the divine Head of the Mystical Body may live in all the members with the fulness of His holiness."[7] Thus perfect union of love with God is ultimately the aim of liturgy and actively disposes a person for it. Mystical experience in itself remains necessarily a free gift of God, always individualized and passively received. In this sense mysticism goes beyond liturgy. But while passive mystical experience is not essential to sanctity, the experience of worship is everybody's ordinary way to God and to sanctity. If God so wills, and St. Teresa of Avila cites such persons, a person may become a mystic and a saint without receiving any gifts of passive contemplation.

It may be noted, finally, that in every age man's pursuit of spiritual growth and sanctity takes on a special emphasis. God sent St. Francis of Assisi to live and preach poverty and penance in an age given to the pursuit of wealth and pomp. He sent the Little Flower to live and to teach simplicity in a time of rationalism and of the dawning complexities of an age of technology. In our time it may well be that lay people, intimately in touch with current needs and hungering for an approach to God that will suit their busy lives in the world, will work out the special direction of spiritual growth needed for the late twentieth century. For whatever it is worth, all the lay movements of today seek in the liturgy their way to God. This is to be expected, since liturgy touches with ease every corner and activity of life in the world. Every day seems to see the development of new ways, often suggested by lay people themselves, of carrying worship into the home and using it there to teach and to live an habitual awareness of God as a loving and all-competent Father. God is evidently forming the homes of saints.

---

[7] *Mediator Dei,* par. 152.

Chapter Nine

Worship is Union with Men in Christ

OUR first vocation as creatures is to worship our Creator. Any particular work we do in any particular place is a secondary vocation and a means of carrying out our primary vocation to worship. Essentially dependent upon God, we feel a necessary subjection to God and a need to express it in worship. A beautiful expression of all creation's duty is the Benedicite Canticle from the third chapter of Daniel. Through that Canticle we urge every sort of creature to sing its hymn to God through the words of miraculously preserved young men. Even the flames about them did not move them to exclude fire and heat as instruments of praise and thanksgiving.

Every creature entering into worship participates in the very life of the Blessed Trinity. The existence of the Eternal Three is an infinitely active life. It is not a static, languid, passive floating in space. The life of the Trinity is an eternally active relationship between three Divine Persons in which the praise of infinite goodness is sung by infinite goodness. It is the in-

timacy of love in which the three Divine Persons are so insepa-
rably one that they have one and the same nature and subsist
only in relation to each other. There can be no Father without
His being related to the Son. There can be no Son without His
being related to the Father. There can be neither Father nor
Son without their pouring themselves out in a Person, a Spirit of
Love. And there can be no Holy Spirit except as proceeding from
the Father and the Son. Each Person's existence is love, a going-
out-to, a relation to the others. Therefore, "God is love."[1]

Creation is a finite extension in time of the life of love and
praise that goes on forever in the Blessed Trinity. New only to
the creature, it is for the creature an entering into something that
has been going on for all eternity. All inanimate creatures, all
animate and vegetable beings, all animals, caught up into the
service of divinity, by physical and chemical law or by instinct
fulfill their duties of service and praise. Each stone and metal
and cloud, each flower and tree and nourishing grain, each bird
and fish and furbearing animal does God's work and sings His
praise in its own order and beauty and power. "All things, by
desiring their own perfection, desire God Himself."[2]

But God was not sufficiently glorified by the mineral and
vegetable and animal kingdoms. So He created man to His
own image and likeness, free to know, free to choose and free
to love like Himself. Unfortunately, after a brief song of fidelity, man chose the smashing disobedience of Eden. And ever
since that fall, man has continued often to choose, by the awful
power of his free will, to be an unfaithful creature, a disloyal
leader of creation's service and praise. He has chosen lesser
goods than God. He has turned persons and things away from
God to his own service and praise. By so doing he has violated
both the rights of God and the rights and nature of man and

---

[1] I Jn. 4:8.
[2] *Sum, Theol.,* I, q. 6, a. 1, ad 2.

things. Man alone has interrupted the eternal canticle of creation.

But there is no point to pitying ourselves or to moaning for a lost paradise. There is no point to stressing, to the detriment of hope, the havoc of sin. Sorrow for sin is not despair but the fruit of hope and the beginning of confidence. It is not the fall that matters; it is the lifting up. It is not the collapse but the restoration that should occupy us. God indeed most wonderfully created this world but He still more wonderfully restored it.[3] We have to say, of course, that it is a more difficult world that we now live in; but it is also an infinitely more wonderful world. We have lost much but we have gained even more. On the one hand, we have taken on intensified temptation and pain and death; but, on the other, through them we are fashioned in likeness to that grace-bestowing mystery, the God-Man, Christ Jesus; and in union with Him, temptation and pain and death become a way of helping Him to redeem the world and build the mansions of heaven. "I am come that they may have life, and have it more abundantly."[4]

Our more abundant life, our more wonderfully restored world that elevates and enriches everything beyond what it was before, began in the order of time with Our Lady, the immaculately conceived, the divinely adorned and enriched, the new paradise of the Incarnation, the mediatrix (dependent upon Christ) of all graces.

And in the order of prime importance there is the Incarnation in which God became one of us and lifted the whole human race to a capacity for divinity.

There is our brotherhood in Christ, our membership in His Mystical Body, our adopted sonship and daughtership in the Trinity through Christ. Our union with and in Him is so marvelously intimate that we are one man with Him.

[3] *Missale Romanum,* Offertory prayer.
[4] Jn. 10:10.

There is the Mass, our infinite Sacrifice, our all-sufficient prayer-medium of infinite adoration, atonement, thanksgiving and petition.

There are the sacraments which channel the divine life into our secret being. And there are the rich sharings in the priesthood of Christ through baptism, confirmation and holy orders.

Therefore, through and with and in Our Lord, by His life and power, we are now by God's mercy more capable than ever before of rendering worship to the Trinity, of participating in the love-life and praise-life of the three Divine Persons. We no longer worship the eternal Three from outside the Trinity but from within, by adoption through God's Son, the Second Person. We understand better those uncompromising words at the Last Supper. "If you ask the Father anything in my name, He will give it to you. Ask, and you shall receive, that your joy may be full."[5]

God shares His very nature with us as a source of power and activity. He gives us the necessary proximate faculties which we call the infused virtues and gifts. These infused virtues and gifts are not mere passive capacities; they are positive inclinations to act.[6]

Thus dignified and empowered, we no longer pray alone. It is now Christ who prays, Christ as Head and members. We no longer pray from outside Christ but from within, as His members. Our worship, centering in the Mass, and the sacraments, becomes the activating and fulfilling of Christ in us by adoption and participation in the same divine life. To us it is given not niggardly by timid dribs and drabs, but inexhaustibly, through the sustaining and unquenchable fountains that are the sacraments. It is ours, not only for the moment's

[5] Jn. 16:23-24.

[6] Herve, *Manuale Theologiae Dogmaticae,* Paris, Berche et Pagis, 1935, V: III, no. 247-248.

activity or prayer, but also through the ages because of the enduring visible society that Our Lord established to channel, protect and guide His shared divine life.

Offering the worship of adoration, atonement, thanksgiving and petition, we have the same end as Christ, which is the glory of the Father.

We even use the very words of Our Lord. The psalms were His prayer book and the Gospels are His spoken words.

We are inspired by His example, His praying in public and in private, His active charity, His suffering and death.

His merit is ours, for everything He did, including His praying the psalms, His praying spontaneously, in public and private, His suffering and dying, all of these merited for us the grace to do the same thing in our own way, insofar as they work to our salvation. The enduring influence of the events of Christ's life, something beyond understanding or calculation, is another reason why we call them mysteries and celebrate them as mysteries.

And always in all worship we are in union with His worshipping members. This union is emphasized by the fact that a person with the obligation of saying the divine office can satisfy his or her obligation by reciting it alternately with a lay person who does not have the obligation. Our Lord insisted on this unity in worship. "If thou art offering thy gift at the altar, and there rememberest that thy brother has anything against thee, leave thy gift before the altar and go first to be reconciled to thy brother, and then come and offer thy gift."[7] That unity is necessary in order to put ourselves in communion with the one Christ, "Because the bread is one, we though many, are one body, all of us who partake of the one bread."[8]

So the secret of appreciating the beauty and power of our worship is the consciousness that Christ is praying and that we

[7] Mt. 5:23-24.
[8] I Cor. 10:17.

are one with Him and in Him. It is the fruitfulness of the branch
abiding in the vine. That is the oneness for which Christ prayed
at the Last Supper: "That they may be one, even as we are
one: I in them and thou in me; that they may be perfected in
unity, and that the world may know that thou hast sent me, and
that thou hast loved them even as thou hast loved me."[9]

St. Augustine speaks of Christ as the "one man who reaches
to the ends of the earth."[10] "There is but one man who reaches
unto the end of time, and those who cry out are always His members."[11] The Mystical Christ, of whom we are members, extends through all space and all time. Even the grace given to
Old Testament people was given in view of Christ's death. He
fulfilled the Old Law in order to make both Old and New Testaments, as well as all peoples, into one living unit, ". . . in order
that of the two he might create in himself one new man, and
make peace and reconcile both in one body to God by the
cross. . . . Through him we both have access in one Spirit to the
Father."[12] And St. John says that Jesus died "that he might
gather into one the children of God who are scattered abroad.[13]

Therefore when you enter a church or a chapel the important
thing is not that you are entering into a place of worship but
that you are entering into a worshipping community, that you
become Christ praying, that you are "putting on" Christ. However important it may be to understand the words we say, it is
much more important to appreciate the one who is saying them.
And the stirring up of one's own devotion means above all an
entering into the mind and heart and will of Him in Whose
name the worship is offered. In the living unity that is Our
Lord the personal responsibility for what is "mine" and "yours"

9 Jn. 17:22-23.
10 St. Aug., *In Ps.* 142.
11 St. Aug., *In Ps.* 85.
12 Eph. 2:15, 18.
13 Jn. 11:52.

merges into the glorious power that is "His." All is "His" and all is "yours" and "mine." From your book and from my book we sing or say together His one prayer, for we are branches of the worshipping Vine that is Christ.

This community praying with and in Our Lord is more real than our community of physical closeness to one another. The supernatural infinitely surpasses the natural and both come from Him who is our Creator as God and our Redeemer as the God-Man. Our fellow worshippers do not give us physical life. And only indirectly do they give us supernatural life, i.e., by meriting and petitioning. But in the Mystical Body at prayer we function with and through one another; we are inspired and helped by one another because the ". . . charity of God is poured forth in our hearts by the Holy Spirit."[14] The Holy Spirit, Soul of the Mystical Christ, makes us divinely one and divinely operative through one another. Through Christ our Head ". . . we have access in one Spirit to the Father."[15]

St. Augustine clarifies this unifying operation of the Holy Spirit by starting with the operation of the human soul in the body. "It is the soul that gives life to all the members; it sees by the eye, it hears by the ear, it smells by the nose, it speaks by the tongue, it works by the hands, it walks by the feet. It is present to each member, giving life to them all, and to each one its office. It is not the eye that hears, nor the ear and tongue that see, nor the ear and eye that speak; and yet they live; their functions are varied, their life is one and the same. So it is in the Church of God. In some saints she works miracles; in other saints she teaches the truth; in others she maintains conjugal chastity. She does one thing in one class, and another in another; each individual has his distinct work to do; but there is one and the same life in them all. Now, what the soul is to

[14] Rom. 5:5:
[15] Eph. 2:18.

the body of man, that the Holy Spirit is to the body of Christ, which is the Church: the Holy Spirit does in the whole Church what the soul does in all the members of one body."[16]

Filled with the Soul of the Mystical Christ, all of us are the whole Christ praying. Each member retains his own individuality and responsibility (which are vastly enhanced by the powers of Christ) and there is a mutual sharing of merits and demerits, of prayers and sufferings throughout the whole Mystical Body. The merits of Christ become our own, for by His human nature He has taken upon Himself the shame and punishment of our sins as well as the burden of our prayers. Both were equally real and present to Him.[17]

"By assuming human nature, the Divine Word introduced into this earthly exile a hymn which is sung in heaven for all eternity. He unites to Himself the whole human race and with it sings this hymn to the praise of God. As we most humbly recognize that 'we know not what we should pray for, as we ought, the Spirit Himself asketh for us with unspeakable groanings' (Rom. 8:26). Moreover, through His Spirit in us, Christ entreats the Father, 'God could not give a greater gift to men ... (Jesus) prays for us, as our Priest; He prays in us as our Head; we pray to Him as our God ... we recognize in Him our voice and His voice in us ... He is prayed to as God, He prays under the appearance of a servant; in heaven He is a Creator; here, created though not changed, He assumes a created nature which

---

16 St. Aug., *Sermo* 267, "In die Pentecostes."

17 "Per ipsum et cum ipso et in ipso." "Through"—because He is the God-man who therefore gives sublime glory to the Trinity and because He is the one Mediator of creature adoration and petition. "With"—because jointly with Jesus, the Father and the Holy Spirit are adored. "In"— because Father, Son, and Holy Spirit are essentially in each other. Therefore through and with the perfect Mediator and in the power, virtues and intentions that are His. (Thus objectively.) Gihr, *The Holy Sacrifice of the Mass,* p. 692.

is to be changed and makes us with Him one complete man, head and body!' "[18]

Thus the whole sweep of tradition and theology is summed up and combined with new force in Pius XII quoting Augustine. And such wide vision makes it sound like small talk indeed (startling and sensational though it may seem) that if, on a particular day we were to pray the divine office or offer the Mass more fervently (because less fatigued, less ill, less tempted) than St. Paul prayed his psalms or Xavier his divine office, then the psalms of Paul and the divine office of Xavier would become more beautiful and powerful through our own more fervent worshipping with Christ and in Christ. This is just one little application of the doctrine of the Mystical Body.

So our worship is not so much a personal prayer as it is pre-eminently a Christian and a Catholic, universal prayer. It is the prayer of Christ that we pray. "We pray therefore to Him, and through Him, and in Him. We pray with Him and He with us; we recite this prayer of the Psalms in Him and He recites it in us."[19] We pray in the name of Christ and in the name of each of His members. Because it is the action of the whole Christ, each member prays in us. Actually, much of the thought of the Psalms often refers, not directly to the person saying them, but to Christ Himself or to some of His members whose prayers they express. They are the prayers of a living community, whatever be the tie of blood, of nation or of common dedication to social or religious purposes. As St. Paul said to the dissenting Corinthians, "Has Christ been divided up?"[20] "The man who works toils with the hands of the man who prays; the man who prays folds the workers hands in his."[21]

[18] *Mediator Dei,* par. 144.
[19] St. Aug., *In Ps.* 85.
[20] I Cor. 1:13.
[21] Houselander, *This War Is the Passion,* New York, Sheed and Ward, 1941, p. 47.

"Let Him rise up, this one chanter; let this man sing from the heart of each of us, and let each one of us be in this man. When each of you sings a verse, it is still this one man that sings, since you are all one Christ. We do not say, 'To Thee, O Lord, we have lifted up our eyes,' but 'To Thee, have I lifted up my eyes' (Ps. 122:1). You should, of course, consider that each of you is speaking but that primarily this one man is speaking Who reaches to the ends of the earth."[22]

If we feel hopelessly unworthy of being used by God so sublimely, we can remember that Jesus and Mary used as their prayer book the psalms that were composed in large part by an adulterer and murderer. Not even our worst faults, if regretted and accepted as our humiliating burden to be steadily whittled down, can prevent God from working through us. As we learn by doing and as God gives His grace through worship, "... thus slowly and laboriously we can transform ourselves 'unto the measure of the age of the fullness of Christ.' "[23]

Once this approach to our worship is understood, appreciated and lived, there will be less concern about the accidental, though real, difficulties that will remain until worship is completely restored. Nothing changes the fact that there is but one Mediator at work for us all, for all the world and for all time. There is but one Priest, Christ Himself; we are, in various distinctive degrees, sharers in His one priesthood. So, too, there is one great worship of that one Priest. After the Mass and sacraments, there is no other way in which we can make that prayer of Christ so much our own as in the official prayer of the Mystical Christ which centers around the Mass.

There is no need for concern if at a particular time the words of official worship do not always apply to one's personal dispositions and circumstances, to the mood of the moment. Actually,

22 St. Aug., *In Ps.* 142.
23 *Mediator Dei,* par. 165.

they are capable, in their full range and variety, of expressing man's every need. The important thing is that they are meant for an application far wider than the merely personal. At every moment they apply to some waiting member of the Mystical Christ in Whose name you are praying. You praise God in behalf of all creation; you thank Him; you beg His grace and mercy, not merely for yourself but for all mankind, for the whole Christ. And throughout worship your prayer to Our Lord becomes more and more, "My God and my All."

Chapter Ten

Worship Bears Fruit

MAN is made for life. Even death itself, however formidable the change it works, does not really interrupt man's vital continuity. Death marks the end of probation and of meriting; but the fear of death is not meant to be a parasite idea that saps and wastes our energy. Death is something that simply is not, as long as there is life. And life is always being alive in the present moment, alive and busy at God's work and at growing in inner union with Him. This sort of eternal now issues in the real eternal now of total union with God in heavenly peace. So up to the very second of death we are busy living, living our vocation of work and worship, living our love-life and praise-life that is the shared life of the Trinity made visible.

It is the continuity of life, coming out of the Trinity and returning to rest in the Trinity, that gives meaning to everything. This continuity provides the essential unity to man's multiple instinctive and sense activities. Hence the need to stress our vital oneness in worship, our oneness as brothers and sisters in

170

Christ. All pursuit of sanctity is essentially a search for unity, the unity of all things in God through Christ our Savior. And the more divided our energies are, because of many duties, many loves, many worries, the more difficult it is to remember the one reason for everything.

That is why the emphasis in our spiritual life should be on putting things together and keeping them together. Even when we divide our faults, it is for the sake of concentrating effectively on one and by concentration to conquer one at a time, while we go on growing to the point of being able to froget ourselves completely. In general, once sins are forgiven, it is better to think of sinfulness than of sins, better to think of abiding sorrow than of counting up so many acts of contrition. It is better to think of one indwelling divine life and power, the Three Divine Persons at work, than of many graces. Although graces are created gifts of God, when we speak of receiving a grace it usually means that we simply have become conscious of something God has already completed in us, of God already at work in our lives for longer than we know. Finally, we are destined for love and joy rather than for many affections, for a state of prayer rather than for many prayers. Each aspect and activity of life has its time and place but the many should not become the enemy of the one.

Putting all the elements of the Church together we have Christ, Our Lord. Whatever else we may say about the complex, vastly rich and many-sided life of the Church, the most important thing that can be said about the Church is that it is Our Lord as He Himself told Saul. The Church is Christ living in the world, living and acting in us, doing His missionary work through us. The most important thing about our worship is that Christ prays, loves, thanks, adores, atones, and petitions through us His members.

The more vividly we realize our union with Christ mediating

and our continuing the Redemption with Him, the less will we bother about difficulties of ceremony and language, fatigue and moods, noises and the clothes people wear. The strength of our faith in this conscious oneness with Our Lord and the rate of its growth depends on two things: first, our frequent exercise of faith and hope and love so that our infused virtues, already given us with divine life, may become an acquired facility. This, of course, presupposes the second essential which is our generous living through prayer, penance and charity in sensitive response to all that Our Lord asks of us. As we live so we pray; and as we pray, so we live. Prayer is a very sensitive thermometer that tells the temperature of our living for God. We are first of all lovers. And our worship is the prayer of love, the work of love. And we are disposed, led and supported in this great work by God's love for us.

It is the very nature of love to express itself by metaphor, by symbols, because love is a giving of self. Self, however, cannot be given completely to the point of annihilation or transformation of substance. We cannot cease to be the personal being that God created us to be, not even in our loving. Therefore, something must take our place and stand for the self that cannot be given entirely. Metaphors, symbols are the language of love.

Besides, the very depth of love makes words inadequate to express its depth. The deeper the love, the less will words express it and the greater the need for symbols.[1]

---

[1] Regarding the use of poetry in our worship through the psalms, hymns and certain passages of Scripture, E. Underhill says: "1. It is the carrying medium of something which otherwise wholly eludes representation: the soul's deep and awestruck apprehension of the numinous. 2. It can universalize particulars; giving an eternal reference to those things of time in and through which God speaks to men. 3. It is a powerful stimulant of the transcedental sense: a function in which the ancient hymns embodied in the Greek liturgy excel." *Op. cit.,* pp. 112-113.

Even the simplest things can be symbols of self and of the depths of love, true tokens of friendship, so long as they are sincere and appreciated. A thousand things speak to a lover of the beloved. Therefore, not only the many beautiful metaphors in the psalms and of the texts of missal, ritual, and breviary can be used as symbols of our love of God, not only the thoughts and events like the Exodus (put into prayer in the Exodus Psalms 104 & 105), but even the very obscurities in the text can be symbols of the mystery of divinity and of the depths of love that is beyond any seeing or knowing. This is not to cultivate obscurity for obscurity's sake nor to encourage excessive allegorizing nor to wallow in the delights of symbolism, but only to take things as they are and use them as our way of the moment to reach God.

This use of metaphor and of the accommodated sense of Scripture should not become a substitute for frequent reading and meditating on the Mass texts, the ritual, breviary (for priests, religious, laity), the psalms and the liturgy in general. Every Christian is a missionary for his faith. He should be able to give something of the solid Scriptural basis for his belief. At least the key texts for key doctrines he should know in their literal sense. For to prove anything, Scripture must be used either in its literal sense or in its inspired spiritual sense. For illustration of something already otherwise proved, but not for proof, passages may be taken in an accommodated sense, metaphorically, by attributing to them meanings other than what God meant to say by His revealed word. It is the difference between identity and analogy. The literal sense or inspired spiritual sense is identity of meaning between what God meant and the way you use the text. Illustration is analogy, something partly similar and partly dissimilar, i.e., you say, "Under one aspect this passage has a similar meaning." In a person's private Scripture reading, of course, God may give light and inspiration through a metaphorical use of a passage. And there is the age-old tradition of such usage that goes back to the Fathers of the Alexandrian School. Still, Pius XII gives a certain caution against the excessive dependence on accommodations, especially in teaching and preaching. What he says applies to meditating the texts of our worship.

The "spiritual sense, intended and ordained by God Himself, must be shown forth and explained by Catholic commentators with the diligence which the dignity of the word of God demands; but they must be scrupulously careful not to propound other metaphorical meanings as though they were the genuine sense of Sacred Scripture. For, although, especially in preaching, a somewhat wider use of the Sacred Text in a metaphorical sense may be profitable, if kept within reasonable bounds, for illustrating doctrines of faith and commending moral truths, yet it must never be forgotten that such a use of the words of Sacred Scripture is, as it were, extrinsic and adventitious to Holy Writ.

"Moreover, the practice is not without its dangers, especially today, since the faithful, and particularly those who are learned in both sacred and profane sciences, want to know what it is that God Himself means to say to us in the Sacred Scriptures, rather than what some eloquent speaker or writer is expounding with a dexterous use of the words of the Bible. 'The word of God ... living and effectual, and more piercing than any two-edged sword, and reaching unto the division of the soul and the spirit, of the joints and also the marrow ... a discerner of thoughts and intents of the heart' (Heb. 4:12), certainly needs no human artifice or manipulation in order to move and stir the soul. The Sacred Pages themselves, written under the inspiration of the Holy Ghost, abound in their own intrinsic meaning; enriched by divine virtue, they have their own power; graced with supernatural beauty, they shine with their own bright splendor ... if only the interpreter explains them so completely and exactly as to bring to light all the treasures of wisdom and prudence latent within them."[2]

Pius XII is particularly interested in repressing the abuse of Scripture which passes off a spiritual application as the first and only sense of Scripture. He emphasizes that we are meant to use Old Testament words (e.g., in the Psalms) as charged with New Testament meaning. Instance Ps. 118: a Christian should consider the Mosaic Law as enriched and fulfilled through Christ, i.e., as including the law of Christ, the Sermon on the Mount, the parables, the new commandment.

Periodically, everyone should re-meditate and re-think the texts of the Mass and the psalms. To neglect to grow in our appreciation of them and in the profit we should derive from them is to be like the person who tries to solve adult problems with an adolescent's knowledge of his faith. We cannot stand still; we cannot rest comfortably in accustomed securities. We are always changing either internally through mental and emotional development, or through external circumstances, or through both. As we mature mentally and emotionally we should also mature in our religious formation. A deeper appreciation of our manner of worshipping God can help.

In spite of everything we do to prepare ourselves for worship, either remotely through meditative reading and a generous life that is unified through our love-union with Our Lord or proximately through meditating the immediate text to be used, seeking God's true word and will in the proper of the Mass or the psalms of the ritual and breviary, there will always be times when we seem incapble of feeling anything. The only thing we may be conscious of is early morning grogginess or the numbness of evening fatigue. Illness, tiredness, worries or the rhythm of spiritual dryness that God may permit for our purification,

---

[2] *Divino Afflante Spiritu,* Washington, D.C., N.C.W.C., par 32-33.

any or all of these things may leave us inwardly numb and seemingly wasting our time trying to pray and worship.

Nevertheless, regardless of personal feelings of devotion, the following is true:

I—The purpose of worship is accomplished. And this is important because every Christian is an apostle of that purpose.

    1. God is adored, thanked, propitiated, petitioned everlastingly by the perfect worship of Christ our one Mediator whom we offer in our place especially in the Mass.

    2. Our brothers and sisters in Christ are strengthened and made better by the satisfactions, the merits (de congruo), the petitions of our sanctified, common prayer. "The salvation of many depends on the prayers and voluntary penances which the members of the Mystical Body of Jesus Christ offer for this intention and on the assistance of pastors of souls and of the faithful, especially of fathers and mothers of families, which they must offer to our Divine Savior as though they were His associates."[3] The breviary alone, Father Parsch calls a "sacred and effective ministry of souls." And St. Paul was not speaking of entertainment but of the apostolate when he wrote to the Ephesians (5:18-19), "Be filled with the Holy Spirit, speaking to one another in psalms and hymns and spiritual songs, singing and making melody in your hearts to the Lord."

II—We do get much out of worship that is an aid to growth in holiness of life.

    1. There is the sublime dignity of being one with Christ in the mission of the total Christ to redeem the world.

    2. We fulfill our vocation simply as creatures. Our natural faculties and energies are dedicated to and employed in

---

[3] *Mystici Corporis,* par. 44.

the highest possible good within man's reach, which is the worship of God. Natural faculties are thus brought to their highest possible perfection. This, of course, requires earnest participation flowing out into sincere fervent living.

3. Worship is the doing of what Christ did and therefore has great power and efficacy for nourishing.

4. We fulfill our membership in Christ. He prays in us and we in Him. It is the great Christ-action springing from Christ-life, Christ-being. Praying from within Christ, as His members, we understand better His pleading for confidence at the Last Supper. "If you ask the Father anything in my name He will give it to you."[4]

5. Our merits (de congruo) and our petitions for our own personal needs are much more effective, partly because of our union with Christ and His members and partly because we are using prayers inspired by the Holy Spirit and hallowed by the usage of Jesus and Mary. "The faithful are to be instructed on the supreme value of the sacred liturgy which always, and especially on these days, far surpasses by its very nature other kinds of devotions and customs, even the very best."[5]

6. We exercise dominion of the spirit over the flesh. We conform ourselves to song or speech or to silence when and as prescribed. Not as we feel like or choose but as directions require, we sing or speak or listen to whatever thoughts and words are to be said and when they are to be said. We follow the ceremonies and sit, stand or kneel or walk as prescribed. This discipline is not less meritorious because it becomes easy or because there is no feel-

[4] Jn. 16:23.
[5] S. Congregation of Rites, *Instruction on the Restored Order of Holy Week,* Nov. 16, 1955.

ing in it. Only one of the conditions for merit, on the part of the object, has to do with the difficulty of the thing done. The far more important conditions are those in the person: degree of sanctifying grace, degree of union with Christ, purity of intention, actuality of intention and fervor of intensity.

Again let it be said that ritual is not for ritual's sake nor discipline for discipline's sake. Worship is not an unavoidable penance but a sacrifice and homage for the glory of God, for the saving of souls and for personal perfection.

7. Our devout reception of the sacraments or attentive witnessing of them, our devout praying of the breviary (by priest, religious or lay person fully employing mind and heart and will) helps towards a more devout offering of Holy Mass.

8. God instructs, inspires and exhorts us by His revealed word, through the Scripture passages, the psalms, through the homilies of the Fathers of the Church and by the examples of the Saints. Even though there may be no immediate stirring of our numbed hearts at the moment, we may find the thought coming back to us when we need it.

9. Not to be spurned as of no importance is the sense of accomplishment, the personal satisfaction, the inner peace that comes from helping, through worship, to bring men to know and love God, to possess and live His life.

10. Finally, there is also the help of emotional balance. The general message of Scripture readings always adds up to the good news of salvation, the victory of Christ and the eternal triumph of all His loyal members. The psalms almost always resolve on a note of hope and confidence and therefore they also help to counteract fears and

anxieties. And by uniting all fears and worries with Christ in His victorious passion and death, you learn the perfect love that casts out fear. Besides, the abundance of affective prayer in worship, as well as its simple beauties and frequent songs make it a normal and healthy outlet for man's affective life.

All these things are true of worship that is participated in by any member of Christ. Where the breviary is said by those who are especially and officially ordained or consecrated to pray, its sacrifice of praise has the added dignity of such ordination or consecration and is further sustained and dignified by the special grace given with that ordination or consecration.

Chapter Eleven

Worship Develops Christian Personality

THE human person without grace is highly vulnerable to pressure and seduction. With grace, life is still a warfare. To be aware of the world-wide and local threats to human security, to see the social and the personal misdirection of human energies is but to open half an eye. And to feel the impact of these forces from without is but the normal reaction of the human passion of fear. Quite naturally, then, there is a distrustful anxiety about things both massive and penetrating that shape our environment by their own weight, without submiting to our immediate control.

Added to these forces from without, are the psychic drives from within that too easily crowd reason into a corner or unhinge it completely. Sometimes the deep impact and inner reaction are so hidden and complex as to challenge understanding; the very mystery of life seems to be involved. To the profound inner disturbance is therefore added a primitive fear of the unknown. As a result, there is a tendency to distrust what seems beyond understanding and beyond control.[1] With the distrust often goes a resentment at the seeming injustice of such power on the loose. The combined fears and anger do not make for a balanced personality even at best. And at worst there is ultimately some disintegration of a person's power to think and will and a serious block to personal sanctity. The brave efforts of some people to live with such a twin-headed monster resolve into oddities of manner and devotion as well as psychosomatic disturbances. But at least they try.

Others try merely to escape, partly by ignoring the difficulty, saying perhaps that other people might be neurotic but not they, and partly by activities and locomotion that at least provide an outlet for the energies released through anxiety. The compromise may succeed for a long time, but only at the price of greatly diminished achievement and of diminished happiness. They do not know what they are missiong nor why. The ultimate tragedy is that they do not know or they know but dimly that part of their trouble is a very proper fear of having offended God whose rights to worship and to obedience they have most ungratefully ignored. The fear that should have been taken as love, love calling them home to be forgiven and healed, becomes instead a fear that is an instrument of justice scourging them for ingratitude and arrogance.

There are some, of course, either professionally or privately, who are preoccupied with trying to understand, manage and blend both the exterior and interior forces that shape personality. And the children of this generation have learned much that can be put at the service of Christian revelation and the sacramental economy of redemption. At times, though, the re-

---

[1] "Man has become distrustful of the mystery which dwells within him. On all sides he suspects infiltration from the pathological and the unconscious." J. Nuttin, *Psychoanalysis and Personality*, New York, Sheed and Ward, 1953, p. 116.

sult of a mountain of labor is either a ridiculous mouse of in-
formation or a misshapen technic that only adds to the confusion
of doctor and patient. For they labor with the hopelessly inadequate tools of reason without faith and science without reason. "In the mere perspective of science and technology we are
at a loss to discover the rational foundations of the dignity of
the human person and to believe in it."[2]

That such things should happen to pagans is bad enough.
A good pagan of long ancestry at least has an accumulation of
religious beliefs and superstitions that give some meaning to
life, even if the meaning is limited and the application as tragic
as human sacrifice. The modern secularist, without religious
roots, is pathetically at sea in a thick fog and all his deep-throated
protests to the contrary only reveal his unrest and uncertainty.
He is filled with fears, and is afraid of fear.

In any case, it is humanly understandable why there should
be a recrudescence of Manichaeism, why people should recur-
rently shape to themselves evil deities to personify the forces of
evil and why they should pay them some tribute of worship.
However understandable, such pessimism is an insult to the
Incarnation. The Prince of Light is not in bondage to the prince
of darkness. Obvious though the evil is, St. John seems to indicate in his Apocalypse that Satan and his legions are in some
way bound and hindered from doing the evil they would and
are to remain so until the final days of the world.[3]

In the meantime, evil is not the dominant reality in the world.
There is no point to sitting like perched vultures waiting for
carrion. In the view of Christian optimism, evil is an emptiness
that hungers for God. Christian optimism is the only true
realism. Where men have created for themselves conflict and
anxiety and pain by trying to settle down in a part-time heaven,

[2] Maritain, *The Range of Reason,* New York, Scribners, 1952, p. 93.
[3] Apoc. 12:7-12.

there precisely the voice of God calls to them to quit the dissipation, the fragmenting of their being for a unifying, meaningful life in Him. In the pit of their distress is the creative love of God filling the void of evil and then stripping away the mask of evil to reveal the goodness behind it. Confused and weakened as we are by evil, we have to believe in the goodness it hides. To God's love we must answer, "I believe."

God did not create the darkness in which we seem to find ourselves. That was the work of man's sin, the original sin and our personal sin. And we try to hide under the darkness we have made. "The light has come into the world, yet men have loved the darkness rather than the light, for their works are evil."[4] Even while we claim to love God and to seek His light, we too often flee from God secretly, into the success, the security or satisfaction or anger that we set up as the junior god of the moment. We ignore our deepest need. "Before any biological or bodily interaction, and even before communion of any kind with his fellow-men, man needs a more universal sort of communication and support and integration; he needs to be able to know and feel himself integrated into an absolute order of existence. Perhaps never before in human history has there been such intense experience of absolute despair and loneliness, such a feeling of utter dereliction, such a lack of transcendental contact, as there is today."[5]

But the dialogue between divine Person and human person goes on without interruption until death. God is always calling us to find the meaning of the multiple in the Almighty One that He is. And our finding Him is simply our discovery that He has loved us all the time, even when we were sinners, and has continued without ceasing to pursue us. All the time He has been giving us the grace to believe and to look within ourselves

[4] Jn. 3:19.
[5] Nuttin, *op. cit.,* p. 229.

to the shared divine life and indwelling Trinity. That discovery of divinity within is life's one great discovery, to which the lovers' discovery of themselves in one another is but a scented whisper. What human lovers find in one another ought to tell them how much more they can find themselves in God. The mystery of creative love and mating should plunge them into the mystery of God indwelling and creatively sanctifying. For as the Fathers of the Church have emphasized, God satisfies our thirst for Him by awakening a new thirst. He gives insight into mystery by immersing us in new mystery. He rewards each trembling departure and abandonment by inviting us to a new desert and to a new mountain of revelation.[6]

But this continual emptying of ourselves is simply an opening of ourselves to becoming truly human through the inflow of activating divinity. God simply will not let us settle down this side of heaven. He will not let us develop one aspect of our personality to the detriment of all the rest. He insists that we achieve internal balance in our natural driving forces. He does not leave us content with an out-of-shape instrument of grace. And He stands ready to aid our inner natural growth towards stability by uniting us with Himself as the eternally changeless One and with fellow human beings as our purification, our comfort and our inspiration. "The aim of the Church is man, naturally good, penetrated, ennobled and strengthened by the truth and grace of Christ."[7]

The Incarnation, God-become-man, is the great and dominating reality in the world. Christ the Prince of Light is advancing inevitably and majestically towards the final revelation of His victory on the Day of Judgment. Nothing can stop that. In the

----

[6] Cf. St. Gregory of Nyssa, *Vita Moysi*, P.G., 44:405; *In Cantica Canticorum, Hom.* V, P.G., 44:876.

[7] Pius XII, "To the Tenth International Congress of Historical Sciences," *The Pope Speaks*, 2 (1955) 208.

meantime, the real self of the Church is Christ Himself, for the Church is the Mystical Christ, suffering in herself what Christ suffered on earth and being every moment the hand of Christ healing and sanctifying His brothers and sisters. Moreover, the Church is incarnated and active in its members, each member being some vital cell of an organism that was born out of Christ's side on Calvary and goes on growing until Judgment Day. Engrafted into Christ by baptism, sealed with a share in Christ's priesthood and spiritually alive only with shared Christ-life, each Christian also is another Christ. "For you have died and your life is hidden with Christ in God. When Christ, your life shall appear. . . ."[8]

We are either Christ or nothing. Therefore, we cannot be content with being a weak incandescence of Christian life and light. We have to be a living fire. There is no substitute for Christian victory, a victory achieved in human persons in spite of imperfections and achieved in human society for the sake of the human person. Goodness is its own authority, whether embodied in a single person or in a community as small as a Christian family section or as large as the Church Militant. The voice of sanctity will always be heard, even if the only response is some quarters is a loud protest.

The call is for balanced Christian leaders who know themselves well enough to be generally objective in their views and decisions, leaders who are strong enough in conviction, habit and emotional balance to hold true against difficulty and the pressure of opinion, leaders who have enough compassionate love to understand and accept people and to deal with them just as they are, leaders who take sanctity as the normal Christian vocation and therefore take also the ordinary means to attain it. In such a person, truth has mastered and emancipated, and

[8] Col. 3:3-4: Cf. Mersch, *op. cit.,* pp. 610-611; Osende, *Fruits of Contemplation,* St. Louis, Herder, 1953, p. 51.

human capacities are free to develop into the glory and beauty of sanctity. Sanctity is the splendor of truth in action, the action of love for God and human beings; it is the inner radiance of being finding outward expression in perfectible existence; it is that humility which is reverence for truth and that meekness which bears all that cannot be changed by truth and love.

The saint is at once the most truly human person and the most dynamic personality, the person of most enduring influence. The perception of that inner dynamism and the response to its radiance depends always on the inner freedom and faith of those who judge him, as it so obviously did in the case of Our Lord. For the Saint respects human freedom in other people. But he also has the patient persistence of God who indwells and activates his being and urges him to service by an impelling charity.

As we proceed then to relate personality development to worship, let it be said at once that liturgy is not a substitute for psychotherapy in correcting serious emotional unbalance. Liturgy can have its effects in helping to correct emotional disturbances but we must normally suppose a reasonable degree of emotional balance. Excessive fears are directly a psychic problem and only indirectly a moral problem. Moreover, a person must bring to worship a hunger for an alert and active participation in its sanctifying functions. If we are filled with our own worldly and selfish conceits, we shall go away empty. Finally, we have to come with sorrow for sin and with enough humility and courage to face ourselves truthfully as we are. We cannot escape into the sublime group consciousness of the Mystical Body nor into the sublime group activity of worship for the sake of hiding a true or false sense of guilt or a sense of personal inferiority. Pride and fear being what they are, such an escape-tendency is a danger for the emotionally disturbed of our times. Pius XII, in his address to the Assisi Congress, encouraged us to face these problems. "Present day liturgy interests itself likewise in many special problems, as, e.g., the relation between liturgy and the religious ideas of the modern world, contemporary culture, social questions, depth psychology."[9]

Whatever is done to integrate spiritual formation and formation in the doctrinal and inspirational aspects of worship, it must be taken for granted, also, that the instructor or the person in charge of the program must first be respected and loved before he or she can hope to instill a respect and love for worship. Therefore, such a person must be sincere, with an attitude of reverence towards people and all things sacred. To teach others to *know* God in worship means to communicate to them the *experience* of God. The teacher must be living that experience of God. In the end, it is not a matter of assimilating truth but of surrendering to a Person. Still, people do not experience God fully except through a full use of their whole being; and that means some part in corporate worship. Corporate worship is the experience of the Whole Christ, the Mystical Christ, whether the group be as small as a family at home, a parish, a community or sixty thousand people in St. Peter's, Rome.

To put this consideration on a proper philosophical basis, it is in place to say that a person in his formal cause in "an individual and incommunicable substance of a rational nature."[10] Union with God is his final cause. His material cause could be defined as his unique talents of analysis, synthesis and action, together with his capacity for union with God. His efficient cause could be set down as his coordinated mental, volitional, emotional and physical habits and acts.

Through the material and efficient causes we come to a notion of "personality." "Personality is the work of a person. . . . Psychologically, personality is the patterned totality of human

---

[9] Pius XII, "Address to Assisi Congress," *The Pope Speaks*, 3 (1956) 286.

[10] Maher, *Psychology*, London, Longmans, 1893, p. 521.

powers, activities, and habits, uniquely organized by the person in the active pursuit of his self-ideal, and revealed in his behavior."[11]

Whatever purposes of understanding may be served by definitions, we cannot forget that we are dealing with a complex vital unit. And when we speak of personality, we are merely taking a specific aspect of the genus, person. Taking personality now in relation to worship, we deal with those more obvious qualities that inspire the good, perhaps irritate the bad and impel many in between to a conversion of life. By personality we do not mean a domineering animal vitality at the service of a selfish or limited ideal nor the actor's charm that can be turned off or on almost at will. We are concerned more with a person's capacity for clear vision in essential things, his deep convictions and self-possession, his simplicity and sincerity, his habitual respect and consideration for people and things and his eagerness to be of service to God and man. This adds up to the authority and influence of personal goodness. Such are the qualities necessary for Christian leadership.

When we face the development of personality through worship, we embrace at once the formation of the mind in Christian values, the formation of the will in Christian virtues, and the formation of emotions in moderation and control.

Lest there be any fright at the idea of maturity meaning sanctity, it is enough to recall that sanctity is meant to be the normal development of a Christian person. Sanctity is the destiny of a Christian, the essence of a Christian brought to full flowering by the full normal use both of natural and supernatural means. Worship constantly recalls that destiny of a Christian and constantly brings a Christian into active participation in the ordinary means of growth towards sanctity. "The true Chris-

[11] Gasson, in Arnold and Gasson, *The Human Person*, New York, Ronald, 1954, pp. 168, 219.

tian, product of Christian education, is the supernatural man who thinks, judges, and acts constantly and consistently in accordance with right reason illumined by the supernatural light of the example and teaching of Christ; ... the true and finished man of character."[12]

Essential to personality development is a right sense of values. And the bent of man to follow the bent of his mind is enshrined by divine inspiration in Ps. 113 which we sing in Sunday Vespers. "Their idols are silver and gold, the work of men's hands. ... Like to them shall they be, who make them, everyone who trusts in them. ... They who fear the Lord, trust in the Lord."[13] Our worship has a strong intellectual content. And the wisdom of it is indicated also by Pius XII in his address to Catholic Journalists: "Character means quite simply a profound love and unchangeable respect for the divine order."

St. Paul broke this down to details when he wrote to his Christians at Philippi, "The things that were gain to me, these, for the sake of Christ, I have counted loss. Nay more, I have counted everything loss because of the excelling knowledge of Jesus Christ, my Lord. ... Whatever things are true, whatever honorable, whatever just, whatever holy, whatever lovable, whatever of good repute, if there be any virtue, if anything worthy of praise, think upon these things."[14] He meant, of course, not an academic but an experienced knowledge of Our Lord.

What are the things true, lovable, holy that are taught through worship? Very prominent is the Trinity. A constantly recurring thought is that God our Father is an almighty and eternal Person who is at once our Creator and constant support, majestic and merciful, just and loving, wise and understanding. "He who

[12] Pius XI, "Christian Education of Youth," *Social Wellsprings,* Milwaukee, Bruce, 1942, V. II, p. 119.
[13] Ps. 113:12, 16, 19.
[14] Phil. 3:7-8; 4:8.

has not spared his own son but has delivered him for us all, how can he fail to grant us all things with him."[15] Orations, psalms, offering prayers, prefaces, Creed—all form our minds and wills in a deep reverence for the Father as our transcendent God who is yet personally and warmly interested in our least thought and need. He is the God whom we cannot look upon and live and who yet holds us in the palm of His hand. On this instilled doctrine rest our reverence for mystery in divinity and our sense of sin as an offense against His majesty which must be repented, atoned for and amended. Before God we admit that "we are justly afflicted for our sins."[16] Sorrow for sin should sink deeper and deeper through repeated emphasis in the Mass, in the sacraments and sacramentals.

The right notion of God the Father attained through liturgy is the natural follow up of a proper respect and love for an exemplary father of a family. In the mind of a child, its father and mother stand for God. But very early the child should be taught the difference, i.e., that any human being is imperfect, even a father or mother, and that there is only one perfect Father and one perfect Mother. A false front is bound to lead to disillusionment and create a psychic hurdle where there ought to be an easy transition.

Where the father is anything but exemplary, since he stands for God in the child's mind, he is likely both to create an insecurity and anxiety in the child's emotional life and to warp a child's whole idea of God. Thereafter it becomes very difficult for the child to respect, trust and love God as a Father. It may take half a life-time to heal the wound and clear away the anxiety. The liturgy can help the healing.

The Father's greatest gift to us is His own Son. We worship the Son as our one Mediator. Because He is at the same time

[15] Rom. 8:32.
[16] Collect of Septuagesima Sunday.

truly the Father's Son and truly one of us, His prayer is certain
to be heard. Our prayer becomes acceptable to the Father because it is joined to His Son's. Christ our Mediator continues
in heaven what He began by His life and death on earth. In
view of what He suffered for us but most of all in view of what
He is and is doing, we plead that Christ be heard in His continuous and living intercession for us.[17] This is the glad tidings,
the good news that forms our minds in Christian optimism and
stays the fires of anxiety. Not evil but the redemption is the
dominant reality in the world. And all doctrines, all virtues and
all practices and exercises are unified and synthesized in our
personal love for Jesus our Redeemer-Brother. From this beginning we grow and grow to "the deep knowledge of the Son of
God, to perfect manhood, to the mature measure of the fullness of Christ."[18]

Worship also forms our minds to implore the Holy Spirit as
the Advocate and Comforter whom Jesus sends to continue His
sanctifying work. He is no longer a shadowy attribute nor a
mere operation as He was in the Old Testament, but always a
Person divinely at work within us and in every act of worship.
Many experience how the Holy Spirit makes Himself seem almost tangibly present at such times as the ordination of priests,
the profession of brothers and nuns, at baptism, confirmation
and marriage. To the Holy Spirit, as to Father and Son, we
give equal adoration, equal atonement, equal thanksgiving and
equal petition. He should not be the forgotten Person of the
Trinity, the forgotten Guest in our hearts.

Adoration, atonement, thanksgiving and petition are woven
into our minds in a hundred ways through offering after offering of worship, always in a concrete and personal form. The
Gloria of the Mass, in particular, expresses the perfect worship

---

[17] Hebr. 7:25.
[18] Eph. 4:13.

of true love, for there we pay tribute to Father, Son and Holy
Spirit, not in exact ratio to our indebtedness because of sin nor
in exact ratio to enumerated benefits of God to us, but more out
of sheer love of God for His own sake, for His own grandeur.
We thank Him just for being the infinitely adorable and loving
God that He is. In summary we say, "Thank You, O God, for
being just You." In this especially we "practice the truth in
love, and so grow up in all things in him who is the head,
Christ."[19] Such gratitude, always a mark of nobility, becomes
our noble estate as brothers and sisters of Christ, joint-heirs with
Him, adopted sons and daughters of the Trinity. Most of St.
Paul's Epistles begin with thanksgiving. And it is repeated in
our minds and on our lips in the prefaces and throughout the
prayers of our worship. This formation of the mind is one of
the purposes of liturgy. "The second end of worship is that
man may be taught by God whom he worships."[20]

The wisdom of this prime emphasis on God is borne out by
the spiritual formation which St. Teresa of Avila prescribes.
In her plan, beginners are to be preoccupied with God Himself,
while emphasis on asceticism and the virtues is to be secondary.
Since beginners are still weak in their vision and do not know
their weaknesses, they could make asceticism a sort of junior
god. Pathetically, when beginners are emotionally immature,
in exact proportion to their fervor and intensity, they tend to
let particular practices of penance, of virtue or of piety absorb
their emotional drive and mental vision. These practices then
become oddities. Liturgy is a perfect example of a dominantly
God-centered life. It is the wise teacher, the skilled molder of
minds.

Since there is no teaching without repetition, worship's power
to form minds is also evident in the repeated summary of Chris-

[19] Eph. 4:15.
[20] *Sum. Theol.*, II-II, q. 92, a. 2.

tian mysteries in every Mass. And the year of worship, with special emphasis on successive mysteries in Christ's life and in the whole plan of redemption, is meant gradually to deepen our penetration and conviction. The actual effect of this repeated indoctrination depends, in part, like all teaching, on the dispositions that each one brings to each act of worship; in part it depends also upon God's free giving of His grace. "In thy light we shall see light."[21]

What about the formation of the will in virtue? Having so divinely transformed the best in us, God has made love the first law of our being. "The rediscovery of the value of existence not only means the rediscovery of God, it also means the rediscovery of love. . . . Love is not a passing pleasure or a more or less intense emotion, but the root tendency and very meaning of his being alive."[22] All the vital drives in us are made to work together harmoniously and flow out to other human beings and through them back to God. And all our love for God is simply our grace-prompted response to His love. "Being rooted and grounded in love, you may be able to comprehend with all the saints what is the breadth and length and height and depth, and to know Christ's love which surpasses all knowledge."[23]

As the mind is formed to direct, so the will is formed to seek and adhere. It adheres through love. But the will is a blind faculty; it is only as strong as the simplicity, the single-heartedness, the strength of the motive. Worship forms the will to follow Christ our one Mediator, to be single-hearted and ardently dedicated, after the examples of the virtues He lived and at the cost of His very life. One of the most obvious things in the Gospels is the complete conformity of His will to His Father's. Almost equally clear is His compassionate love for people, a love that

---

[21] Ps. 35:10.
[22] Maritain, *op. cit.,* pp. 91, 92.
[23] Eph. 3:18-19.

healed the sick and the lame, freed the possessed and wept over the destruction of His people within the besieged walls of Jerusalem. And when He asked that we learn of Him to be meek and humble of heart, He was drawing us after Him to see ourselves and be ourselves sincerely; that means also the willingness to pay the price in self-control, tolerance and patience, without either childish helplessness or bitterness at inevitable opposition and sometimes defeat.

Jesus who centers our worship is not only drawing us with love and with desires to be like Him; He is also constantly giving us in worship the grace to form our will in habits of virtue. Besides, the very acts of worship are themselves exercises in the virtues of obedience, reverence, gratitude, faith, hope, love and sorrow. Above all, we are trained in constant, courageous victimhood with Christ. "While we stand before the altar it is our duty so to transform our hearts, that whatever sin there is may be completely blotted out, while whatever promotes supernatural life through Christ may be zealously fostered and strengthened even to the extent that, in union with the Immaculate Victim, we become a victim acceptable to the eternal Father."[24]

There is another part of every human person that comes under the molding hand of worship and that is the affective life. As difficult to understand as they are to manage, emotions are the inner driving forces; they trigger energy for thinking, willing and acting. Habitually out of control, they warp personality. Even momentarily in the saddle, they play embarrassing tricks on a person who usually is balanced and reasonable, for they tip our thinking and misdirect our willing. They are too important to be ignored, even while they are part of the humiliation of being human. We are neither angels nor disembodied spirits. Under control, emotions are most valuable servants. They are

---

[24] *Mediator Dei*, par. 100.

bad masters but very good servants. What can liturgy do for them?

To begin with, worship fulfills certain important basic needs of a human person. One of them is a sense of integration with the great central realities: God, human beings and the material world of animal, vegetable and inorganic things. "The true personality, far from being suppressed, only comes to light at the moment when the union with Christ is consummated."[25] It is precisely through the Eucharist as sacrifice and sacrament that everyone achieves his or her strongest sense of closeness to God. And through the year's successive Masses God reveals both His plan for man's redemption and the mystery that remains in each part of His plan. Through worship man learns to know the three ages of enlightenment in God's revelation: (a) The Old Testament which was clear enough for man's immediate needs and yet held the mystery of a coming Savior; (b) The New Testament in which God spoke clearly enough to explain and fulfill the Old Testament and to indicate that Christ henceforth was to be the perfect model to follow, even while it held the mystery of the coming Holy Spirit; (c) After Pentecost God made clearer the meaning of Our Lord's words but there remained the mystery of eternal life and of God's own inner nature. So we have many contacts with God and yet keep a proper sense of awe before His mysterious depths. This is important for our basic religious instinct.

Therefore our strong personal need for happy, successful and significant relationships with divinity is fulfilled in worship. On our part this relationship must also embrace the fact of our sins. The feelings of guilt we have after sin are a very proper fear of having offended God; they are not unhealthy. Those

[25] Bouyer, *The Meaning of Monastic Life,* New York, Kenedy, 1955, p. 102.

feelings release energy and thus create an inner tension that, under grace, is meant to be released through sorrow, confession, atonement and amendment. The psalms and other texts of the liturgy inculcate the awareness that evil is due to sin, proximately or remotely. Therefore the tendency to fight evil is turned in upon the capital tendencies to sin and upon the consequences of sin, rather than outward upon people and circumstances. That is the antidote to projection and escape. Adversity, therefore, will be accepted as deserved punishment for sin and as a reparation for sin, our own sins and the sins of others.

With guilt and fear taken away, sorrow remains, sorrow springing from love and progressively deepening through worship and through the deepening of love. Then the need and desire for reunion with God finds its realization in holy communion. This momentary corporal union strengthens the divine indwelling.

The inevitable conflicts of life that are the consequences of original sin and of personal sin often create disturbing anxieties in those who do not resolve their meaning, especially if they are the delicately wrought thoroughbreds who should be great saints. The doctrinal fact of being baptized in Christ, of being able to suffer meekly and still go on loving for His sake, can do much to check the excesses of fear and anger by rechanneling their released energies into love. The exercise of such victimhood with Christ in every Mass is a daily establishing of emotional balance between fear and love. Every crucifix is a recall to that purifying and fruitful victimhood. At the same time, the repeated insistence in the texts of worship on the dignity of each human person because of divine life shared with him is a constant appeal to the positive emotions of love, confidence, trust and hope. Besides, the inner reality of grace, everyone's capacity for sanctity, the purchase of souls by the death of the God-Man and the eternal destiny of human persons, these are all inspiring parts of the reality of redeemed man that every developing personality wants to accept and embrace.

A further and sustained awakening of healthy positive emotions springs from the victory of Christ over evil that is exercised in every Mass. Again the great annual feast of His resurrection and its frequent recall as the pledge of our own resurrection is a light of joy that can steady us during reverses and stimulate affective prayer. Finally, the ever-recurring psalms embody thoughts of hope, confidence and joy as the dominant and resolving notes of worship. There is never any resolution in despair nor any unmitigated fear of darkness, not even in the dark nights of the saints. Even Christ had His angel of the agony.

Then take the sense of community exercised in worship. Not only with God but also with fellowmen, each person needs to have a measure of happy, successful and significant relationships for personality development. These are never more fully achieved than on the sublime level of corporate worship, the corporate singing of God's praises, the corporate offering of the one divine Victim of sacrifice and of all of us together with Him and, finally, the completion of the sacrifice by eating together the one Bread that unites us in the very core of our being. There is a sense of belonging to a vitally active and purposeful community. There is also the sense of accomplishment through engaging in sublime action that is infallibly successful where the proper dispositions are present.

Thus we come from worship with the awareness that we are alive spiritually, precisely and only in relation to one another, through the one divine life we all share. Renewed and strengthened in union, we can know the joy of companionship in spite of the burden that imperfections put upon charity. In fact, formed and strengthened through worship, we are strong enough to let those very personality-conflicts purify us and aid the growth of our personality. The peace with God and with one another, re-established and made stronger in Mass, flows out into peace and cooperation in work and social relations. Of high importance in this regard is the consecration of love in the sacrament of marriage and the graces that are given to live its difficult obligations.

Not to be passed over in the healthy outlet and growth of positive emotions through worship. Most important, of course, is the affective prayer that assures the interior sincerity of corporate worship and should normally accompany it. But there is also the beauty of song and ceremony, of vestment and decoration, of the very house of God. And that emotional control which is essential for personal maturity is embodied and exercised in the beautiful restraint that is a mark of everything sacred.

Let it be said with emphasis that all this is not to advocate an emotional approach to worship nor emotion for emotion's sake, least of all the blasphemy of worship for emotion's sake. It is simply to say that we are human beings and that all human forces can be helped toward maturity through enlightened and sincere living of worship. Besides, as Maritain says, "A new age of civilization will realize again that the descent of the divine plenitude into man matters more than the ascent of the man towards self-perfection. In this new age the movement by which the human being answers God's movement of effusion would not take place, as in the Middle Ages, in a childlike, ignorant-of-itself humanity. Its new simplicity would be a mature and experienced, self-awakened simplicity, enlightened by what might be called a free and evangelical introspection."[26] The clock cannot be turned back.

Since the human person by his social nature is inevitably committed to develop within and through association with his fellow-

---

[26] Maritain, *op. cit.*, p. 95.

men, and since by his supernatural and eternal destiny he is committed also to take proprotionate means to such an end, he is called to communal worship and to all its formative power. Man's whole being must be subject to the creative action of God even while man accepts sin as his own doing and knows the imperfection of his offering. This humility which is truth, this humble supplication which purifies, far from destroying or cramping personality, rather deepens and enriches it. As Guardini says, Christ living in a person guarantees that person's most individual personality. "The more powerfully Christ activates an individual, and the more completely He penetrates his being, the more clearly that individual attains his own inherent personality."[27]

Moreover, "As he kneels in communal worship and shares in the expression of the common needs and universal aspirations, he grows in the knowledge of God's supremacy and solicitude which now becomes so comprehensive as to extend infinitely beyond the narrow confines of his own person. . . . Above all, it is in the common life of the spiritual family that he comes to realize the social implications of religious living, the obligation to 'bear one another's burdens.' "[28]

This spiritual formation through deliberate and active participation is all the more important in a civil order of democracy where the presumption is in favor of freedom and where constraint must prove its own case. There is an unconscious carryover of an habitual attitude and habit of acting from civil and social life into religion. While freedom is presumed to be freedom under God and therefore bound by moral law, in practice, laws are obeyed because they merit and receive the consent of the civil community, because they express the community's own

[27] Guardini, *The Lord,* Chicago, Regnery, 1954, pp. 449-450.
[28] Giguerre, *Social Value of Public Worship,* Washington, D.C., Catholic University of America Press, 1950, p. 62.

convictions as to what is just or unjust, good or evil. This habit of thinking and acting, transferred to religion, puts a great responsibility upon democratic man to abandon himself voluntarily to formation in sanctity through living a life centered in worship. His constant return to Christ's sacrifice and sacraments is not a refuge nor an escape but a continual rebirth to new divine life, new courage, new strength in Christ's battle and Christ's victory. "The essence of Christianity, of its grandeur and obscurity, is that Christ lives in the Christian."[29] "For me to live is Christ and to die is gain."[30]

"Not that I have already obtained this, or already have been made perfect, but I press on hoping that I may lay hold of that for which Jesus Christ has laid hold of me."[31] This pressing on with unshakeable hope is the work of every Christian. Christ has laid hold of us and given us a Christian being that is Christian greatness. We do not have to do extraordinary and sensational things to prove our existence. God has put greatness in us. To live what we believe is to the sign that our disillusioned and frightened world needs. "The path of the just is like shining light that grows in brilliance till perfect day."[32]

That path of the just will be full of the contradictions that marked the path of Christ. And the reason for carrying a cross is to be nailed to it. On the cross we are most powerful because most in union with the redeeming death of Christ. To redeem men the Christian saint must be as opposed to their diseases of the spirit as he is deep in his love for them. "If a new age of civilization is to come rather than a new age of barbarism, the deepest requirement of such an age will be the sanctification of secular life, a fecundation of energies and brotherly love."[33]

[29] Guardini, *op. cit.,* p. 448.
[30] Phil. 1:20.
[31] Phil. 3:12.
[32] Prov. 4:19.
[33] Maritain, *op. cit.,* p. 116.

This is the work of Christian personality brought to fervor and sanctity. We cannot set the timetable but we know with the certainty of faith that "What God proposes 'that comes about, that happens; even though it happens slowly, it happens ceaselessly' (St. Augustine). God is truly the Lord of history."[34] We are therefore committed to hope. And we are committed to joy through the hope of entering into God's eternal peace. We are committed to be that wonderful somebody with vast influence, the somebody we call saint. We can never give way to bitterness, nor despair nor flee like a child from opposition. "God has not given us a spirit of timidity but of power and love and discipline."[35]

[34] Pius XII, "To The Tenth International Congress of Historical Sciences," *The Pope Speaks*, 2 (1955) 206.
[35] II Tim. 1:7.

Chapter Twelve

Worship and the Mission of the Church

SINCE the Church is the Mystical Christ, the mission of the Church must finally be the mission of Christ Himself. What are the purposes of the Incarnation? God became incarnate to atone for the sins of the world, to transform the people of God into a new people and to bring men to mystical union with God through grace on earth and through the light of glory in the mansions of heaven.

This mission of the Church can be summarized in various ways. It must, first of all, achieve the purpose of all creation and render to God the perfect worship of the people of God. For such a sublime, over-all purpose there is the basic sanctity and dignity given to men through their Redeemer, a grace that is also expansive and missionary. "The perfection conferred on Christ's humanity by the hypostatic union makes that humanity, as it were, universally human, so that Christ can reach out to all men, contain them in Himself by grace, and raise them to the supernatural state. This mystic fullness enables His humanity, which was made the unity and head of the race, to be the instrument that is perfectly equipped to purify and sanctify all mankind."[1] Thus the Church is revealed in its apocalyptic consummation as "the completion of him who fills all with all."[2]

While every expansion of the Mystical Christ is a growth from within, quiet but vitally forceful like the leaven and the mustard seed, there is also an expansion that reaches by exterior agents over the earth's curve into the remotest village and human heart. That is what Jesus meant when He promised at the Last Supper, "Amen, amen, I say to you, he who believes in me, the works that I do he shall do, and greater than these he shall do."[3] Jesus did not refer to miracles but to the world-wide apostolate. He limited Himself to Palestine but His Mystical Self was to convert the world and to transform the inner being of men through the Holy Spirit whom He would send.

Still, the apstolic work of the Church is really the work of Jesus Himself. It is His doing. "Whatever you ask in my name, that I will do, in order that the Father may be glorified in the Son."[4] Therefore it can be said under another aspect that the mission of the Church is to make known the mystery of Christ. "Her whole end is to show us Christ, lead us to Him, and communicate His grace to us; to put it in a nutshell, she exists solely to put us into relation with Him. She alone can do that, and it is a task which she never completes."[5]

Pius XII has made this aspect of the Church's mission more specific. "The object of missionary activity, as all know, is to bring the light of the Gospel to new races and to form new Christians. However, the ultimate goal of missionary endeavor,

[1] Mersch, *op. cit.*, p. 610.
[2] Eph. 1:23.
[3] Jn. 14:12.
[4] Jn. 14:13.
[5] De Lubac, *The Splendor of the Church,* New York, Sheed and Ward, 1955, p. 148.

which should never be lost sight of, is to establish the Church on sound foundations among non-Christian peoples, and place it under its own native hierarchy."[6]

So the immediate mission of the Church is to make disciples of all nations, to form a world family in Christ. Through the Church all men are to receive the mind of Christ the divine Teacher, the life of Christ the divine Sanctifier and the will of Christ the divine Ruler. This mission to evangelize, to sanctify and to rule is as visible and lasting, as mediatorial and universal as the work of Christ. Jesus said, "You shall be witnesses for me . . . even to the very ends of the earth."[7] Again to Saul, "I am Jesus, whom thou art persecuting."[8] Jesus chose to speak through the visible lips of His Mystical Body. And He guaranteed the endurance of His work, for He said, "I am with you all days, even unto the consummation of the world."[9] Like Christ the one Mediator, the Church also is at once the indispensable and the unobtrusive link of communication between God and man. There is no other. "Without me you can do nothing."[10] All salvation is through the Mystical Christ. Finally, the mission of the Church is a mission of all its members to all people and to all things, each one doing his or her part according to office and occupation.

Against so vast a purpose there stand formidable obstacles. The prince of darkness has many witting and unwitting allies in his warfare against the Prince of Light. His original deception has left deeply penetrating consequences. Personal sin has increased the havoc. These disturbances have been compounded during the centuries by an accumulation of misconceptions and

---

[6] Pius XII, "Evangelii Praecones," *Catholic Mind,* 53 (1951) 579.
[7] Acts 1:8.
[8] Acts 9:5.
[9] Mt. 28:20.
[10] Jn. 15:5.

antipathies. Christendom has suffered a triple division that began with the Jewish people when some of them accepted Christ
and some rejected Him. After a few centuries of expansion came
the great schism between east and west. Then the glory of the
Middle Ages passed into sunset with the religious revolt of the
sixteenth century. In the field of meeting social problems the
early Fathers of the Church preached some revolutionary principles. Later, as Pius XII has recalled, "Everybody knows the
social reforms of St. Elizabeth of Hungary, of St. Ferdinand
in Castile and of St. Louis of France."[11] But to our confusion
we must admit that atheistic humanists, under the inspiration
of Hegel, Marx and Nietzsche, took over all too largely in setting the direction of social changes. Perhaps their hopeless inadequacy and bungling, protected by ruthless force, will serve
as the scourge of God upon the practical atheists who have worn
the name Christian but ignored its teaching.

In any case, God's glory will yet be served. His arm is not
shortened. He began the mission of redemption by entering
into sacred history. He personally spoke to Abraham, to Isaac
and to Jacob and told them how to guide His people and where
to settle them down. He spoke personally to Moses and the
other prophets and told them how to prepare His people for
the coming of the Redeemer. And a part of that long preparation was a detailed worship that embodied the theology of God
as the Father and King of all nations whom all kings and nations
were to adore and serve. He was also a God of tenderness who
wanted above all to be loved and served out of love, as Pius
XII has indicated again in his recent encyclical on the Sacred
Heart. The tenderness of the Father was nowhere more clearly
shown than in the divine delicacy of the Incarnation. He could
have sent us a fully grown majestic Savior who would have
cleansed the world of its sin by a sweeping gesture. Instead, He

[11] Pius XII, "Evangelii Praecones," *loc. cit.*, p. 583.

predicted and prepared a virgin mother who would bear the
Redeemer as her own Child in the casual simplicities and incon-
veniences of census-taking. Then she became the Queen of apostles and missioners both in her grace-filled dignity and office
and in the order of time when she took her Redeemer-Son on
that first precipitous trip into foreign lands. But she guarded
and raised Him till He left her home to choose and form the
nucleus of His new visible society.

Through passages from the historical books, the psalms and
the prophets, which are read in our worship, we learn and relive the history of our salvation in its long beginnings. With
the actual coming of our Savior, every major event in His life
took on both an importance and a sanctifying power in our salvation and has been enshrined in a Mass celebration. When
He prepared for the total sacrifice of Himself on the cross He
left Himself with us both in the very act of sacrifice and in the
living substance of His body and blood united to His total divinity. He established His Church and its mission and went to
heaven. But He also remained with us in an act of unbloody
sacrifice, in a corporal presence, in an active sanctifying power
that somehow extends from the moment of each redeeming event
in His life to its sacramental presence in each feast that cele-
brates that event. His self-oblation, His wounds, His living
intercession, and His acceptance by the Father have not ceased;
they become present in every Mass.

Pius XII deepens our understanding of how Christ carries
on His sanctifying mission in worship. "Along with the Church,
her Divine Founder is present in every liturgical function: Christ
is present at the august sacrifice of the altar both in the person
of His minister and above all under the eucharistic species. He
is present in the sacraments, infusing into them the power which
makes them ready instruments of sanctification. He is present,
finally, in the prayer of praise and petition we direct to God,

as it is written: 'Where there are two or three gathered together in My Name, there am I in the midst of them' " (Matt. 18:22).[12]

Jesus chose human instruments to perpetuate His mission of redemption. He empowers them for their destiny by giving them a share in His one priesthood by baptism, confirmation and holy orders. To prepare and complete the work of priesthood, Christ also gives them a share in His work of teaching and governing in His name. These powers to sanctify, to teach and to govern all center in worship, for worship is both the prime creaturely duty and the prime and indispensable source of life. But His human instruments do not exist nor function apart from Him. Always it is Our Lord at work in His Church and in His ministers. "All her teaching is a lie, if she does not announce the Truth which is Christ; all her glory is vanity if she does not find it in the humility of Christ. Her very name is something foreign to us if it does not at once call to mind the one Name given to men for their salvation. If she is not the sacrament, the effective sign, of Christ, then she is nothing."[13]

In view of an apostolate that increases with increase in population, with the success of the enemies of Christianity and with means of communication that takes us everywhere quickly, we can again love the wisdom of the Holy Spirit that awakens missionary zeal in the baptized and confirmed. This is another sign of vitality in the Church. They are ready to accept the command of Pius XII: "Cooperation in the spread of the kingdom of God . . . is a command incumbent on everyone who has been . . . called in Baptism to citizenship of the kingdom of God."[14] As an encouragement in this sharing of Christ's mission, the Holy Father cites sacred history. "The Gospel followed the great Roman roads and was spread not only by bishops and

[12] *Mediator Dei,* par. 20.
[13] De Lubac, *op. cit.,* p. 160.
[14] *Summi Pontificatus,* Washington, D.C., N.C.W.C., p. 34.

priests but also by public officials, soldiers and private citizens. Thousands of Christian neophytes, whose names are today unknown, were fired with zeal to promote the new religion they had embraced and endeavored to prepare the way for the coming of the Gospel. That explains why after about 100 years Christianity had penetrated into all the chief cities of the Roman Empire."[15] He gives the laity a large share of the credit for the spread of early Christianity. This is also our hope in an age when history is being reshaped with frightening speed and when the means for giving it a Christian shape need to be greatly multiplied.

The laity also play an increasingly important part in what Pius XII calls "the manifold power and the apostolic effectiveness of sacred music. . . . All who use the art they possess to compose such musical compositions, to teach them or to perform them by singing or using musical instruments, undoubtedly exercise in many and various ways a true and genuine apostolate. They will receive from Christ the Lord the generous rewards and honors of apostles for the work they have done so faithfully."[16]

Our Lord's sharing of His mission with human persons brings us back to what He prayed for at the Last Supper: "Sanctify them in truth."[17] That includes all His members, even though in its immediate application it meant those at table with Our Lord. The fact remains that "The body of the faithful as a whole, insofar as it puts the gifts it has received into act, is the cause of the life and radiance of the Church."[18] There is no enduring vitality in the Church without a vital laity. Since saints are the great triumph of the Church, it can be said also that

---

[15] Pius XII, "Evangelii Praecones," *loc. cit.,* p. 582.
[16] *On Sacred Music,* par. 38.
[17] Jn. 17:17. Cf. Confraternity Commentary on the New Testament.
[18] Journet, *op. cit.,* p. 19.

the great mission of the Church is to spread sanctity. Quoting St. Paul's reference to the Church as "a holy temple, a habitation of God in the Spirit,"[19] Pius XII has said, "Thus the society founded by the divine Redeemer, whether in her doctrine and government, or in the sacrifice and sacraments instituted in Him, or finally, in the ministry, which He has confided to her charge with the outpouring of His prayer and the shedding of His blood, has no other goal or purpose than to increase ever in strength and unity."[20] For everyone, worship is the prime source of the sanctity that so much increases the strength and unity of the Church.

Since all creation is to be redeemed and "Will be delivered from its slavery to corruption into the freedom of the glory of the sons of God,"[21] the mission of the Church extends to things as well as to persons. Missioned to "preach the gospel to every creature,"[22] the Church purifies the best in every culture and nation, restores it to the divine order through Christ and remains the enduring meeting place of Creator and creature. Therefore, everything that surrounds and concerns human persons, everything in everyone, his religious and social life, his work and intellectual life, his worries and joys must be reached and transformed. Nothing is beyond the mission and power communicated by Christ to His members.

The mission of the Church to all peoples and all things, therefore, puts a quality of reverence into her approach to the mission world. There is an immediately practical reason for this. "Respect for what is authentically religious, for what bears marks of religious promise, must carry with it respect for all the human and cultural heritage bound up with it. It is irreligious to de-

---

[19] Eph. 2:22.
[20] *Mediator Dei,* par. 19.
[21] Rom. 8:21.
[22] Mk. 16:15.

stroy or upset the praiseworthy elements of a human culture, for
by so doing we diminish some rich aspect of the Church's future
heritage."[23] In this age when everything is at the crossroads
of international influence it is doubly important to let the vitality
of essential Christianity flow into the accidental but necessary
forms of expression that are native to each nation and culture.
Shining through these multiple human facets of east and west,
north and south, Christ's atoning and sanctifying love will be
at once more penetrating and more glorious.[24]

In reaching out to all peoples, therefore, the Church has no
intention of leveling all native differences into a single way of
life and of worship. That is indicated again by the instruction
on the new Holy Week Ordinal.[25] The intention is rather to
reverence those differences and to bring them to their highest
perfection, because through them the full universality, the full
catholicism of Christian purpose will be realized. It is highly
important also that this adaptation of native cultural riches be
made in order to use their good qualities in making easier and
more fruitful the preaching of the Gospel.[26]

Pius XII gives the profound reason for this broad realistic
approach. "Human nature, though, owing to Adam's fall, it
is tainted with original sin, has in itself something that is naturally Christian (cf. Tertull. Apologet., cap. XVII; ML, I, 377A);
and this, if illumined by divine light and nourished by God's
grace, can eventually be changed into true and supernatural
virtue. This is the reason why the Catholic Church has neither
scorned nor rejected the pagan philosophies. Instead, after free-
ing them from error and all contamination she has perfected

[23] Hasseveldt, *The Church: A Divine Mystery,* Chicago, Fides, 1954,
p. 176.
[24] Cf. Danielou, *The Salvation of the Nations,* London, Sheed and
Ward, 1949, p. 36.
[25] S. Cong. of Rites, Nov. 16, 1955, par. 23.
[26] Cf. *Summi Pontificatus,* p. 19.

and completed them by Christian revelation. So likewise the Church has graciously made her own the native art and culture which in some countries is so highly developed. She has carefully encouraged them and brought them to a point of aesthetic perfection that of themselves they probably would never have attained. By no means has she repressed native customs and traditions but has given them a certain religious significance; she has even transformed native feast days and made them serve to commemorate the martyrs and to celebrate mysteries of the faith."[27]

There is no need to stress further the obvious relation between the sanctifying mission of the Church and the sacrifice, sacraments and sacramentals that are the source of all sanctification. Be it enough to sum up by saying that Jesus Himself chose persons and used things to continue this central purpose of His coming. There is normally no maintenance of spiritual vitality, let alone its expansion, without the usual channels of worship regularly and actively exercised. The exceptions, such as the Nagasaki Christians and how they kept the faith with only a limited worship, suggest that God must have compensated in His own divine way.

One way to point up the governing mission of the Church in relation to worship would be to catalogue the heresies and undesirable practices that have stemmed from worship or to the temporary expedients that found their way into worship throughout Christian history. Such an approach could turn out to be either very tiresome, or discouraging, or so alarming as to engender panic at the least thought of adaptations; it could also be just plain morbid. Pius XII has indicated clearly enough in Mediator Dei the abuses that spring both from excessive attachments to ancient rites and from the introduction of new rites without proper sanction.

[27] Pius XII, "Evangelii Praecones," *loc. cit.,* p. 588.

It is of more lasting value and a greater inspiration to take the positive approach and recall the close connection between doctrine and its expression in worship as the two developed together through the centuries. That has already been treated.[28] It remains to state the obvious conclusion that since *doctrine* must be so carefully developed and defined on the basis of scripture and tradition, so also must the forms of worship that express doctrine be carefully governed for accuracy and suitability. It is an oblique tribute to the teaching power of liturgy that it can shape worshippers in wrong ways as well as in right.

The very mission to govern is established through worship. Only through baptism and confirmation do the laity enter into their very real power to govern the formation of their charges in worship, and to lead them in worship, whether those charges are children in the home, or children in school and social welfare institutions, or choirs under the hand of directors. And only through holy orders do priests and bishops enter into their power to receive and apply in details the prescriptions for worship that come from the Holy Father. Only to such chosen and consecrated men is given the supernatural power to consecrate the Body and Blood of Christ and to absolve from sin; only to them is given the authority to govern worship in Christ's name; only to them is given the indelible character of holy orders and the grace needed for their clerical functions and clerical state of life.

In this connection it should be recalled again that the Holy Father is not a substitute for a Christ who has ceased to exist but the vicar and voice of the living ressurected Christ. Neither is the priest at the altar a substitute for a non-existing Christ but a minister for the one Mediator-Christ who lives and goes on making intercession for us in heaven. "Prior to acting as

---

[28] Cf. supra, pp. 62-84.

representative of the community before the throne of God, the priest is the ambassador of the divine Redeemer."[29] So the exercise and governing of worship is still the continuous mission of Christ carried on in a person-to-person command and a person-to-person communication of life and power.

It remains for us to deal with the teaching mission of Christ and His Church in relation to worship. Teaching must begin with holding and preserving the revealed word of God. Pius XII numbers the sacred science of liturgy among the "theological sources" from which Popes and Councils ". . . have not seldom drawn many an argument." Then he adds that liturgy helps the clarification and development of doctrine. Finally, he states that liturgy teaches doctrine. "Since the liturgy is also a profession of eternal truths, and subject, as such, to the supreme teaching authority of the Church, it can supply proofs and testimony, quite clearly of no litle value, towards the determination of a particular point of Christian doctrine."[30] Moreover, Archbishop Pietro Parente gives the sacred liturgy as one of the principal instruments by which divine tradition has been conserved.[31] And in reference to Mary's universal mediation, Garrigou-Lagrange lists liturgy as the first of the ways in which the ordinary teaching office of the Church proposes this doctrine.[32]

A thousand texts could be cited to illustrate different points of doctrine that set like jewels in the worship of the Church through the centuries. But it is more to our point in speaking of the mission of the Church to cite precisely those texts which embody the universal reach of Christ's kingdom. We will instance only a few. In the Didache, or Doctrine of the Twelve

[29] *Mediator Dei,* par. 40.
[30] *Ibid.,* par. 48.
[31] Parente, *op. cit.,* p. 285.
[32] Garrigou-Lagrange, *The Mother of the Savior,* St. Louis, Herder, 1949, p. 197.

Apostles, which dates from the end of the first century or the beginning of the second, there is this prayer before the consecration of the bread: "Just as this broken bread, formerly scattered on the mountains was gathered to become one whole, so may thy Church be gathered from the extremities of the earth into thy Kingdom." Then after Holy Communion: "Remember thy Church, O Lord. ... Gather her from the four winds, this sanctified Church."[33] In the Apostolic Constitutions, which was composed in the second half of the fourth century but included very ancient liturgical traditions, there is a prayer which implies the triple mission of governing, sanctifying and teaching: "Let us pray for peace, tranquility of the world and of all the holy Churches of God. . . ; let us pray for the Church holy, catholic and apostolic which is spread out from one end of the world to the other. . . ; let us pray for our brethren, the neophytes, that God may consolidate and strengthen them. . . ; let us pray for those who live in error outside the fold, that the Lord may convert them."[34] Through the ages the cry of John the Baptist has been our preparation for Holy Communion, "Behold the Lamb of God who takes away the sins of the world." And the Messianic Passion Psalm has always been on our lips. In it we pray, "All the ends of the earth shall remember and turn to the Lord; all the families of the nations shall bow down before him."[35] Every Mass and office of an apostle is filled with the apostolic mission of the Church. This is a sample of how doctrine is both contained and taught through official corporate prayer.

There are reasons both profound and practical why worship is intimately related to the teaching mission of the Church. St. Augustine said, "A man speaks wisely in proportion as he is

[33] *Didache*, IX-X.
[34] *Apostolic Constitutions*, Bk. 8, c. 10, *P. G.*, 1:1086-1087.
[35] Ps. 21:28.

steeped in Holy Scripture."[36] The scripture readings and psalms in each Mass are thrust into our hands for our meditation and study and as texts for teaching and preaching. All the mysteries of redemption are contained in the successive Masses of the Church year. There is a concentration on essential truths and all truths hold together around the mystery of Christ and His Mother. All that God's love has done and will do through all the different stages of redemption becomes the good news of salvation.

The teaching of the scripture passages in the proper of the Mass is dominantly dogmatic and therefore needs to be supplemented by systematic instruction in the commandments and in the applications of doctrine and morals to every phase of life. But as much as possible this systematic instruction should be related to the temporal and sanctoral cycles of the Church year, mainly by illustrations. Above all, all such Christian teaching should keep the unified, joyous, hopeful, personalized quality of the texts of our worship. "The Christian feast achieves to an eminent degree . . . the demonstration of the Christian values in a luminous and attractive manner. Christianity is no longer considered and practiced as a troublesome obligation, but lived as a free gift and a sacred mission."[37]

It may be said also that liturgy serves as a model for teaching in certain respects. There is a beautiful dignity, a restraint and objective depth to its thought and its manner of expression. It is neither bombastic nor banal, neither sentimental nor cold. Moreover, vivid word pictures and stories, ceremonies, symbols and pictures gives concreteness and directness, implicity and drama to thought and presentation. And there is the repetition of essential points which all good teaching requires.

Very intimately related to the effect of teaching through wor-

[36] St. Aug., *De Doctrina Christiana,* 4:8.
[37] Hofinger, *Lumen Vitae,* Vol. X, no. 2-3, p. 246.

ship are the motives and dispositions of all participants. The very act of coming to worship normally presupposes at least a desire to do God's will. Within the service itself, instruction, song and prayer awaken a sense of dependence upon God, a sense of sorrow for sin, and a desire for union with God in prayer, in holy communion and through the hours and days after the service ends. This makes for the repentant, humble, eager dispositions that open the heart to the word of God. And all the while, the very worship itself is the immediate source of the grace that prompts such dispositions and brings them to full fruit.

In line with the power of God's word to stir the human heart when received in the context of official prayer, our present need brings forward to the present moment the force of the Council of Trent on this point. The Council "Commands all pastors and those having the care of souls to explain frequently during the celebration of Mass in person or by others from among those things that are read in Mass, and among other things something also of the mystery of this most holy sacrifice, especially on Sundays and feast days."[38]

To be more specific about the direct teaching that is woven into our feast day worship, there is something very personal and almost tangible about religious truths that are embodied in concrete forms. The very house of God is a sanctified place apart, a holy of holies. The altar is the place of sacrifice where God is offered to God. The Stations of the Cross surround the worshippers like a crown of thorns and recall their vocation to fill up what is wanting to the sufferings of Christ. And in crib and crucifix, in statues and symbols, in the sacred vestments and ceremonies, and above all in active participation in the holy mystery of Calvary made present, truth is made visible.

God and the whole world of the supernatural thus become

[38] *Council of Trent,* Session **XXII**; Denz. 946.

not merely a contact with truth but also a personal experience of God as a Person to be adored and loved with mind and heart and body, as well as a Person who is actively at work in the depths of a person's soul and who is welcomed there. This religious experience gives a unity and fullness to life that helps to quiet the turbulence of conflict within and without, even while it transcends such conflict. All the fascinating mystery in any experience of a person is infinitely deepened in the experience of God. And we end on our knees immersed in the abyss of our nothingness. In that abyss we are still more baffled by the thought of our magnificent destiny. That is the moment of grace towards which God has been leading us all the time. To the extent that we are prepared to give our all, to that extent God is prepared to overwhelm us with the giving of Himself.

This relationship with God which is lived in the depths of the soul in adoration and love is experienced also within the living community of the Mystical Christ at worship. In the mystery of celebrating Christ in His great act of redemption, all His members are one great community in Him, with a single mind and heart united in a common purpose of glorifying the Father through union with one another in His Son. Within this unity there is still a conscious hierarchy of gifts and offices and functions which merit both mutual respect and cooperation. This sense of belonging to a vital supernatural organism engaged in a sublime and successful action answers to a deep psychological need in our times.

Thus each feast becomes a solemn profession of faith, an acceptance of truth that is learned by a sacred doing, by a joyous religious experience. The wavering and weak are strengthened and deepened in their faith and fervor. Supported by their local community, they feel themselves one with the brothers and sisters of Christ everywhere at worship, in heaven and on earth. This builds community spirit. All together truly experience the mystery of the Church with an awe and love that calls to their devotion and cooperation. It is a foretaste of the Church in its final stage of triumph.

The Christian feasts, therefore, make us share in the mystery of salvation which is celebrated. In that sense they give what they signify. In each feast a faraway time and place and Person suddenly become alive and active in the present moment and place, bringing grace, courage and happiness, a deeper insight into the mystery and a deeper desire to live its message. Pius XI said that nothing would serve better to make the Kingship of our Savior recognized and understood as widely as possible than a special feast in honor of that Kingship. "For people are instructed in the truths of faith and brought to appreciate the inner joys of religion far more effectually by the annual celebration of our sacred mysteries than by any official pronouncements of the teaching of the Church. Such pronouncements usually reach only a few and the more learned among the faithful; feasts reach them all. The former speak but once, the latter speak every year—in fact forever. The Church's teaching affects the mind primarily; her feasts affect both mind and heart, and have a salutary effect upon the whole of man's nature. Man is composed of body and soul, and he needs these external festivities so that the sacred rites, in all their beauty and variety, may stimulate him to drink more deeply of the fountain of God's teaching, that he make it a part of himself, and use it with profit for his spiritual life."[39]

For the sake of implementing the teaching mission of the Church, all services should be as easy to understand and as easy to learn as possible, with the parts for the people either simple but forceful responses and affirmations or easily divided and recited texts. Hymns, prayers and ceremonies should appeal to the best that is in people and thus form them to appreciate

[39] Pius XI, *Quas Primas, loc cit.,* Vol. II, p. 39.

and desire the best. In many places this may mean beginning with something that is only second or third best but which really appeals. In any case, variety and dramatic impact are necessary to any sort of appeal. The very solemnity of worship heightens the impressiveness, suggests awe for God's majesty, gives vent to spiritual joy and thus helps the inner disposition of the worshippers. Of course, everything possible should be done to prepare for each Sunday and each feast by oral or printed explanations and by encouraging confession and communion, with more elaborate preparations for greater feasts.

Happily, the changes in worship that have been made give hope for more and more of the vernacular. The language of the people greatly strengthens the teaching power of feast day celebrations by making everything more vivid and understandable. With the vernacular, great spontaneity will be added to the grandeur of the celebration; and the appeal to come and take part will be stronger. A Lutheran minister wrote in a letter to the editor of AMEN:[40] "A liturgical life such as one can find in Catholicism, when presented in the vernacular, can offer to the entire realm of Protestantism the media of worship and living which they seek but somehow cannot find. I can say this with the conviction of experience, since I found this to be so in my own life."

Whatever we may say about the teaching power of liturgy we cannot forget that its direct and essential aim is not to evangelize but to render adoration, thanksgiving, atonement and petition to God. Its purpose is not knowledge of divine mysteries but a deeper faith in them and an active participation in their celebration. A feast day or Sunday is not a mere solemn catechetical lesson nor an exceptionally favorable occasion for explaining and creating a love for Christian doctrine. Always

[40] *Amen*, February 1, 1954.

and above everything else, the liturgy is the whole Christ in the action of prayer.

This action of prayer is part of the whole dynamic, expansive action of a Church that is made to grow and grow till the consummation of days. The expansion takes place first within the individual soul when transformation into Christ empties and frees the soul for the inflow of divine life and joyous charity. Ransomed and redeemed by Christ, each Christian is henceforth committed to spend himself for Christ and the purposes of His mission. "Not only the sacred ministers and those who have consecrated themselves to God in religious life, but the other members as well of the mystical body of Jesus Christ have the obligation of working hard and constantly for the upbuilding and increase of this Body."[41]

To plunge so deeply into the mission of Christ can mean to plunge also into His passion and death. It may be that God will ask an individual or a whole group of His members to save souls by their failures. It may be that some are chosen to be crucified with Christ for the salvation of their very persecutors. "They shall look upon him whom they have pierced."[42]

In any case, through the light and strength and solidarity gained from worshipping together, we shall be able to carry on Christ's mission and "To walk in a manner worthy of the calling with which you were called, with all humility and meekness, with patience, bearing with one another in love, careful to preserve the unity of the Spirit in the bond of peace: one body and one Spirit, even as you were called in one hope of your calling; one Lord, one faith, one Baptism; one God and Father of all, who is above all, and throughout all, and in us all."[43]

[41] *Mystici Corporis,* par. 96.
[42] Jn. 19:37.
[43] Eph. 4:1-6.

Chapter Thirteen

Worship with Voice and Hands

IN view of the mission of the Church to all peoples, we will consider the relation of worship to singing and making . We may hope: 1. To increase appreciation of everything good in native cultures. 2. To prepare for leadership in encouraging good native artists, composers and singers and in teaching people to appreciate the best in their own native culture. 3. To guide native artists in the embodying of Christian mysteries and ideals in native media of expression. 4. To see and encourage Christian singing and making as an act of prudence, the choice of the right means to the right end, and therefore as formation in virtue.

Singing and making can be treated together, for as Pius XII says, "Sacred music obeys laws and rules which are no different from those prescribed for all religious art, and, indeed, for art in general."[2]

[1] Pius XII.
[2] *On Sacred Music,* par. 22.

The Holy Father also gives the relation of all art to worship from the viewpoint of the person acting. "The artist who is firm in his faith and leads a life worthy of a Christian, who is motivated by the love of God and reverently uses the powers the Creator has given him, expresses and manifests the truths he holds and the piety he possesses so skillfully, beautifully and pleasingly in colors and lines or sounds and harmonies that this sacred labor of art is an act of worship and religion for him."[3]

He calls the "sacred labor of art . . . an act of worship." All of you probably will agree with me when I say that all of you are workers, because everybody does some kind of work, whether it be with a tool, a pencil, a vacuum-cleaner, a typewriter, or books or anything else. But do you agree when I say that all of you are artists? Probably not. It depends on what you mean by an artist. There is little chance of agreement about anything unless you get down to essentials. Take an artist for what he is essentially. An artist is simply one who makes things well. What is made well gives pleasure. Art is that which when seen gives pleasure. As we commonly say, "That is a beautiful piece of work. That is a beautiful tool, or a beautiful table." Things are well made when they are true and good and therefore beautiful. Whatever you may think of art, you will in some way think of it as something good and true and beautiful.

What makes it that way? That is where you face things in their essentials. And that is why you can use the phrase, "philosophy of art," because philosophy is the study of things in their ultimate causes. We will come back later to the purpose for which a thing is made, to its formal distinctiveness, to the material that is used and to the tools and skills and moral integrity that go into the making. These are the ultimate causes of making things well.

But the ultimate cause of causes, the first cause of everything

[3] *Ibid.,* par. 28.

is God. That is why you can talk about a "Christian philosophy of art." Christ, the God-Man Redeemer, came to remake the souls of men and to lead them to remake the earth, all for the glory of the Father and the happiness of men. Christ is the Head and you are His members. You have to help Him in the remaking that we call redemption. You have to cooperate in remaking yourselves and in remaking the earth. "All creation groans and travails in pain until now. And not only it, but we ourselves ... groan within ourselves, waiting for the adoption as sons, the redemption of our body."[4] Our full, perfect final adoption, our full, perfect redemption, and the final unchanging, incorruptible permanence of things will come only when we enter body and soul into final glory. But it begins now with everything we do to live as adopted Christians and responsible apostles and co-workers of Christ and in Him and under Him. And we must begin now to help all creation to share in our partially unfolded redemption. Creation, rightly ordered to the service of God and man, will help us to love God and man. Therefore we have to put order and harmony and goodness back into the world where God meant it to be.

God made man to His own image and likeness and that is the greatest beauty in man. He made the earth to be an image of heaven. Therefore the first home of Adam and Eve was called Paradise. But already in heaven there had been trouble and a great battle. It began with an angel, an archangel, but an angel who had a resentment and who rebelled against God. He led other angels in a great battle and lost. That was the end of heaven for them and the beginning of devils and the kingdom of hell.

When God made a perfect earth, He placed a perfect man and a perfect woman in a perfect home, called the Garden of Eden. They had things to do and to make there because "The

---

[4] Rom. 8:22-23.

Lord God took the man and placed him in the garden of Eden to till it and keep it."[5] "It is not good for man to be alone; I will make him a helper like himself."[6] And there was so much harmony and beauty and happiness there that the devil envied man. Besides, that fallen angel was still an outlaw from heaven and a rebel against God. He was a troublemaker and he successfully tempted Adam and Eve to pride and disobedience.

"The woman saw that the tree was good for food, pleasing to the eyes, and desirable for the knowledge it would give."[7] "Good for food, pleasing, desirable for knowledge." Knowledge, pleasure, usefulness. You can almost hear Eve talking herself into taking a bite. But all her excuses were against the command of God. So it was not innocent knowledge nor innocent usefulness but rather the excesses of pride and sensuality and avarice. (Avarice is the inordinate love of earthly goods.) In any case, Adam fell for the bait, too, and at once their perfection their peace and harmony and happiness were gone. They had rebelled against God and the world rebelled against them. Their own natural instincts also rebelled against their reason. Anarchy was on the loose and with it came disorder and ugliness and suffering. And we have been trying ever since to undo disorder and ugliness and suffering.

This background must be considered because the only real world is the world in which God is the center of everything. If God is not the center of everything, then everything is off-center, out of balance, ugly in some way or other. Christ came to re-center, reorder all things in God. Therefore the only normal life is the Christ-centered life, the full Christian life. And only a normal man will do things and make things in a normal way. Man does not have to think of God every minute of the day

---

[5] Gen. 2:15.
[6] Gen. 2:18.
[7] Gen. 3:6.

but He does have to obey God every minute; and he has to respect God's real world in everything he does. He must love God and love his neighbor as himself. He cannot be a secularist who ignores God nor an individualist who ignores his neighbor. In all his doing and making he must be fully a man all the time, a person who subjects this bodily instincts to his reason. And he must be fully a Christian who lives after the teaching and example of Christ and who manifests outwardly the Christ who dwells in his soul. In this is man's splendor, for he is made in the image and likeness of God. "The virtue of art is to be predicated peculiarly of God, like Goodness and Justice, and the Son, plying His poor man's trade, was still the image of the Father and of His action which never ceases: 'Philip, who sees Me sees the Father.' "[8]

If Christian living is necessary to right making, then what of the ancient Greeks and the beautiful things they made? What about the art of the orientals? To begin with, they were not a godless people. The Greeks had a limited religion but in the days of their great art their religion extended into much of their lives. Even their athletic contests were originally conceived in honor of some god. "Paul stood up in the midst of the Areopagus, and said, 'Men of Athens, I see that in every respect you are extremely religious.' "[9] Besides, they were men of great natural vision and skill. Their work had great physical harmony and beauty. But when you look at the best of it, there is nothing of Christ's prophecy fulfilled therein, "And I, if I be lifted up from the earth, will draw all things to myself."[10]

The old Greeks manufactured their mythical gods according to their own human likeness, with human weaknesses. And their art is also a glorification of the human. Christ is not its center

[8] Maritain, *Art and Scholasticism*, New York, Scribners, 1933, p. 21.
[9] Acts 17:22.
[10] Jn. 12:32.

nor does it center our attractions in Christ. But, of course, they could not be influenced by a Christianity they did not have. What they did, however, was so well done that, under the skill of thorough Christians, it might have become a Christian art, with a Christian purpose, a Christian symbolism and a Christian spiritual quality. What they did was so well done that we as Christians can learn much from them. The early Christians learned from them by building basilicas on the model of Greco-Roman architecture. And they took the beautiful young Hermes and used his figure as a model for Christ the Good Shepherd. Gregorian chant also was a blending, made from the fourth to seventh centuries, of Jewish solemn chanting, the melodies of the near East and the melodies and modes of ancient Greece and the Mediterranean world. This was the finest fulfillment of pagan art. "Wherever art, Egyptian, Greek or Chinese, has attained a certain degree of grandeur and purity, it is already Christian, Christian in hope, because every spiritual splendor is a promise and a symbol of the divine harmonies of the Gospel."[11]

But we are not ancient pagans of the Grecian or Roman world. We claim to be twentieth century Christians. While we try to learn from the wisdom and skill of every age and country, we cannot forget that we are first and always empowered and committed to be living, active members of Christ. We must not make the mistakes that began with the Renaissance and which continue in their effect until this day.

Until the fifteenth century in Italy and the sixteenth century elsewhere in Europe and the Mediterranean world, whatever was taken from ancient Greek and Roman culture was Christianized and served Christian purposes. Then people fell grad-

---

[11] Maritain, *op. cit.*, p. 69. And in *Creative Intuition in Art and Poetry*, he says, "Oriental art is essentially religion. . . . In actual fact, religion, not art, has lifted art to that level of life which is the very life of art." New York, Meridian Books, 1955, p. 10.

ually in love with the interest and beauty of the ancient classical sculpture and literature and architecture for their own sake. Much of their thinking and living and making was modeled on it. Classicism was in great vogue. "This new intellectual world of the Renaissance pretended to be truly age-old, but it was actually nothing but an artificial veneer of a culture. . . . It craved the supra-human instead of the supernatural, as witness the paintings of Michelangelo. . . . This was the period when Leonardo da Vinci could paint a Bacchus and a St. John that are almost indistinguishable from each other."[12]

"The 'new learning' was attended by 'humanism,' the belief that the charm of the classics resides essentially in their humanness, their humanity, and that everyone who would recapture the greatest charm in life must not prize the supernatural, the theological, or the ascetical above the natural, the human, and the sensual. Satisfaction is better than sacrifice, and self-gratification, than self-denial."[13] "There can be no doubt that a kind of assertive individualism was admired and practiced by humanists in sharp contrast with the self-abnegation of the medieval monk, who, without personal property or family, was vowed to obedience and humility. It was of a kind, indeed, with the individualism which was contemporaneously displayed by hardy explorers and colonists, by daring pirates and freebooters, and by gambling middlemen, investors, and bankers, and which was shortly to be exemplified in a widespread repudiation established tradition and authority."[14]

Coupled with this external influence was the inward tendency of man to become so absorbed in a means that he makes it his

---

[12] Bouyer, *Liturgical Piety*, Notre Dame, Ind., University of Notre Dame Press, 1955, p. 6.

[13] Hayes, *A Poltical and Cultural History of Modern Europe*, New York, MacMillan, Vol. I, p. 103.

[14] *Ibid.*, Vol. I, p. 106.

end. "The artists of the early Middle Ages began as symbolists for whom nature was not so much a text as a pretext. Gradually symbolism lost its interest, or rather the interest in it was swamped by the greater interest in nature for its own sake. The study of nature for its own sake became a passion as men awoke to the beauties of the world. No longer was it a book of instruction but a book of pleasure. It was no longer a schoolroom but a playroom, wheore he came to find not lesson at all but delight."[15]

So when men underrated their God-centered Christian tradition and became enamored with the human in the ancient classics and in nature, they ended up by loving thmselves and nature more than God and by making their own ideas and likes and dislikes the measure of right and wrong. You can call such people atheistic humanists or secularists or something similar. The point is, they began to live and to make things too much for enjoyment or self-expression or reputation or profit. Their making was no longer centered in Christ and His members but in sensuality and pride and avarice. Enjoyment and reputation and profit are things that should follow Christian making as effects, but they cannot be the purpose of art.

Renaissance art was the result of Reniassance thinking and living. Art is always a part of all life. If the way people think and live is normally sound, so will be their art. But no amount of natural vision or technical skill or new discoveries about materials can make up for the spiritual poverty of a people and its art. If anyone wishes to ask why there is not a better art, he should first ask why there is not more of normal Christian living. And in redeeming the black sheep he should, of course, always start with himself. From the great difficulty he finds in changing himself he will be able to judge the difficulty of

[15] Jarrett, *Social Theories of the Middle Ages*, Westmister, Md., Newman, p. 258.

changing an entire people. Developing vision and technical skill and discovering new uses of materials is far easier than raising mental and moral habits.

There is another difficulty which even a thorough Christian and competent artist must face and that is the general bad taste or the docility (and I think it is more docility than anything) which makes people too ready to accept poor art. But this particular problem seems to be the easiest to solve. When good things are available people either spontaneously or with little help come to appreciate them. It is a known fact that primitive and backwoods people are quick to appreciate classical music. You begin by learning to appreciate things that are well made and by learning also to make them well. Your appreciation will grow by casual contact and most quickly of all by your own doing and making. Aristotle said that only by doing and making can a person learn to appreciate what is done and made. If your work is good and done for a good purpose, you will find a satisfying joy in it.[16]

Unfortunately, for a long time, things that are supposed to be useful have been made in factories, entirely for profit. Such things may or may not be beautiful. Pius XI said, "Dead matter leaves the factory ennobled and transformed, where men are corrupted and degraded."[17] When factories make things efficiently and beautifully, it is to make them more saleable and profitable. Their ugliness, if not in the things, is in the purpose for which they are made, or in the corrupting and degrading effect which their making or use has upon men. No human act or product can be wholly acceptable if wrong in its purpose or effect, even if it is tolerated for serious reasons. As human

[16] Cf. Sister Mary of the Compassion, "Notes on Modern Art," *Today,* Dec. 1949, p. 20.

[17] Pius XI, "Reconstructing the Social Order," in *Four Great Encyclicals,* Paulist Press, p. 161.

beings we are responsible for each other. We cannot pretend that we are vacuum-sealed individualists.

Another unforunate fact: the things that are supposed to give the thrill of enjoyment are made in studios. Such things are not supposed to be necessary and useful. And the purpose of the people who make them may or may not be right: it may be for the thrill of enjoying the things themselves, or the thrill of having a great name as an artist, or merely for profit. In any case, there is often a great deal wrong with their thinking; and thinking and willing, in actual practice, go together. Therefore, among the people we call "artists" there are erroneous extremes of thinking and doing. There are the extremes of excessive realism and of excessive idealism and all the variations of each.

In the realists the imagination is not developed and they say that we should simply copy the works of nature or the works of other men. Represent literal facts but do not select subjects nor arrange details according to any special idea or mental image. To the realist, beauty depends on appearance, not on meaning. The principal kinds of realism are:

1. Classicism (Derivative art) concentrates on the mere imitation of acknowledged masterpieces of art.

2. Naturalism wants to represent living facts and sensations, physical as well as moral deformities. It gives much attention to the nude.

3. Impressionism (The painters, Edouard Manet and Claude Monet) represents the immediate sense reaction, i.e., mere external appearance, without any analysis or study of characteristics.

4. Functionalism (In mechanical and structural making—Le Corbusier, architect, defined a house as a machine to live in) says that the purpose or use of a thing, and only the

purpose, must control the design. Imagination is left out and the result is an ultrabareness of things.

Idealism, on the other hand, concentrates on the imagination and on selecting or shaping things according to preconceived types or images or moral and mental concepts. The principal kinds of idealism are:

1. Romanticism, or escapism, runs away from the discipline of formal classicism and literal fact and usefulness and puts the tools of making into the hands of imagination and feeling and supposed "significance."
2. Gothicism appeals to the mind rather than to feeling and represents symbolic and mystical subjects after the manner of the Middle Ages.
3. Abstractionism (Picasso, Klee, Braque) says that form is everything and that a thing has no purpose other than its own perfection. The resulting form is usually understandable only to the artist and is of no use to anybody else.
4. Post-impressions (In painting—Paul Cezanne) gives itself to self-expression rather than to literal fact, to meaning rather than to form. This group will paint a watch draped like a pancake over the edge of a book to express the idea of the fluidity of time. There are several interblending variations:
   a) Cubism advocates depicting everything of significance that comes to mind about a particular object.
   b) Futurism represents simultaneously a number of consecutive movements and impressions.

From these two and others like them you get that strange conglomeration of objects and angles that look more like somebody's nightmare than anything else. They completely ignore the fact that art is one of the means of communication and that it must communicate something for the usefulness and ennobling of man. If a work of art "needs to be explained in verbal lan-

guage, it loses its value as a sign and can only serve to procure
for the senses a physical pleasure, which does not exceed their
own level, or be for the spirit a subtle but vain toy."[18]

As we wade through these abnormal and morbid forms of
art and come out into fresh air again, we still, with shame, have
to admit that some Catholic artists have been influenced by them,
just as some Catholic educators have been influenced by Deweyism and Catholic scientists by materialism. Among the "serious
errors" of the "age in which we live," Pius XII puts down the
"montrosities of art which even pretend to call themselves Christian."[19]

It is extremely difficult for anyone to disengage himself from
the habits of his social environment. It takes a great spiritual
vitality to clear a person's vision and strengthen his will enough
to stand apart from his environment and see things differently,
as God made them and as God wants them for the good of man.
Fortunately, that spiritual vitality is beginning to show itself
in many countries. In the 1950 Holy Year Exhibit at the Vatican, the art from mission countries consistently surpassed the art
from supposedly civilized and Christian countries. So everywhere
we may hope for a more rational and Christian making of things.
We are at the beginning of a new age in many things, including
art. We must not despair. There is nothing so tough and resilient
as human beings. And God's arm is not shortened.

Every period of artistic development is divided into three
parts:

1. The primitive stage which is marked by great vigor of ideas
   but limited technic.
2. The golden age in which there is perfection of technic to
   express noble ideas.

[18] Pius XII, *Address to the First International Congress of Catholic
Artists,* Sept. 3, 1950.
[19] *Menti Nostrae,* par. 118.

3. The decadence which is given to slavish copying and profusion of refinements. This copying and profusion are abuses of a perfected technic that is no longer dominated by balanced ideas.

At present we are seeing the decadence of Renaissance art and the birth of a more thoroughly Christian art.

And mixed in for good measure are those who still are trying to distort the human figure in order to express Christian doctrine in various geometrical shapes and patterns. It is a part of the idealist heresy that subordinates fact to fancy. And the result is either obscurity or a dragging down of sublime ideas to earthy levels and leaving them there, instead of using earthy materials to lift men up to the divine.

Not everything in modern art is wrong. In fact, to be genuine at all it must be contemporary. Some already are beginning to use the best in it and are dedicating it to holy purposes. Fortunately, the living voice of Christ guides us in this matter. Pope Pius XII told us in *Mediator Dei*:

Recent works of art which lend themselves to the materials of modern composition, should not be universally despised and rejected through prejudice. Modern art should be given free scope in due and reverent service of the church and sacred rites, provided that they preserve a correct balance between styles tending neither to extreme realism nor to excessive "symbolism" and that the needs of the Christian community are taken into consideration rather than the particular taste or talent of the individual artist. Thus modern art will be able to join its voice to that wonderful choir of praise to which have contributed, in honor of the Catholic Faith, the greatest artists throughout the centuries. Nevertheless, in keeping with the duty of Our office, We cannot help deploring and condemning those works of art, recently introduced by some, which seem to be a distortion and perversion of true art and which at times openly shock Christian taste, modesty and devotion, and shamefully offend the true religious sense. These must be entirely excluded and banished from our churches, like "anything else that is not in keeping with the sanctity of the place" (Canon 1178). Let artists be capable and willing to draw their inspiration from religion to express what is suitable and more in keeping with the requirements of worship. Thus the human arts will shine forth with a wondrous splendor, and contribute greatly to human civilization, to the salvation of souls and the glory of God.[20]

As a practical expression of its interest, the Vatican Museum opened in 1958 a special pavilion for modern art.

At what point then does Christian making take its start? It begins with living the Gospel and that begins and grows in the home. In the normal Christian home where play and work and worship are a united family affair, with every person taking part, right there is the beginning of a Christian world of right living and making. That is where it started in the first place, in the hiddenness and simplicity of Nazareth where Mary and Joseph made things and did things well for the love of Jesus, our Redeemer. Their home was the first Christian studio. And every since then the production of rare works of art has depended upon the broad base of general right making, just as the rose must depend upon the whole bush and upon the root hidden in the soil. As Graham Carey said in a lecture at Harvard University in 1938: "The great artistic civilizations of the past were as glorious as they were, not through their possession of a few great artistic geniuses, but on account of the myriads of little artists all going about their daily tasks. They were glorious through the labor of countless weavers and dyers and embroiderers that made their daily clothing what it was, through the woodworkers, and the stone-carvers, and the smith, the wagoners and boat-builders, the leather-workers and the potters. The air was full of music because hearts were full of music, and the weavers sang at their looms, the sailors at their ropes, the wagon-

---

[20] *Mediator Dei,* par. 195-196.

ers along the dusty roads. The great artistic civilizations of the world have been so, not through the efforts of a few great men, but through the efforts of many little ones, when the many have been on the right track.

"And the right track has always consisted, and always must consist, in making things of use to man, the consumer, in a manner normal and natural to man the producer."[21]

God gave each of you a reason to analyze and work out conclusions. He gave you an imagination to conceive new pictures and shapes. He gave you a will to desire what is right and the intuition to see directly and immediately the inner rightness and wrongness of things. In your normal living, more unconsciously than consciously, you regularly use all these faculties of reason and imagination and desire and intuition. And only when you are able to use all of them is your doing and making completely human. Only then do you feel satisfied and happy with your way of life.

Very few men in their work-life have the full use of their God-given powers. Women in their homes are more fortunate. They have more chance to be themselves, if only they will forget about what other people think and glory in their freedom. A man's best outlet is in his family-life and in the things he can do around his home. In our Catholic worship and in the teaching and dramatizing of our faith the opportunities are endless. Parents need the full use of all their faculties in order to teach their children a sense of the all-pervading God, to guide them spiritually, to train them in a sense of responsibility and to awaken them to a sense of apostolic mission within their particular vocation in life.[22] So to help you to be in your own way an artist, a good maker of useful things, is to help you to be completely human, a human master of God's created things

---

[21] Carey, *Pattern,* Newport, John Stevens, 1938, p. 8.
[22] Cf. *American Bishops' Pastoral Letter,* Nov. 1950.

insofar as they touch your own life. And to help you be fully human is to make it easier for you to be more Christian and more holy, to worship with your voice and hands.

Go back, then, to the beautiful, the true and the good. Start with the beautiful. And take beauty first from the viewpoint of personal enjoyment. Beauty can be defined as "the intuitive realization of the essential rightness of things."[23] Either you like a thing or you do not. You do not have to line up reasons in a row. But why is it that some people appreciate beauty more than others? That depends on two things: one of them, in greater or lesser degree, you have in common with everybody and that is your inborn human power to see and enjoy the true and the good; the other depends on how much you as an individual have developed your power to see and enjoy.

Do not for a moment underestimate your God-given ability to see the essential rightness of things that makes them beautiful. There is plenty of evidence to show that if you are left to yourself and have contact with things well made, your ability to appreciate and to make things will come out. The 1950 Holy Year Exhibit of Art is one evidence. In any museum that has a good display of native household utensils and ornaments from various parts of the world you will find a great wealth of things made beautifully by all kinds of ordinary people. These people were not geniuses. They were ordinary people on the right track. "Little minds on the right track do more in building a happy society than great minds on the wrong track."[24] Folk songs and folk dances spring from the people and are enjoyed by the people. The rug-making and colorful dress of North and South American Indians, their pottery and their silver ornaments, the spontaneous singing of the Negro, the handmade knitted wear of the Aroostok Valley in Maine that is marketed

[23] Carey, *op. cit.,* p. 47.
[24] Carey, *Thoughts and Things,* Newport, John Stevens, 1937, p. 43.

in New York are all signs of everybody's ability to make and enjoy beautiful things. In the Middle Ages, when men made chests to keep their clothes and tools in and keys to lock them with, they made them so beautiful that we now put them in museums and admire them.

But you take what God gave you and develop it and help it to grow. This does not mean wading through a heavy book on the history or philosophy of art. Nor does it mean limiting your ideas of what is beautiful to a few masterpieces and looking down your nose at everything else. It is one of the blessings of this age of transition that we are forced to face fundamental realities and that we want to face them.

Start with the real world in which you live. You do not have to know everything in order to appreciate something. It is true, of course, that a skilled cabinet-maker can best appreciate a beautiful table, just as Jascha Heifetz can best appreciate superb violin playing. But you do not have to be told that a sunset or a well-set table is beautiful. You do not have to be bold that a rightly built church, a tool or a landscape is beautiful. You only have to stop and look at them and wonder at what God and man can do. Of course, men and women each find a special joy in certain things that are more familiar to them. But that is precisely the point. As St. Augustine says, good taste comes from contact with good work.[25]

God has placed good work all around you. Start with that. And He has given you a natural sense of wonder at the marvelous proportion, the endless variety, the intricate unity, the graceful lines of things. You had it as a child and you should have developed it into a priceless maturity and treasured it as something that would enrich your life and be a natural help to supernatural living. Unfortunately, most people fail to value it as a lifelong joy and let other things preoccupy them and they

[25] St. Aug., *Christian Instruction.*

lose the spontaneous use of that sense of wonder as well as its enjoyment. But it can be re-awakened and developed because it is a part of your natural being. It is not entirely dead but only dozing or sleeping. Convince yourself that everything God made is good and has something of God Himself in it. Know that He did not mean life to be utter misery and boredom. He meant only that you should use things with moderation and restraint and not wallow in them. Besides, there is misery enough without adding to it by our own bad handiwork. Your love of neatness and order and cleanliness, your desire to ornament houses with paint and rooms with furniture and curtains, your delight in dancing or singing, your thrill at a beautiful dress or a fine car is all in the right direction. Go on from there to know the simple things that make for beauty. And you will find that it is their truth and goodness.

First take truth. Normally, it is easier to appreciate truth than it is to live by it. More people see the truth of Catholicism than are willing to embrace it. But it is also a fact that unless we try with some success to live by the truth we know, our appreciation of it will be dimmed and perhaps lost altogether. That is why people who stop living their faith end up by losing it altogether. Life is a principle of activity. You are made to act. And, to encourage you, God has given a certain pleasure to all activity that is normal and rightly directed to a worthy object. You have perfect natural enjoyment when the essential rightness in you discovers an essential rightness in things or puts that truth and goodness into them. This natural pleasure is a faint suggestion of the joy of holiness that comes when a person centers all his actions and being in God and finds the beginning of heaven in a love that is both an active possession and a passive surrender.

This is a way of saying that there will be a better Christian art when there are more Christian people. For "a work is Chris-

tian when it clearly shows that it has issued from a mind formed
in the dogmas of Holy Church. It does not matter whether the
subject is religious or secular. A work, no matter how good
as a work of art, which shows a purely material conception of
life or interpretation of a mystery is not Christian—even if the
titue is 'The Holy Family.' "[26] Persons who think doctrinally
as Christians and who are innocent and good find joy in the
rightness of simple things. And sinners can be bored by masterpieces. The more there is in you of the integrity and proportion
and clear light of a God-centered life, the more quickly will you
respond to the integrity and proportion and splendor of form
that you find in things. Something of this you must have for
a start or you will find no real pleasure in anything, except the
dulled sensation that still remains after excesses and satiety or
the weak stimulus of passive entertainment that sends you seeking after sensationalism and forced stimulation.

Now one part of a wholesome joy, the part that is a disposition and preparation for something better, you will find in the
senses; and that depends upon their natural sensitiveness and
upon your not being already overstuffed with sensual pleasure.
Part of the joy is in the imagination and all the associations it
suggests; and that part, presupposing as a necessary condition
that the imagination is kept wholesome, depends much on age,
sex, temperament, character, experience, etc. The best part of
your joy depends upon an intuitive knowing of the proportion
and unity and right embodiment of an ideal that you find in a
work of nature or man. You can increase your power to appreciate and to make beautiful things by forming the right associations in the imagination and by sharpening your intuitive
knowing of what is right proportion and unity and a right embodiment of an ideal. That is why we are looking for truth.
Art cannot be Christian art at all unless it is first good art.

[26] Sister Mary of the Compassion, *op. cit.*, p. 20.

At the moment our concern is not the organization of truth which is called a science. We are concerned with the truth of making and of the thing made. "Art is the imposition of an original FORM upon a MATERIAL by the use of certain MEANS to achieve a given END."[27] There you have the four causes that make something beautiful: the formal cause, the material cause, efficient cause and final cause. You can best understand what a thing is by understanding the causes that make a thing. And there is beauty only when all the causes are in harmony and balance.

The form is that which constitutes the life, the essence of a thing and makes it distinct from every other. The form you look for in appreciating something beautiful is the special, distinctive aspect or image that its maker has grasped and tried to embody. The form you try to express in making something beautiful is that distinctive aspect of being which awakened joy in you. In each case, it is some truth, some radiation of being, some dominant characteristic, some ideal that becomes the very soul of the beauty in what you are seeing or making or singing. It comes from something real, something in a person or in nature. But to make that radiance of being, that splendor of truth stand out more clearly you rearrange lines and parts and colors and and objects (still in harmony with their essential nature, and not with violence and distortion) and you eliminate unnecessary detail that may distract from the clear beauty that must dominate.[28] That is called idealizing the real for the sake of realizing the ideal. It is called, also, the creation of the ideal type. It demands sufficient completeness or integrity to suggest the perfection of an ideal. And in the subtle arrangement of

[27] Carey, *What is Christian Art?*, p. 11.
[28] Hyperbole is a legitimate figure of speech in any language. Exaggeration of certain details for the sake of effect is equally legitimate in art.

significant detail there must be unity in diversity, i.e., the right proportion, so that a single point of view, a single aspect of truth will dominate. The distinctive beauty, the splendor of form must spread its radiance over everything. "Radiance is the essence of beauty."[29] "The essence of the thing (philosophically called 'forma') beautifies it, and beauty is nothing else than the essence of the thing showing through its material, intelligently arrayed."[30] This harmonious dominance of form is the reason why classic art is simple to the point of severity and Renaissance art is often little more than glorified photography. In Fra Angelico and Rouault the brilliance of form is clearly dominant; no one can mistake the spiritual quality of their work.

The splendor of truth you see or make should be clear but should not have the details of a photograph or blueprint. It should say what it says clearly but it should suggest even more than it says. The rest is left to imagination, to dreams, to movement, to sound. Your enjoyment of art will depend greatly on your ability to fill in. This power to suggest and symbolize what cannot be expressed is true of every form of making, whether in music or dance or things or words. Song begins where speech breaks off, "the exultation of the mind bursting into voice."[31] That is the cry of Jeremias, "A, a, a. Lord God, I know not what to say.[32]

Another thing about the truth of form is that you do not come by it through reasoning or mathematics but through intuition and imagination. By intuition you directly and immediately see as a shining truth some aspect of the inner rightness and perfection of someone or something. The imagination stores

---

[29] St. Thomas, *De Divinis Nominibus,* VI.
[30] Jarrett, *op. cit.,* p. 246.
[31] St. Thomas, *Commentariaum in Psalmos,* Prol.
[32] Jer. 1:6.

and arranges and sifts the many ideas and pictures and aspects of being and beauty that have come to it, all unconsciously. The artist is not so much a creative thinker as he is a creative organizer. He reveals rather than invents. His invention is in the manner of revealing. "Art responds very faithfully to the general outlook of its period. The artist is always a man of his own time."[33] The intuition sees the rightness of appreciation or selects the rightness in the making of something given to it by the imagination. Very little creative work can be done by analysis or by rules based on analysis because the perfection of every individual thing made is different from every other. Beauty is a very delicate balance of many elements. Rules and analysis help appreciation more than they help making, but conscious comparison with classic models must be limited. The greater time and effort must be given to frequent casual contact with good work and to frequent making of things.

Where does reason come into appreciation and making beautiful things? In practice it works alternately with intuition. Intuition conceives and reason checks up on the conception. Reason must harmonize the form, the image, the aspect of truth with the nature and ideal of each thing. It must guide the right choice of materials and tools and purpose. Intuition also has its part in speeding up the rechecking of essential rightness. This rechecking is necessary. As an activity of the person appreciating or making, art is a habit or virtue of the intelligence which perfects the practical understanding. And because it is a human activity, it is subject to rules and moral precepts. If the mind does not guide choices and make revisions and keep the purpose dominant, the result is likely to be obscurity and uselessness. Art has a certain autonomy of its own, in the harmonious operation of its four causes, but it does not have a license to suicide. The artist must always act as a rational person. In this con-

[33] Jarrett, *op. cit.*, p. 236.

nection it is worth mentioning that you can take a miniature score and beat out the measures with Toscanini. Yet within this regular timing he achieves tremendous life and power.

To continue the four causes, the image or aspect of beauty that shines in your mind and awakens joy must be embodied in some material. In relation to materials, art is the reshaping of existing materials by imposing upon them some human idea or image. It may be one of hundreds of different materials. Starting with wood or words, movement, or marble, cloth or clay, or sound or paint, or anything else, you must judge and choose the right kind of material that will best embody the splendor of truth that has awakened in you. The essential beauty and right use of each kind of material must be understood and its limits must be respected.

This raw material has to be worked on and shaped and arranged until it becomes alive with the shining image that is alive in you. This is done by the efficient cause. That efficient cause may be a tool or an instrument or a voice or training in writing and dancing and in any kind of making. Each instrument must be understood in relation to each material so that it can be mastered for expressing perfectly the inner image. The great Renaissance artists were masters of their materials and tools and that is why they could reproduce things with a photographic exactness. Their weakness was in their formal and final causes. Their fallacy was the "optimism of technic" that Gabriel Marcel applies to scientism.

The right use of materials and tools is what we call technic. A certain time and training are needed for each, depending on the maker and the thing made. You can learn technic by formal training in an art school, or by informal apprenticeship under a person with know-how, or by the trial-and-error method of personal experimenting plus private reading. Informal apprenticeship is probably the ideal.

What is the final cause of right making? What must be the purpose? To begin with, there can be no such thing as art exclusively for art's sake, for the simple reason that in a created, contingent being the perfection of a thing requires that its purpose be extrinsic to the thing itself. It is the nature of love and the life of all living to lose itself in something greater than itself. "Each single being is perfect in the measure in which it reaches up to its own origin."[34] "All things, insofar as they have being, aim at likeness to God, who is being itself."[35] "Everything in its own way naturally loves God more than itself."[36] Art is not a love and a law unto itself. It was the Renaissance giant, the dying Michelangelo who said: "Now do I realize how my soul succumbed to error in making art its own idol and sovereign master."[37] Making must serve man the immediate maker and consumer and God the ultimate Maker.

Making, like everything else, has a certain independence in its own distinctive process of making (conception of form, choice of material, use of tools, etc.). But its final cause must be something beyond it. This is where the heresies that began with the Renaissance most clearly show themselves. But, like all heresies, they are exaggerations or misapplications of things that are true. They are due in part to Renaissance secularism and in part to fallen human nature.

One of these exaggerations insists that art is essentially imitation and copying, the transfer of a beautiful appearance to a permanent material. This was due partly to their misunderstanding of what Plato and Aristotle meant by "imitation." Copying is a proper purpose of photography. And some of the

---

[34] *Sum. Theol.*, I, q. 12, a. 1.

[35] *Ibid.*, II-II, q. 34, a. 1, ad 3.

[36] *Ibid.*, I, q. 60, a. 5.

[37] Quoted by Proudhon, *Du principe de l'art et de sa destination sociale*, Paris, 1875, p. 46.

arts, like painting and sculpture do include an element of copying. We learn from models, animate and inanimate. But the
models are only conditions, helps to guide (but not enslave)
the mind in its own original embodying of its fresh inner vision
or image.

Reacting violently against extreme slavish imitating, some
of the idealists go to another extreme and say that self-
expression is the only purpose of art. It is true that in any
genuine living work there will necessarily be personal characteristics. They are necessary effects of sincere work but they cannot
be its purpose. Self-expression ignores our responsibility to God
and to man and to the nature of materials and tools. It is likely
to end with distortion and obscurity.

And neither can making a name for yourself be a final cause
and reason for making things. That is a legitimate effect and
when it comes you may enjoy it within whatever limits your
humility will permit. In its own way it can keep you from doing careless work because of laziness. But pride can lead you
to waste time basking in praise when you should be doing more
work. It can lead you to make things, not in the way that is
best for their purpose, but in the way that best shows your skill
and originality, or in the way that will best set off the desired
acclaim.

Equally wrong as a purpose is the enjoyment of beauty, the
seeking of thrill for the sake of thrill and enjoyment. Joy is
a necessary effect of beauty and an artist must make a thing so
perfectly that, as an effect, it will please. But he must aim at
the perfection and not at the pleasure it gives, just as we must
aim at the God-given purpose of our instincts and not at the
pleasure that accompanies their satisfactions. To seek pleasure
for its own sake is a kind of sensuality.

Where does this error leave its mark? The heresy of enjoyment shows its effects in the ultra-prettified, over-painted and

over-decorated things or in their sensual lines. As a result of this heresy, over-decoration of churches led to over-decorated canopies around the altar.[38] All such things, moreover, by their multiple sense impressions are a dissipation of the senses, a confusion for the mind and a hindrance to the spirit in its seeking of the splendor of truth. It is no wonder that St. Bernadette was shrank in horror from the Renaissance Madonnas. Father Martindale in his "Bernadette," says that "St. Bernadette was shown an album containing pictures of Our Lady. At the sight of some, she shut the book with a cry of horror (those of the Renaissance period). It was in the old Byzantine painting known as St. Luke's Madonna that she found something...well, that she could recognize. Where all realism had abdicated, there she found the nearest approach, among all of them, of the Real."[39]

Next, can profit be a motive? This motive has become so engrained in our whole web of life that straight thinking about it is extremely difficult. Still it must be said that in right making, the profit should not be a primary motive but should follow as a normal effect. Every workman has a right to a reasonable reward for the goods he produces for other men. Making a living is a proper secondary motive, insofar as a person must assume his social responsibilities to family and society. But in relation to what is done or made, it cannot be the principal and immediate motive.

These heresies show how selfless and conscientious a person must be to do good work. The immediate end of right making must be the good of the thing made. That, quite simply, is the final cause of art. It takes great self-discipline, at least during the actual conceiving of an image and the putting of that image

[38] *Catholic Encyclopedia,* 1:363.

[39] Editor of *London Catholic Herald* answering a correspondent who claimed religious art should normally be naturalistic. Cf. *Orate Fratres,* April, 1951.

into its material medium. "The artist must be forever on his guard not only against the vulgar attractions of easy execution and success, but against a host of less subtle temptations, and against the slightest relaxation of his interior effort, for habits diminish, if unexercised, and ever so much more by any careless exercise not proportionate to their intensity.[40] In the sphere of making and from the point of view of the good of the work, he must be humble and magnanimous, prudent, upright, strong, temperate, simple, pure, ingenuous."[41] "The Christian Faith, when cordially accepted and lived is the one thing capable of inspiring the finest work of art."[42]

What, then, is the "good of the thing made"? It is simply to be made well. Unless a thing is well made, it can serve no further purpose, either Christian or otherwise. It is well made, when it properly represents the original idea in suitable material rightly worked by the right tools. Then it will be useful for man's spiritual and bodily needs, in his worship of God and in his vocation in life. The things that are used for satisfying bodily needs will have about them a goodness that gives a certain joy in their use. Other works, called fine art, will serve to refresh mind and body simply by the enjoyment which their beauty gives. (The refreshment is the thing to be sought, not enjoyment for enjoyment's sake). Still other works, called sacred art, serve man in worshipping God. And in these sacred objects the self-discipline of the artist must be the greatest of all, for the beauty and delight must not distract the worshipper but rather lead him by the tranquillity and joy produced through the sense impression, into the spiritual calm of communion with God and His saints.

For these same reasons, St. Pius X laid down the qualities of

---

[40] Cf. *Sum. Theol.*, I-II, q. 43, a. 3 and q. 42, a. 3.
[41] Maritain, *Art and Scholasticism*, p. 82.
[42] Pius XII, "Evangelii Praecones," *loc. cit.*, p. 590.

music for worship. "Sacred Music should consequently possess, in the highest degree, the qualities proper to the liturgy, and precisely sanctity and goodness of form, from which its other character of universality spontaneously springs."[43] Pius XII gives the deep purpose for these qualities: "Sacred music enters more intimately into divine worship than many other liberal arts, such as architecture, painting and sculpture. These last prepare a worthy setting for the sacred ceremonies. Sacred music, however, has an important place in the actual performance of the sacred ceremonies and rites themselves. . . . Its special power and excellence should lift up to God the minds of the faithful who are present. It should make the liturgical prayers of the Christian community more alive and fervent, so that everyone can praise and beseech the Triune God more powerfully, more intently and more effectively. The power of sacred music increases the honor given to God by the Church in union with Christ its Head."[44]

Within the immediate end of good making and good composing and singing, the maker, composer, singer has all the freedom he needs to rightly use his material and tools for the expression of the original image within him. If there is in him the tranquility of order that comes from virtue, wherein all his mental faculties and bodily senses are subject to reason and the reason to God, then, given technical skill, his mind and hands will spontaneously coordinate in producing things that are genuinely useful, enjoyable and inspiring. In the production itself, however, his main concern will be to do his work well, whether it be ceramics or carving, or singing or carpentry.

Such freedom in working requires high personal integrity. Some such integrity, at least within the sphere of making, was required to achieve the natural harmony of ancient Greek or

[43] Pius X, *Motu Proprio,* no. 2.
[44] *On Sacred Music,* par. 30-32.

of the perennial Chinese art. It is theoretically possible for a murderer or pervert of any sort to master a craft or fine art and turn out a good piece of work. For it is the quality of his work that for the moment absorbs him. But how completely can it absorb him and for how long? Life is complex and most intricately unified. (The contradictions that are found in great persons are a limited exception to this rule. When their tremendous energies are poured out in a single direction worthy fruit often results. Our concern is with the work of a Christian community). "In order that a man may make good use of the art he has, he needs a good will which is perfected by moral virtue ... for it is evident that a craftsman is inclined by justice, which rectifies his will, to do his work faithfully."[45] "The piercing perception of beauty rises from the marriage of goodness and truth ... and the marriage takes place with God as witness during His visitation to the artist on the natural level at the moment of inspiration."[46]

In his making, as in everything, the artist is subject to the limitations of materials and tools and personal skill and he is subject to the limits of the rights and needs of other human beings. He must be moral in his making, as in everything else. That is why his liberty and obedience must be blended in love. If his whole being and all his energies flow out into love of God and man, he will work humbly before God and he will make nothing and do nothing that would normally stimulate sensuality or glorify man's pride or feed restlessness and hate. Through the tranquillity of order that is within him and that allows him freedom of thought and expression, he helps other men to reorder their being and free their thinking and acting for love and worship. He will not forget that he is part of fallen humanity and that he works in the material of fallen humanity

[45] *Sum. Theol.,* I-II, q. 57, a. 3, ad 2.
[46] McCauliff, *Renascence,* Vol. III, n. 2, p. 153.

and of unredeemed creation. But through the gifts of nature and redemption he will try to embody some image of natural order or revealed rightness. Through his hands he will have part in redeeming the world. But the man and his work will reveal the splendor of order.

This divine, universal purpose, breathed in an air of glad freedom, is doctrinally stated by Dom Herwegen in "Liturgical Arts."[47] "It is the highest and greatest mission of the art of the Church to lead the Christian community to Christ, and to dedicate its highest and best to Him as the Head of the Church in Heaven and on earth. Only he who breathes and lives in and with the Church can grasp this exalted thought and practice it with humble reverence. . . . Only the spirit of worship in the Church, which becomes articulate in the union of priest and people by sacrifice and prayer, can reveal to earthly pilgrims the vision of the Heavenly Jerusalem." Such a breath of purpose, even if it were consciously held, would less likely hamper originality than a particular human purpose. Even such a particular purpose need not destroy greatness, as Lucretius proved in spreading the philosophy of Epicurus, Virgil in writing his Georgics to bring labor back to the land, and Wagner in glorifying the teutonic religion. Still, in a Christian artist, the universal purpose is something that directs his whole life rather than an immediate directive in his work.

Where does originality come in? What makes a thing original? Originality starts with the fresh image that a person conceives and wishes to embody. It is not a seeking of novelty for novelty's sake nor a preaching of eccentricity for attention's sake. It is simply the necessary result when a person thinks out and works out his idea according to the material and tools he uses and according to the vigor and tone of thought and feeling that

[47] Herwegen, *Liturgical Arts,* Fall, 1931, p. 6.

moves him to act and work. The differences in any instrument blend in a new image each time we do or make something. So originality and perfection flow from the same source, the mysterious, unified blending of the four causes of art.

A difference in national culture is a part of the difference in persons. But the basic humanity of the maker and our basic human needs will move him to so embody the universal in the particular that all men will see the rightness of his making and doing. His product must spring spontaneously from the whole man and end as something outside of him, made at once for a definite time and for an immediate end, but also for the ages and for the needs of all. "Art needs to be localized in order to cross the world, to be individualized to appeal to all, to be nationalized to move all nations."[48] As for sacred music, "It must be universal in the sense that while every nation is permitted to admit into its ecclesiastical compositions those special forms which may be said to constitute its native music, still these forms must be subordinated in such a manner to the general characteristics of sacred music that nobody of any nation may receive an impression other than good on hearing them."[49]

If you want an example of how the four causes can perfectly blend in beautiful making, take the Scriptures, and the Gospels in particular. The spiritual, eternal aim and the selflessness and holiness of the authors have imparted a great tranquility to their writing. There is strength and simplicity in their use of the material and efficient causes, i.e., the doctrine and narrative material and the language as they knew it. And there is originality in the form each gave to his Gospel.[50] The Magnificat of Mary is another example of the same thing. Both Mary and

---

[48] Jarrett, *op. cit.,* p. 248.

[49] Pius X, *op. cit.,* no. 2.

[50] Cf. Huby, *The Church and the Gospels,* New York, Sheed and Ward.

the Evangelists worked in pre-existing material and each wrought
a distinctive creation. I make a point of this because if divine
inspiration did not hamper originality and beautiful making,
then neither should Christian morality. We are fortunate, of
course, that great discernment has guided the translations of
the Sacred Books. Usually, translations, like copies, lack the
power and freshness of the original precisely because there is
not in the translator or copier that vital spontaneous blending
of the four causes that worked in the originator.

All this sums up to the fact that a philosophy of art is also a
philosophy of work. There is no reason why useful things and
useful tasks should not be beautiful and enjoyable. Nor is there
any reason why beautiful and enjoyable things should not serve
a useful purpose. "I wept in Thy hymns and canticles, touched
to the quick by the voices of Thy sweet-atuned church."[51] God
has told us of wisdom, "Her ways are beautiful ways and all
her paths are peaceable."[52] And in the Book of Ecclesiastes[53]
He says to us, "I perceive that there is nothing better, than that
a man should rejoice in his own works; for that is his portion."
And this in spite of original sin. The counterpart of that
thought is given by St. Thomas Aquinas, "No man can live
without pleasure. Therefore a man deprived of the pleasures
of the spirit goes over to the pleasure of the flesh."[54] Such sensuality is the whirlwind we have been reaping from the sowing
of industrialism and scientism which have taken most of the
pleasure out of work, and from passive entertainment which
leaves people dissatisfied and bored. In part, of course, religious
deficiencies are also repsonible.

In speaking of the natural function of beauty in man's life,

[51] St. Aug., *Confessions,* IX, 6.
[52] Prov. 3:17.
[53] Eccles. 3:22.
[54] *Sum. Theol.,* II-II, q. 35, a. 4, ad 2.

we are not forgetting its limitations. If you want it in the form of a striking case history, take the master of masters, Michelangelo, who said in his old age, "Painting and Sculpture will lose their charm for the soul turned to that divine love which opened its arms upon the Cross to welcome us."[55] That is the ultimate unity and order and harmony to which all of us must grow. The hyperbole of Michelangelo, of course, does not contradict the saints who found great joy in natural beauty, for it was God's beauty they saw there.

Bring this back to yourself. What can you do yourself? How can you judge what is well made? Begin with yourself. Very prosaically, be neat; keep things clean and in order. Start with your room, your home, your backyard, your work and the tools or machines or materials you use. Do thoroughly and well and honestly whatever you do. Do it for good and honest reasons. Let there be no sham or pretense in anything you do or say. Be impatient with slovenly work or covering up of any sort.

Do not be afraid of being distinctive, for if you are honest and thorough you cannot be otherwise than distinctive. It is only a sick and weak society that is afraid of the originality that springs spontaneously from strength and honest vitality. Insecure tyrants and machine-minded people demand identical conformity. Be as quick to respect honesty and distinctiveness in others as you are quick to cooperate and to show love. If you poke fun at vital originality, you condemn yourself out of your own mouth; you are weak in your thinking; you are in need of stronger spiritual health.

Stop long enough and reverently enough to see the distinctive beauty in every separate creature that God has made. No two of them are exactly alike. Know the beauty of the natural grain of each kind of wood and you will never cover it up with paint

[55] Cf. Maritain, *op. cit.,* p. 85.

unless you absolutely have to for protection out-of-doors. Know the beauty of stones and cloth. Study the best uses of different kinds of wood and stone and cloth. Learn at least the elementary color circle and its simple harmonies. Learn the elementary symmetrical and occult designs. See what you can do to bring the year's sacred Feasts into your home by colors and symbols and little programs. Lead and urge people to the healthy joy of active, creative recreation. And your life will be filled with hope and joy and your apostolate among men will be vastly more fruitful. Besides, by appreciating and dedicating the natural good of things you will avoid the errors of ultra-supernaturalism, angelism, puritanism. "Every creature of God is good, and nothing is to be rejected that is accepted with thanksgiving."[56]

Since we cannot understand a work of art unless we understand something of what the artist thought and felt, so we have to meditate the text which prompted the melody and gives life to our singing of the melody. This is the beginning of a service of worhipping with your voice.

How deeply we will enter into service of sacred song depends also upon the prayer, the charity, the discipline in our whole life. Since practice itself is an act of worship, far more significant than all the acts of all the creatures summoned in the Canticle of Daniel, we should dispose ourselves also for practice by fervent prayer. Through prayer and through conscientious intelligent practice we enter into the beauty of sacred music and learn to love it. Through love, in turn, we enter into deeper understanding; and "song becomes the lover."

We become identified with sacred music in its purpose, its thought and its feeling. Our whole being becomes engaged as the connatural instrument of worship. Through training we perfect our connatural instrument. Then each song, each note

[56] I Tim. 4:4.

means that our personality, our personal relationship with God, our prayer becomes embodied in our voice. That song, that note, becomes our work of art at the moment—at once unpredictable and unique; it can never be repeated.

We find a joy in this personal prayer-art in which we pray twice by singing well. We are doing what we like best. We find that the joy of singing also coordinates our voice mechanism and perfects our singing. We are one in a community worship.

Everything possible should be done to discover and encourage anyone with a bent for composing songs and music. Out of a broad base of many little composers will rise the great composers who will write the sacred music of tomorrow.

As a final thought, in judging work for decoration or worship, look for these things:

1. A certain tranquillity and peace and restraint which in turn begets calm within you. All material things, like all truth, should lead us to the contemplation and love of divine truth and beauty.

2. Simplicity, with enough details to make clear the central idea, with no deails that detract attention from it. This springs from unity and from a respect for the limits of each material medium of expression.

3. Strength, which is a part of simplicity and so necessary for tranquility.

4. Originality, which grows out of tradition and respects tradition and which also respects the subject represented. Because of the great needs for better sacred art and because of the limited number of persons to produce them, we must often be content with reproductions. Then make sure they are good ones by the standards of honest materials and workmanship and by the impressions of serenity, simplicity and strength.

In your doing and making, in your praising and procuring, be faithful to the leadership of Pius XII, "Cause to smile upon the earth and upon humanity the reflection of beauty and of divine light; and in the helping of man to love all that rings true, all that commands reverence and all that makes for right, all that is pure and all that is lovely, you will have contributed largely to the work of peace 'and the God of peace will be with you' " (Phil. 4:8-9).[57]

[57] Pius XII, *Address to the First International Congress of Catholic Artists*, Sept. 3, 1950.

Chapter Fourteen

Mary is the Queen of Worship

WE have to think of Mary, the ever active Mediatrix, within the context of the very real world in which we live. She was a practical person who, with the help of St. Joseph, had to adjust herself and her child to the pressures and tensions of living in an occupied country. She is at home therefore, with the harassed people of every generation.

In the prisons and concentration camps of the world, crucified men and women are telling their Aves to Mary on Rosaries of cord and by counting sticks and stones. They whisper ejaculations to the rhythm of shuffling feet and pounding tool as well as to the unrhythmic inner rumblings of perpetual hunger.

These barred and wired confinements are become the grim cloisters of Mary's prisoners. They are Calvary where Mary stands with them and sees her Son crucified again in them, for they are the Mystical Christ. From those cloistered Calvaries God receives their holocaust of prayer and suffering for their very persecutors, for their own families, for their priests and

257

Sisters and benefactors, for all the members of Christ. Through their prayers and suffering everyone is made better.

Mary sustains the thoughts of the world's sufferers as she sustains our own. Nothing can take away the happiness of thinking about and talking about someone we love, especially when that someone is the Mother of God. The delight is deepened by the pervading sense of her presence.

Mary remains for us a living presence who sums up in herself and fulfills all the heroines of the Old Testament, from Mary, the sister of Moses, who saved his life, through Judith who risked her life to save her people, through queenly Esther who braved mortal danger to intercede for her people, to the mother of the Machabees who looked upon the martyrdom of her seven sons. The very types of Mary seemed to involve her in a great holocaust. And the first word about her in Genesis (3:15) involved her with her Son in the battle against the prince of darkness for the redemption of the world.

But from the first moment of her conception, the Trinity made Our Lady the Queen of Light, immaculately radiant with a great fullness of divine life. Being this world's most perfect image of the Trinity, Mary was most perfectly prepared to join in the Trinity's battle to win back the souls of men. We sing her preparation in the Feast of the Immaculate Conception.

And after that awesome moment of the Incarnation, in which Mary found miraculously combined in her small person the twin glories of virginity and motherhood, she was the bearer of that still greater mystery, God become man, God become her baby within her chaste being. That decisive moment in history is our meditation and our song as we worship in the Feast of the Annunciation.

Then a few days later, as she stood on the doorstep of Elizabeth's home, it was not the shadow of conflict nor of Calvary that filled her mind and heart. She was rather bursting with radiant joy that the Savior, the Prince of Light was come and that she was His Mother.

When Mary had set out from Nazareth, it was not that her mind doubted Gabriel's words about Elizabeth being with child. She did not come to Judea to verify them. She believed Gabriel. And Elizabeth confirmed and praised her faith. It was the Holy Spirit speaking through her. "Blessed art thou among women and blessed is the fruit of thy womb. And how have I deserved that the mother of my Lord should come to me? The things promised her by the Lord shall be acomplished."[1]

No words were needed, then, to tell Mary's secret. The Lord God Himself had been her herald. He had spoken for her. She wanted to speak for Him. Since the hour of the Annunciation and all through the days coming down from Nazareth to Ain-Karem, praise of God, gratitude to God and joy had risen within her, thought on affectionate thought. The words that came were the familiar prayers of Samuel's mother, Anna, and of the Psalms. But they poured out freshly minted in the distinctive form of Mary's own unique hymn, her Magnificat. The ideas conceived and gestated for days came spontaneously to birth in a new creation. Mary was at once the poet of the moment, the authentic Lady of Letters, the religious historian of her people and the prophetess of her Son's new kingdom. She was, in fact, the Queen of prophets. That is why she is often represented with a book in her hands.

The big thing that stood out in her mind was that God had exalted her because she was of no importance. His hand was at work and no other. He lifted her in His arms for all the world to see. And all generations would sing her glory and call her Mother. Her thoughts were not the musings of girlish vanity but the full flower of a mother's responsibility. This was no momentary celebration but a unique destiny. She took her destiny

[1] Lk. 1:45.

in both hands, a mother's active hands, and accepted the swords of all its unknown ways. Mary's happiness was the solemn, deep, awesome happiness of young motherhood, a happiness like no other because her innocence and love and destiny were like no other. She had no Confiteor to say but could begin at once with her Gloria. Like a whispered antiphon came the thought of Ps. 111:9, "Holy is his name." But God has mercy and the joy of salvation for all "those who fear Him."[2]

As the Lord had scattered the military conceits of proud Pharaoh by drowning his armies in the Red Sea, as He had put down the mighty Canaanite kings to protect and homestead His desert-weary people in Palestine, so He would finally exalt the hidden and oppressed and feed the hungry of body and the hungry of soul. As the Father had kept His promises to Abraham and to Israel, He would be merciful to all generations who would fear Him. The fear He prefers is the fear called tenderness, the lover's fear of hurting the beloved.

In this poem of Mary, patterned in parallel phrases, the Old Testament is fulfilled and the Gospel is summarized. It is the victory hymn to God's mercy and power and fidelity. Her joy is the supreme fruit of her Son's spiritual kingdom. Her poem is the supreme fruit of her wise religious mind.

The heart of Mary that poured out so spontaneously in gratitude and joy in her Magnificat, and thus set the dominant note of all Christian worship, that same mother's heart poured out just as naturally and spontaneously in protesting grief when her Boy remained behind in Jerusalem at the age of twelve. "Son, why hast thou done so to us? Behold, in sorrow thy father and I have been seeking thee."[3] Those words were like the momentary human protest of her Son in Gethsemani and on the cross. "My God, my God, why hast thou forsaken me?"[4]

[2] Ps. 102:17.   [3] Lk. 2:48.   [4] Mk. 15:34.

Later in the more tranquil circumstances of the wedding at Canaan, Mary found her Son just returned from the desert and His conflict with Satan. Jesus was lean from the fast and tan from the desert sun and wind. He had with Him a few chosen apostles. This time, as the Mother of the Messiah, she approached her newly announced Messiah-Son, not to command but merely to tell Him the need. That was her new relationship of intercession. It was the hour of enlightenment about her new role as the co-redemptrix.

"The Mother of Jesus said to him, 'They have no wine!' "[5] Mary's petition was the prayer of perfect holiness, the prayer of absolute trust. With great delicacy she simply explained the need and left to her Son His own way of answering it. If the answer meant a miracle, that was within His power. The time for manifesting His mastery of the universe was determined precisely by that implied request of His Mother; except for that request, it was not the moment to show His divinity; except for Mary, there would have been no miracle.

"Jesus said to her, 'What wouldst thou have me to do, woman? My hour has not yet come.' "[6] The solemnity of the moment was indicated by the way Jesus addressed His Mother. He used the respectful and somewhat formal title of "Woman." And He gently suggested to her that He was now her Messiah-Son, going about His Father's business. It had been His tentative plan to delay the showing of His power. But Mary was not at fault. Jesus did not rebuke her nor did He speak harshly. There was a kind of refusal in His words but it was only momentary and conditional. What He said was not clear to Mary but her Mother's heart read more in His looks than He said in words. What she saw meant that for her sake He would do what He would otherwise not have done. Jesus let Mary

[5] Jn. 2:3.
[6] Jn. 2:3.

know that her implied request had, from all eternity, advanced the beginning of His public ministry.

That was the mightiest and most important prayer ever said by anyone other than Christ Himself. And she alone was made to say it. Mary was the Trinity's first love (after Christ's humanity) and in her matchless beauty of holiness and total love she held the key to divine power. We have to recall that for centuries there had been no miracles in Israel. And not even John the Baptist was given the miraculous touch, despite the fact that he was the greatest of the prophets because the precursor of the Savior. Only the mighty Woman, the Lady Mary, was to begin this new submission of the material world to her Son. The beginning of miracles at that moment was conditioned upon her prayer, just as Our Lord's other miracles were to be conditioned upon the requests of the sufferers or their friends.

Leaving to Jesus the manner of relieving the wine shortage, Mary quietly told the waiters to do anything He asked. "Do whatever he tells you."[7] She had begun to act on the higher plane of her Son's divine mission.

That is the heart of Mary we know, close to her Son and close to us. She was the Mother of God and a Mother who was one of us. Nothing about the life of her Son was too small to claim her full heart. Nothing about any of us is too small to claim her intercession.

> "O Mother of the Word Incarnate
> Never was it known that anyone who fled
> to thy protection was left unaided."

We can learn from the heart of Mary the perfect prayer of Cana, the prayer in which we tell Mary our needs and leave to her how to fill them. That is the prayer of De Montfort's

[7] Jn. 2:5.

consecration to Mary. "Delight in the Lord, and he will give thee the requests of thy heart."[8]

We can learn from the heart of Mary how to receive her Son's commands. In every part of our day, in everything we are asked to do, we can think of Our Lady standing there and saying to us, "Do whatever he tells you."

Within a few months after Cana, the death plot against Christ was already in the weaving. Remembering how Our Lord sought the company of His friends at Bethany, we think also of our best known Madonna, Our Lady of Perpetual Help. The picture represents a moment when angels appeared to the Child Jesus with the instruments of the Passion in their hands. And the Christ-Child was frightened and ran so fast to His Mother's arms that He nearly lost a little sandal. He is holding on to His Mother and looking back in fear. That baffling mystery of the almighty and transcendent God running in a fright to its mother could be just as real as the cries of Our Lord in Gethsemani and on the Cross.

In the sense that His human nature shrank from the cross, precisely because He was so perfectly human, in that sense of wanting to run away from suffering and death, it is true to say that even Christ Himself dreaded the cross.

That is a consolation that makes the Christian life more real and more livable. It means that we are not an impossible coward when at times the cross of life seems intolerably heavy. But it is one thing to dread the cross and quite another to be scandalized at the cross. Scandal is being drawn to evil. In a comfortable country and in a war-weary generation we are in serious danger of being scandalized at the cross. It can become for the people of our time a stumbling block and a foolishness. This scandal can take a thousand forms but they sum up to peace at

[8] Ps. 36:4.

any price. Hence the lives of sin. Hence the broken homes that make a holocaust of the children. Hence the failure to appreciate the vocation to virginity and the very uncomplimentary attitude that celibate chastity is impossible. We rebel at the difficult command to love our enemies and we walk out on unlovable people. We rebel against pain as something uncivilized, something that serves no good purpose but only warps and destroys a personality. We are scandalized at the cross.

This is a time when we need the "courageous and even audacious will" of Mary mentioned by Pius XII. We need to run to Mary as the frightened Christ-Child ran to His Mother. We need to remember the grown Son who cried out in anguish to His Father. From her strength of will we shall be renewed in our strength of will, because from her we shall learn simplicity, the total giving of ourselves that conques all conflicts. From her we learn the invincible confidence and the joy that releases the energies of love. From her we shall catch an apostolic zeal for the establishment of her Son's kingdom.

Every thought of Our Lady returns us to her Son. And the work of Our Lady and her Son is centered in the Mass. For Calvary is not a distant memory to us but always a tremendous moment. Christ lives it on each altar at the beginning of each day or in the evening or at midnight. But we are always aware that He goes on living it at every moment on some altar as the spinning earth turns mile after mile of its surface to be lighted an warmed by the sun.

At those altars and around those altars, sometimes stealthily improvised, stand parish priests and missioners and heroic priests in prisons, our apostolic brothers in Christ. And with them are the Christians who have been brought to Jesus and His Mother through prayers and sacrifices and missionary work. At Mass we are most intimately one great family, most obviously one in Christ. Distances mean nothing. Close to Our Lord, we are close to each other. As Pius XII says in His Encyclical on the Mystical Body: "The more we become 'members one of another,' 'mutually one for another,' the closer we shall be united with God, with Christ; as on the other hand the more ardent the love that binds us to God and our divine Head, the closer we shall be united to each other in the bonds of charity."[9]

That is why it is so right that the world should pour its troubles into the lap of worship and prayer and ask that the members of Christ take the world's distress and heal it in the infinite mediatorship of Christ exercised by the Head and participated in by His members.

Everyone has at times the experience of sinners confiding as if in God Himself, even though the confidant knows himself to be weak and wounded with sin. Anyone may be asked to give strength to others when he feels at times his own helplessness and inconstancy. Anyone may be asked to speak or write of the love of God when only by will power in the midst of spiritual darkness, is it possible to keep alive the flame of love in one's own heart.

"I do not the good that I wish, but the evil that I do not wish, that I perform ... I am delighted with the law of God according to the inner man, but I see another law in my members, warring against the law of my mind."[10]

But no one, least of all a Christian, has the right to throw up his arms in despair. Never for a minute may a person step out of his Christian character. There is no such thing as a process of "unbaptism." Pius XII speaks of this "deep mystery: that the salvation of many depends on the prayers and voluntary penances which members of the Mystical Body of Jesus Christ offer for this intention."[11]

[9] *Mystici Corporis*, par. 73.
[10] Rom. 7:19-23.
[11] *Mystici Corporis*, par. 44.

In other words, the Christian road we walk leads only in one direction. It is a straight road and it goes us to Calvary and to the tomb of resurrection. There is lo legitimate road of return.

Every Christian goes up to Calvary by baptismal dedication to Christ and to His work. And as he goes he burns behind him all the bridges that lead away from Calvary, all the bridges of sin. "If anyone wishes to come after me, let him deny himself, and take us his cross daily and follow me."[12] "All we who have been baptized into Christ Jesus have been baptized into his death."[13] "Always bearing about in our body the dying of Jesus so that the life also of Jesus may be made manifest in our bodily frame."[14] "If we have been united with him in the likeness of his death, we shall be so in the likeness of his resurrection also."[15]

The only way to come down from Calvary is by the road of sin. Sin is always a turning of one's back on the crucifixion of God. It is an escape from Calvary, from the salvation of the world and from the salvation of one's own soul. It is flight from the company of Jesus and Mary.

By baptism and by every apostolic and religious dedication, a person is committed to stay on Calvary. No Christian can go away and leave Our Lord hanging alone on the Cross, with only His Mother beside Him. Everyone belongs there because he has been called and signed and sealed for that cruel place. Everyone belongs tthere because Christ wants our company and cooperation. Everyone belongs there because he wants to be there with Jesus and His Mother.

But no one comes suddenly to the Calvary of conscious dedication. It takes a long time to learn what baptism means. It is

12 Lk. 9:23.
13 Rom. 6:3.
14 II Cor. 4:10.
15 Rom. 6:5.

one of the principle objects of the new Easter Vigil service to help us understand and to live the meaning of baptism, to see that it is so intimately a preparation for the Calvary of Mass. As we grow in the fervor of Christian life, that consciousness becomes more vivid. In the same way, it takes a long time to prepare for a conscious adult consecration of life to Jesus and Mary.

Our Blessed Mother did not suddenly come upon her Calvary. There were the moments of pain all along. Holy Simeon had warned her of them. And the flight into Egypt, the massacre of the Innocents, the loss of her Boy in the Temple told her something of what Simeon meant. After He left Nazareth and began preaching, the news came back to her that Jesus talked of the sufferings and death that He must endure. All that she had meditated in the psalms and in Isaias was suddenly an urgent, present and personal thing, centered in her Son. And it was not something that was just happening to Him; He said that He was deliberately choosing His ordeal. "The Father loves me, because I lay down my life that I may take it up again. No one takes it from me, but I lay it down myself."[16] Mary knew that He chose to hide His divine power when He walked into the hands of His enemies and let them do as they would.

Then there was that way of the Cross when the two most lonely persons on earth met and looked at one another in utter inconsolable loneliness. There was nothing either one could do about it. There was only the love and the courage to witness and endure.

It was the same on Calvary. In spite of her love, Mary could not help at all. And she suffered the more deeply because of her very love and helplessness. But at least she was a note of

[16] Jn. 10:17-18.

tenderness in that cruel, bloody place, a contradiction to the mockery and hatred that eddied in black tides around her.

Mary's presence on Calvary makes her a part of every renewal of Calvary in the Mass. As it was for her Son, so it was for the Mother, the climax of what they suffered together for the redemption of the world. The offering she made of Him there she continues to make in every Mass. And it is a wise preparation for Mass, and a helpful thought during Mass, to ask Mary to give us her mind and heart and will so that we can offer her Son to the Father through her hands. We feel her presence there very much. As history has it, there was no Calvary without the Mother. In every Mass, Mary takes us and offers us to the Father with her Son, for we are her Son's Mystical Body. She says to the Father, "This is my Son's Body; this is my Son's Blood."

Another thing, on the first Calvary John stood for all of us, as Leo XIII and Pius X have said, when Jesus gave John to His Mother to be her son. St. Pius X even said that we all rested with her Son beneath the heart of Mary and were born of her with Him who is our Head. This union of all in Him was declared to the world from the Cross. She was to be the Mother of everyone whom the Trinity, through her Son, would adopt as sons and daughters, the generations upon generations who would call her blessed when they called her Mother.

Were it not for this new prolific life born out of her Son's death, the Magnificat of Mary might have seemed like a terrible illusion. Where could be the joy, where the gratitude that welled up within her as she stood on Elizabeth's doorstep? In actual fact, her Magnificat remained true, not only in spite of Calvary, but precisely through Calvary. The mourning on Calvary would be the song of the suffering members of Christ through all generations. All sorrow for sin and all suffering would feel at home on Calvary with the crucified Redeemer.

God would be faithful to His promises. He would fill the hungry with good things.

Our Lady's Magnificat is forever echoed in the Calvary of each Mass. The Savior's worth we celebrate. God has indeed done great things. As St. Paul says, "Jesus, having offered one sacrifice for sins, has taken his seat forever at the right hand of God. . . . For by one offering He has perfected forever those who are sanctified. Thus also the Holy Spirit testifies unto us. . . . 'Their sins and their iniquities I will remember no more.' "[17] The bloody cruelty, the hatred and mockery of Calvary are not visible in the Sacramental offering of the Mass. And they do not need to be. The reparation is complete in the Person of Christ. But He wills that the one sacrifice of reparation be renewed to the end of the world. The application of Calvary takes place especially through the sacraments.

The ends of the Mass which are given special prominence are adoration and praise of God and thanksgiving for the graces of redemption. So Mary's thoughts in the Magnificat are constantly recurring in the Mass. The very name, "Eucharist" means thanksgiving. It is truly a celebration of thanksgiving and of praise. It is Mary again giving us her mind, her heart, her will. She sang first her thanksgiving and then praised the mercy, the power, the faithfulness of God in keeping His promises. As she sang her hymn of thanksgiving and praise in the majestic parallelism of Hebrew poetry, we sing our thanksgiving and praise in the majestic cadences of Chant. As Mary sang her thanksgiving that God had kept His promise and sent a Savior, we sing our thanksgiving that the Savior is with us all days even to the consummation of the world, offering Himself at every moment through one of His ministers and through the members of the Mystical Body.

[17] Heb. 10:12, 14, 17.

There is another thing that makes Our Lady so much a part of every Mass, and that is holy communion. There was no communion of Calvary, of course. And we cannot be sure of her presence at the Last Supper. It was the custom for the lady of the house to light the Passover lamp. And Mary may have been there for that. But on Calvary Jesus committed His mother to a newly ordained priest. (He might have entrusted her to Salome. He surely knew that John would be a busy apostle and bishop.) Thereafter, when John renewed the Calvary Sacrifice, through the anointed hands of John, Mary became again the immaculate tabernacle of her Son and her God. With the fervor of each communion, more and more her union with Jesus became like the living union of the divine and human natures in Him, and even like the life-oneness of the Trinity.

Dispensing all graces that come to us through Mass and communion, Mary is with us, wanting to give us her mind and heart and will so that we will receive her Son with something of the spiritual profit that came to her. Asking her for such a favor is one of the ways of living our consecration to her and of keeping our childlike dependence upon her. In moments of distraction we can ask her to let us think of her Son.

One of the natural things to ask of Mary is to request something of her mind and heart and will as we offer each Mass through the hands of the celebrant and offer ourselves as co-victims with Christ. In the offering of the Mass, everyone can feel that Mary is the leader of our worship. Even though she was greater in dignity than St. John, because she was the Mother of God, Mary did not have the priestly character and could not bring her Son to earth under the form of bread and wine. But when St. John offered Mass surrounded by his people and in her presence, Our Lady could penetrate more deeply than the celebrant into the mysteries of the altar. Better even than John, she knew that her Son is always the principal offerer as well as Victim in each Mass and that the heart of each Mass is the offering made in her Son's heart. She knew that when the world would be ended and the Mass would not need again to be offered, the inner offering of her Son would go on forever, not as reparation or petition but as thanksgiving and praise; for He would be for eternity the Head of the Mystical Body worshipping the Trinity.

In the Mass of St. John that Mary offered with him and with her Son, she prayed as the mediatrix and co-redemptrix of the world. The prayer she gave us at Fatima was in her heart then: "O my Jesus, lead all souls to heaven. Help especially those who are most in need." She prayed especially for the work of the apostles and for their courage under suffering. She was the perfect victim-soul and offered all that she herself suffered, especially on Calvary.

In her heart the burning of Calvary's pain would never cease. And each Mass was not a simple ritual but a vivid renewal of all the horrors and the blood and the blasphemies of those dark hours. To her mother's heart it was all as clear and real as two minutes ago. That Mass of St. John, with Mary present at it, was the most perfect reliving of Golgotha that could ever be. And the giving back to Mary of her Son's living Flesh was the completion of the eucharistic Sacrifice. Resting again in His Mother's immaculate being, Jesus found the perfect rest and perfect love that He always seeks.

We ask Our Lady to make us at home on Calvary. We have to be at home there because we stand on a Calvary of our own making. At every Mass we come again to a Calvary that we have made. It is always a living Calvary, alive with Christ the Victim and alive with our personal sins. It is not something that happened in a dead forgotten past. The sins of 2,000 years before Christ were no more and no less present to the Father than the sins of 2,000 years after Christ. We do not point fingers at other people. It is not the sins of somebody else. It is our own sins that put Him to death. His death is our doing. Through His death each of us has the grace to be a prodigal returning to the Father, if only for a single venial sin.

All foolish human pride ought to break against the crucifix. How can we be proud as we stand before the crucified Son of God and know that we have been His murderers? We can face that awful fact only because we know that God's murdered Son has already forgiven us and by His very death gives us new life, even eternal life. We can face it because we know that Mary stands there with us, pleading our forgiveness and pleading for grace. She makes her own the words of her Son, "Forgive them, for they do not know what they are doing."[18] By the grace she obtains for us, her Son's crucifixion becomes a call to sorrow and repentance and atonement.

But we also know that He is showing us the cost of mediatorship and victimhood. We might cry out against that cost and say that it is too much, if it were not for the woman who stood there on Calvary, the woman who was the most innocent of all, most involved of all because His Mother, immaculately sinless and yet suffering the cost of redemption with her Son more keenly than anyone. She suffered with her Son in order to give life to the world.

That is our great hope. Calvary is not a hopeless, bloody, meaningless confusion. It is not merely a death but also a birth that we have part in. Because that death accomplishes our redemption, it is our life, our sweetness and our hope. So in each Mass and through the day we remain on Calvary with Mary who is our life, our sweetness and our hope.

"O God, who in a wonderful manner didst create and ennoble human nature, and still more wonderfully hast renewed

18 Lk. 23:24.

it, grant that . . . we may be partakers of His divinity who vouch-safed to become partaker of our humanity, Jesus Christ Thy Son." Mary was the one most nobly created, and with her Son she renews the world.

Chapter Fifteen

Sacramentals Prepare Us for Worship

WHEN God created the material world of seas and dry land, and heavens and the fruit-bearing earth, the multiplying fishes and birds and animals, He "saw that all that he had made was very good."[1] Everything was meant to work together for the service and happiness of man. But sin crippled the harmony of the material universe and put it in partial rebellion against men. And man, suffering in himself the consequences of his fall from grace, found his relations with things vitiated to the point that they easily distracted and seduced him from his primary vocation to worship and to achieve heaven.

Indeed, the material world may seen at times to dwarf man, but never successfully. "He is not a big as a mountain nor as beautiful as a sunset, yet the ungainly dwarf manages to overshadow them both. It does not matter how nature favors or fortune serves him. You can give him gray hair and fallen arches, fling him on a park bench without a penny in his pocket,

[1] Gen. 1:31.

stand him on a street corner with a tin cup, bury him in the jungle, and he will still remain the center of the universe. Find him in his cradle; put a bib around his neck and a rattle in his hand. Cover him with loathsome disease. Reduce him to any state you like, but he will everlastingly preoccupy you more than all the constellations. The world is but a stage for this chief actor. All drama is here, and all history. The curious creature has a soul."[2]

Though the whole world is man's stage, it has to be more than his playroom; it has to be also his schoolroom and his workroom. Because of the internal disorder created by sin, things tend to draw man away from God to the satisfactions they give. "The wisdom of the flesh is hostile to God, for it is not subject to the law of God, nor can it be."[3] Following desire, man tends to preoccupy himself with a row of things as if they were junior gods in a part-time heaven. He wants to settle down somewhere short of his full-time heaven and coddle the illusion that he has reconciled the irreconciliable opposition between the law of God and the warring law of our members.[4] He wants to think he has eliminated the need of penance and restraint.

Therefore, to bring man to his senses and to restore order and the right use of things, God entered into the material world, took a material body to His divine Person and used material instruments to redeem both man and the world man inhabits. Henceforth, the world became sacramentalized. Things became the instruments of grace in the sacraments and sacramentals.

It was nothing less than the free submission of His humanity to terrible suffering and final destruction by crucifixion that made possible the redemption of man and things. And that was only the climax of centuries of preparing people to believe that only the

[2] Bishop James E. Walsh, *Field Afar*, Maryknoll, N.Y.
[3] Rom. 8:7.
[4] Rom. 7:23.

truly poor man is acceptable to God, for that is the meaning of the suffering servant in Isaias and the meaning of the psalms. By His life of disciplined labor and simplicity Jesus emphasized the truth that we must come before God with the sense of having no right to anything. His public ministry, with no place of His own to lay His head, taught us that we cannot settle down anywhere this side of heaven.

But in Himself Jesus also reconciled and personalized all the seeming contradictions between the dignity and humiliations of man. All suffering and loss is redemptive through our oneness with Him and through our suffering all things for love of Him. Since He has undone the greatest evil, which is Adam's sin, He also turns all lesser evils to good purposes. He taught us, finally, "That the sufferings of the present time are not worthy to be compared with the glory to come that will be revealed in us."[5] In this redemption the material world also is to share. "The eager longing of creation itself also will be delivered of the sons of God. . . . Creation itself also will be delivered from its slavery to corruption into the freedom of the glory of the sons of God."[6]

But, again, He did not say it would be easy. "Now you have not received a spirit of bondage so as to be again in fear, but you have received a spirit of adoption as sons. . . . But if we are sons, we are heirs also: heirs indeed of God and joint heirs with Christ, provided, however, we suffer with him that we may also be glorified with him."[7]

This understanding of the redemption of man and things at great cost is necessary both for the true Christian humanism of St. Francis de Sales and Maritain and for a proper understanding and use of sacraments and sacramentals. Without this

---

[5] Rom. 8:18.
[6] Rom. 8:19, 21.
[7] Rom. 8:15, 17.

sound sacrificial basis, sacramentals especially can easily degenerate into illusion and magic. Sacramentals can never be separated from asceticism and human effort. The sign of the cross is used in every sacramental. Christian asceticism rests on a proper esteem for all created things; but, aware both of their dangers and their possibilities, the Christian prefers the spiritual to the material and eternity to time and therefore uses created things for higher and eternal purposes. Our adjustment to and our balance with material things can only be relative and cautious this side of heaven, "for the flesh lusts against the spirit, and the spirit against the flesh; for these are opposed to each other, so that you do not do what you would."[8]

This healthy Christian realism not only makes Christian life and sanctity possible and practical in every vocation but it also pleads for the sanctifying of things and the sanctified use of things through sacramentals. We are utterly dependent upon God for everything and we deserve nothing. We are capable of abusing anything and everything. Therefore, the use of things needs to be made holy. This consciousness, truly lived, amounts to being poor in spirit. So Christian poverty as well as Christian asceticism are closely related to sacramentals. Besides, in this conscious dependence, and weakness, we welcome, not just some of the means of grace nor merely the occasional use of them, though they be as great as the sacraments, but we welcome every means of grace and therefore also the frequent use of sacramentals. Some day, at the end of time, there will be a "new heaven and a new earth."[9] In the meantime, we have to live with the one at hand. We have to seek God coming to us and leading us to Him through the things of this present world. Thus the whole world will become sacramentalized.

Sacramentals can be taken both in a broad and in a restricted

[8] Gal. 5:17.
[9] Apoc. 21:1.

sense. "Sacramentals in a broad sense are all those rites and ceremonies which accompany the observance of the divine cult and
the administration of the sacraments."[10] In a narrow sense, they
are "certain rites, actions, or particular things which the Church
customarily uses, in imitation of the sacraments, in order to
obtain, through her intercession, certain effects, especially of a
spiritual character.[11] They are instituted by the Church and
produce their effects because the Church, in her dignity and by
the power of her intercession, obtains from God those spiritual
effects for the individual in proportion to the individual's worthy
disposition.

"The sacramentals are divided into two classes: exorcisms
and blessings or benedictions. Exorcisms consist in the imposition of hands and the recitation of certain prayers for the purpose of expelling the devil from the soul and body of the
believer. They are applied to irrational creatures also, so that
the devil may not use them abusively to harm man. Benedictions are divided into constitutive and invocative. The constitutive benedictions are applied to men and to irrational
creatures to consecrate them to God (e.g., blessing of the virgins,
consecration of chalices). The invocative are imparted to man
for the purpose of obtaining some divine benefit (e.g., the blessing of St. Blaise), and to irrational creatures that their use may
be beneficial to man's soul and body (e.g., blessing of the
table)."[12]

Sacramentals are instruments of redemption but their effect
is not automatic. There could be nothing wanting, of course,
in the merits that Jesus won for us on the cross. And there is
no blocking the prayers of the Church which seek to apply the
merits of Calvary. These two sources of life and power, chan-

[10] Parente, *op. cit.,* p. 246.
[11] Can. 1144.
[12] Parente, *op. cit.,* p. 247.

neling grace through sacred actions and sacred objects, make sacramentals just worlds apart from the automatic magic of superstition. There is something more that makes them a person-to-person medium of communication between God and man and that is the necessary disposition of the individual who is to receive the effects. That worthy disposition must begin with the basic creaturely attitude of dependence upon God, of being obliged to render God due homage and of sorrowing and aton-ing for sin. This attitude, as well as the desire to receive the spiritual effects, may be implicit. The desire, in turn, will be largely in proportion to our sorrow for sin and our sense of de-pendence upon God. This is especially true of our desire to gain the indulgences that are attached to certain sacramentals. The most important dispositions, of course, are the state of grace, the degree of sanctifying grace, the actuality and purity of inten-tion and the fervent love of the person receiving the spiritual effect. Implementing love, sacramentals also deepen it.

Sacramentals are not necessary for salvation but, rightly and frequently used, they help anyone to grow closer to God and to persevere in love for God unto the end. Consciously linked with sorrow for sin, they do much to deepen sorrow and humil-ity. Expressing love, they deepen its tenderness and all-pervading power. Sacramentals do not supplant the Mass and the sacra-ments; they express and intensify the dispositions needed for a more fruitful reception of the sacraments. Knowing as we must that they depend primarily upon Christ's suffering and death, we are prepared through them to unite ourselves with His sufferings, to enter into and live those sufferings in our flesh. The sacramentals bring the sacrifice of Christ into every point and activity of life and stimulate us to live a sacrificial life.

We may link sacramentals directly with worship as we enter a church and make the sign of the cross. This richly indulgenced sacramental pulls our thoughts and our whole being together for praying to our Redeemer-Brother in this house of sacrificial worship. And we remind ourselves of the reason for that cross when we begin by dipping our fingers in holy water, for the meaning of water is first of all cleansing, a cleansing from the sins that are the reason for Our Lord's crucifixion. But the blessed water also gives us protection against the devil and his temptations, especially during prayer. The sign of the cross and holy water are meant to serve the same inspiring purposes at home and in many things we do and use. In the church and in the home there is also the crucifix which pictures the cost of our redemption and disposes us to think of entering into worship by lives of sacrifice, a sacrifice that respects the goodness of everything God made but renounces the lesser for the greater and prefers the eternal to the temporal. This price of redemption has to be emphasized because we too easily seek a comfortable Christianity and are too quickly scandalized at the Cross.

The very church building is a place of mediation between God and man and is itself blessed. Within the church is a whole world of things made sacred by blessing: Chalice, ciborium, altar cloths, bells, candles, vestments, stations of the Cross, statues, organ, etc. In church, also, palms, ashes and incense, medals and scapulars are blessed. Everyone comes to church for the blessing of throats and young mothers for the blessing before and after childbirth. There abbots are blessed and there virgins take their vows with a blessing. These manifold benedictions orchestrate the whole human person in the blended depths of worship.

Families share in the use of many sacramentals. There is the nuptial blessing that begins family life. The very home itself is blessed each year as the protective dwelling place of the "little church," the little Mystical Body. Father, mother, and children take their blessed rosaries and say together their family rosary. There are special blessings for eggs, bread and cake, cheese and butter, bacon or lard, grapes, fresh fruits and wine, and for food in general. As the mother was blessed before and after childbirth, so the child itself receives a special blessing. Sick children and sick adults have separate blessings to invoke God for a speedy recovery. Medicine and wheel chairs, linens and wine for the sick come under benediction. Through the blessing of our country's flag, religion and patriotism are united as twin virtues in the minds of the children and indicate that each child and adult must be at once a citizen of God's spiritual kingdom, His Church, and of His temporal society, the nation. Finally, a "Blessing for All Things" leaves nothing untouched, makes everything sacred. When mortal life suddenly or gradually passes into the life that does not change, prayers for the dying prepare for the transition that is death and prayers are said over the place where the body sleeps until its resurrection.

As the family is united in many great and little duties, so also it is united in many joys and pleasures. And sacramentals enter into our recreational life and bless our need for refreshing mind and body. As there is a deep inner joy in working together with those we love, so there is added pleasure in recreating together. The family meal together can be a daily and refreshing joy, in spite of the spilled milk and the clash of emerging personalities. Food is necessary to life. Therefore God meant everyone to eat. Preparing food is work and eating could be bothersome. So God made it a pleasure to eat and drink. The various blessings upon food and drink sanctify both their power to sustain the body and the pleasure they give. Wine, ale and beer may also know the touch of benediction. Besides, the sense of unity that comes from sharing in legitimate pleasure is heightened by the thought of God's blessing upon everything. Since He made us that way, God intended also that there should be such a natural help to community charity, perhaps to offset the inevitable frictions between people who live so close together. These holy purposes, plus the fact of our de-dependence upon God for food and pleasure, are good reasons for the prayers that go before and after the family meal.

In a highly electrified age the blessing of the essential dynamo brings God into all the many ways that light and power serve for family enjoyment: radio, television, movies, lights over the family table and for reading, the mixers that prepare food, the heat that cooks food, etc. The blessing upon the family car is a sacramental that figures in many pleasant rides and vacation trips. The airplane, too, and ships and trains are blessed for their part in both business and pleasure jaunts. And God's bene-diction is invoked upon the very journey itself. Even tools for scaling mountains have their benedictions. Sacramentals in recreational life not only help to safeguard our using them but also, through the sanctification of joy and pleasure, dispose us to enter into the very real joys and pleasures of corporate wor-ship. Worship is not meant to be a begrudged obligation that must be fulfilled to keep out of mortal sin. Worship is above all a joyous celebration and we should come to it physically refreshed and relaxed and ready to give our best, our whole being. Then we will leave it spiritually refreshed.

"The whole body is the tool and the expression of the soul. The soul does not merely dwell in the body, as if it dwelt in a house, but it lives and works in every member and every fiber. It speaks in every line, and form, and movement of the body."[13] Therefore, not only worship and family and recreation but also work should have its measure of sacramentals to complete the consecration of the human person in all its activities.

This is especially important in our time. For one thing, with little or no idea of sacred history, very few look to Genesis to

[13] Guardini, *Sacred Signs,* London, Sheed and Ward, 1937, p. 5.

find that Adam and Eve worked in their Paradise. "The Lord God took the man and placed him in the garden of Eden to till it and to keep it."[14] So it is not work that is the result of original sin but only the disagreeableness of work. God meant work itself to be a part of the many pleasures in that heaven on earth which He made for our first parents. Many even now feel a joy and satisfaction in their work if they are temperamentally and mentally suited to it, take pride in doing it well and are able to see both its creativeness and its service to God and man. Sacramentals that bless the instruments of work at least help to recall God as the source of all power and the final purpose of things. They keep in mind the human beings who are to be served, fed, clothed and housed by the instruments of work. But sacramentals still depend upon the disposition of those who use them. Their effects can be nullified if the primacy and dignity of the human person and of human society are subordinated to technology for technology's sake or to wages for wages' sake. Work can be prayer and the tools of work help man to fulfill his destiny of completing God's creation. But the prayer must be welcomed and willed. And the work must be a voluntary offering. Made sacred by prayer and offering, the disagreeableness of work becomes atonement for sin and the productiveness of work becomes a sanctifying duty.

There is another reason for sacramentals in occupational life. The machine is a marvelous servant. Machines do so much and such intricate work that they may seem to substitute for intelligence itself. But their delicate and rapid computing still require the human person with intelligence to design them in the first place and to stand by, understand, judge, select and act. The machine is only as clever and as dependable as the human mind and will which control it. And the human mind can nod and the will can be pulled in wrong direc-

[14] Gen. 2:15.

tions. Therefore, the bigger the machines, the more tragic the consequences of human error. Trains, ships and airplanes collide because somebody misjudges. The dependence of the machine upon man ought to suggest the dependence of man upon his Creator and Sustainer. A pilot or engineer who lives his responsibility to God and man is an alert pilot and engineer. And the sacramentals can bring those decisive hunches that save lives and could be called graces. Rightly, then, do we have blessings upon planes, trains and ships, automobiles and fire engines. Dynamo and blast furnaces, lime kiln, and flourmill, bridge and ambulance can be blessed. And there are sacramentals for the telegraph, the printing press, the typewriter and the library. Sacramentals, therefore, can have their part in keeping the thought of God in factory and shop and store and thus dispose the mind and will for full official worship.

Although the dominant thinking of the western world is in terms of industry and urban life, we cannot forget that two-thirds of the world's people work the soil and produce the world's food and grain and much of its clothing. Quite naturally, then, there are sacramentals to bless the farm, the fields, the seeds and the meadows, the orchards and vineyards. Draft animals, cattle and sheep, whether sick or healthy, may be blessed. And there are benedictions for bees and silkworms. The essential well, too, can be blessed. So may the stables and the granary. Through these blessings and the ones for food and for all the modern means of transportation, Christ's work of redeeming creation to the service of God and man weaves through rural ways like daylight and dark, sun and rain, summer and winter.

Thus the sacramentals extend and radiate the sacraments. In their own way they apply the merits of Calvary. As Christ became the lamb who was slain to take away the sins of all men, so His Mystical Body unites its prayers for the efficacy of all the sacramentals that are used all over the world. And the user of each sacramental knows that it is not so much his individual use as it is the prayer of the Church and his own worthy union with her prayer that give the sacramental its effect. In sacramentals, therefore, Christ our Redeemer, all Christians with their prayers and their needs and all creation are united in a great and continuous sanctifying act. They make the Ritual more than a book of sacraments and bring the ritual into home, and field and factory, onto the highways and railways and into the air. Always their purpose is to make the better Christian who is better disposed to enter mind and heart and soul into worship. They are not baby food for primitive inclinations to superstition nor are they a vulgarization of things sacred. They are not a scattering of piety nor a watering down of piety nor a "gimme" cash-and-carry piety that distracts from the great central acts of worship. Rightly understood and rightly used, they help greatly to heal the cleavage between religion in church and religion in life.

Steeped in the understanding and use of sacramentals, a Christian looks at the familiar world about him and sees beyond the surface of things. He is not looking at their metaphysical essence. As he handles and uses things he looks beyond them to the powers and influences that produce them, to their functions and influences and to their capacity to receive impact and influence and transformation. The sacramentals reveal a dynamic world in ceaseless movement, a world engaged in an endless ebb and flow of forces, influences and action in which the sacramentals are divinely employed instruments and not helpless victims. In their own way, they reveal and implement the struggle, the warfare of God that runs through all of Scripture.

This wonder-world is treated partly on the natural level, where causality is still much shrouded in mystery, partly on the preternatural level of the devil and his "illusions, machinations, snares and assaults," partly on the level of angels, and, most important of all, on the supernatural level in which health of soul and body leads to everlasting life. Things do not stand alone nor do they stand still. In this world of gigantic activity, there is a mighty flow of good forces and evil, of good effects and evil; there are unsuspected presences, love that proffers help and hatred that sets snares. Such a world of mystery might frighten a person were it not that it can be entered, to begin with, only by faith. Besides, the sacramentals enlighten and transform everything into the voice of God speaking love and protection and the voice of man responding with adoration, love and thanksgiving.

This divine-human dialogue reasserts man as the center of God's creation. Planes and ships, food and clothing are not blessed for their own sake but for the sake of man whom they serve. Of man alone it can be said, "There are sermons in stone and books in running brooks, but there are poems in people, and also symphonies, grand operas, and sometimes three-ringed circuses. In all the universe there is no dream comparable to the life of the humblest man. The woods may move to Dunsinane, and the stars falter in their courses, but these things are only footnotes to his career, and their cosmic importance is measured by the degree in which they affect him. Let the very sky tumble about his head, and the main thing we want to know is how it found him, what it did to him, and in what situation it left him."[15] Sacramentals teach this wondrous human being to wonder also at the mystery of things and then to look beyond their forces to adore a Person. They teach him to wonder at God's gratuitous tenderness and unvarying kindness in making all things for the unpredictable human person. They teach him, finally, to love, to reach for God with his whole being, for even though God is infinitely separated in power, He chooses to be joined to us in love.

[15] James E. Walsh, *op. cit.*

Let it be repeated for emphasis that through the sacramentals the whole world becomes a sublime conversation in which God and man speak to one another their reciprocal love. Thus the sacramentals become an excellent school of theology. And the God they teach us to know is the transcendent God who yet stoops compassionately and full-handed to His adopted children and draws them in awe to a most intimate personal union. He He is more than Creator; He is the tender One who disposes all things for the good of His sons and daughters, for only God could give creatures a power that is so much beyond their natural capacity. But the effects of sin remain; the redemption is not yet complete in its transformation of man and the world. So the conflict between the prince of darkness and the Prince of Light goes on until the end of time. The mysterious interplay of forces in material things is simply ammunition in this cosmic conflict. Entering with faith and hope and love into this battle, under the leadership and by the strength of Jesus whom we love, we are ready to look with respect and compassion upon things that give their own being in a divine cause.

Chapter Sixteen

The Father is the Leader of Family Worship

WOULD it be an understatement to say that there seems to be a lessening of the natural leadership which the father should exercise in his family? There are those who accept it, endorse it and are ready to fight any change in the unnatural relationship. And there are others who take a second look and see quite a few complications. Some in a professional capacity try to mend the disturbing effects of the imbalance on husbands, wives and children. Couples in the Christian Family Movement and Cana Conferences have some ardent discussions on this point.

Fortunately, there is a healthy re-examination of the matter both on the part of men and women. Taking it first from the viewpoint of the husband's weakness, Dr John R. Cavanaugh, Washington, D.C. psychiatrist, told the Family Life Convention in Boston (March 1956), "At the present time man has to a large extent adbdicated his position as head of the family. He may still provide the necessities of life but even in this he is frequently helped by his working wife. This has left to the wife the active direction of the family and the raising of the children. Thus the children are deprived of paternal discipline which is so necessary for their complete development. And the woman is projected into a situation in which she must be dominant. This frustrates her need to be dependent and passive. As head of the family she must assume the male qualities of independent action and aggressivity which she does not naturally possess."[1]

On the other hand, women are being just as frank. Sidonie M. Gruenberg, a famous feminist, looks at the other half of the picture, "Most of my life I have been fighting for women's rights. Now I find I must stand up for men's rights. For I detect a danger signal in many young families today: the growing tendency of wives to exploit their husbands. Yes, I mean *exploit*, in its strongest sense: to use selfishly for one's own ends. I am not talking about the nagging women who chip away at their husband's self-respect, nor about women who hound their husbands for fur coats, cars and cruises. I am talking about perfectly nice young wives—not lazy, not vicious, not overly grasping, and not at all stupid—who are taking unfair advantage of the fact that today's husbands are willing to help at home. These young wives are shifting their household responsibilities onto their husbands. And in many instances they are using their men as outlets for their own frustration."[2]

Lest we think this matter too much of a sudden crisis, it helps to recall that Henry Adams once wrote to his friend Charles Milnes Gaskell, "She (my fiancee) rules me as only American women rule men."[3]

[1] Cavanaugh, *Boston Pilot,* June 16, 1956, p. 9.
[2] Gruenberg, *Catholic Digest,* June 1956, p. 18.
[3] Adams, *New York Times Book Review,* April 8, 1956, p. 2.

In any case, the degrees of diminished male leadership in the home differ no end and so do the causes. There is no one cause. And the job of relating cause to effect is entangled in a national culture which everyone breathes and reflects unconsciously.

To some extent you could point to the social, economic and political independence of women and say that their independence and forcefulness in the home is all of a piece with the whole pattern. It is a habit. Everybody does it. And no one should be surprised if eligible bachelors need extra courage to take a wife. Or is it that they fear fatherhood?

Books have been written about "momism," its causes and effects. But who would care to suggest that we give less respect to our mothers? No one, I'm sure. Let there be all possible respect of the right kind and in the right place. Let the boys grow up with full devotion to their mothers. But is such regard in its right place when it carries over into marriage and prompts the young husband to give his young wife the deference that belonged to the authority of his mother? The taste of power is sweet and, like leaven, the appetite for it grows. The wife says, "Let's have more of it."

The problem of "momism" is also related to man's abdication of leadership and is aggravated by school and work life. Dr. Cavanaugh says on this point, "It also leads, too frequently, to the mother assuming a matriarchal jurisdiction in the home. The tendency toward matriarchy is already pronounced in this country. We have only to realize that in recent years the majority of high school teachers are women. This places the boy under the domination of women through high school. Even into college the young man may be supervised by women; and when he gets a job his boss may again be a woman. Because of this domination of woman in both family and school life, a boy has no opportunity to learn independence of female domination. He accepts control and automatically obeys his female preceptor."[4]

Does urban life have something to do with undermining male leadership? The father works away from home and his wife and children do not see him as the skillful fashioner of raw materials into useful products, the master of merchandise, the competent professional counselor and technician. They see him too much as the servant who provides a pay check and runs errands. There is a noticeable difference in rural areas where the father is the he-man who plans his fields and handles his livestock and puts muscle and brains and mechanical skills into a whole long day of useful work, all under the eyes of wife and children. His leadership is naturally evident and naturally respected.

Is there so much rush and fatigue in a man's work-life that he gladly leaves the raising of the children to the mother? That is the way it often works out. Perhaps it is also the extra activities and recreations away from home that eat into his remaining time and energies. In any case, the wife is left emotionally starved. And it is no surprise to find her compensating by exercising great authority and fastening excessive emotional bonds upon her children.

Could a poisonous materialism have something to do with it? Everybody breathes it in and exhales it; and lucky are we if we do not live by it in unsuspected ways. How many fathers are conscious of their spiritual power and leadership? How often do wife and children look to him for spiritual leadership and respect him for it?

This is being long on questions and short on answers. But before we look for answers we may profitably call the roll on what the unhappy imbalance does to family life.

---

[4] Cavanaugh, *op. cit.,* p. 9.

For one thing, the female domination that has shaped a man's family and school life tends to leave too many men emotionally weak and passive. The natural aggressive tendencies remain and may rebel in marriage against feminine control. If the rebellion does not succeed it may become a smouldering neurosis or be acted out in delinquency and infidelity. This frustration, emotional insecurity and neurosis do not make for a good husband-wife relationship. "The failure of men to play their natural role as head of the family is one of the greatest hidden causes of divorce."[5]

It is bad enough that a husband feels a sense of frustration because he does not sufficiently exercise his natural leadership in the family. But the home difficulty is often further complicated by the sense of dissatisfaction and frustration that he already feels in so much of factory and business employment. If home life were in balance it would at least help to offset work-life. But as it is the husband often does not develop normal confidence nor his full ability.

Born of frustration, concealed emotional storms help to drain away a man's energy and shorten his life. It cannot, of course, be calculated mathematically that every time a wife wins an argument she shortens her husband's life by a day. But a relaxed and contented husband is less liable to cerebral hemorrhage and heart ailments.

It is not hard to see the unhappiness of the wife when she steps out of her natural role of dependence and obedience into executive dominance. Neither mentally nor emotionally is she made to so function.[6] She gets too little of the protective love

---

[5] Cavanaugh, *Associated Press,* March 14, 1956.

[6] The man has greater muscular strength, is heavier boned and taller for his active, working life, and for his role as aggressive protector and persistent builder. His emotional reactions are slower, which makes for more objective thinking in a crisis and a generally greater capacity for seeing all the aspects of a question. He is more direct in speech and

and attention that she needs and that bring out the best of her tender qualities. And she gets too much of the submissive attention that tends to harden her in pride. It is often said that American wives are at once the most pampered and the most unhappy wives in the world.

Where there is tension between father and mother from misplaced authority and leadership, or from any other source, the children sense it inevitably and absorb it as an atmosphere. It tends to make them overserious, possessed of excessive anxieties and emotionally unstable. Besides, father's too frequent absence from homes adds up to just one thing for the affectionate boy or girl: "Daddy doesn't love me! Daddy doesn't care what I do!"

On the positive side it can within proper limits be said, "The interest that young husbands take in today's home is one of the great gains of modern family life ... I'm all for this new kind of father and what he does in the new household. I'm particularly glad the change came about gradually and amicably. The 'revolution' required no parades, placards, nor aggressive demands from us women. It happened as a part of pervasive social change in all aspects of living. Today, young men and women share the same activities, and our family living is the healthier for it. But now I'm afraid that too many young women are

more independent in thinking and acting. Besides, man has a greater readiness to laugh at himself. God gave man these qualities in order to make him the natural leader. That also is why men sometimes envy the independence of bachelors and why women pity spinsters.

Woman, on the other hand, is more frail, more inclined to dependence and passivity and more oblique in speech. She is quicker to react emotionally in order to tackle and solve the dozens of family needs that call her to be the educator and spiritual mother, physician and nurse, umpire and counsellor, housekeeper and cook. And every woman in her better moments recognizes her husband as the natural leader. No woman wants to be married to a man she cannot admire, upon whom she cannot depend and whom she cannot want as the father of her children.

taking unfair advantage of their husbands' cooperative spirit."[7]

The beginning of a happy balance between the father and mother in a family is that they try not so much to equal each other as to be worthy of each other, the father being fully the man in prudence and delicate reserve and the mother being totally feminine in cooperative obedience. A mother's duty of subordination does not come from any womanly inferiority but from the very nature and glory of her motherhood. In the essential rights of fidelity and conjugal fulfillment there is no subordination but necessary equality. Obedience is not a degradation but an exaltation; it is the surrendering of a lesser freedom of choice by natural impulse in order to gain the greater freedom of choice by God-given authority. Obedience is simply the free and noble acceptance of duty; it is expansion into something bigger than one's self, into the family; it is fulfillment in a social, community spirit; it is realism and sanity.

A mother retains her own endless ways of strengthening and influencing her husband simply by being utterly the woman God made her to be. Every advantage of friendship is heightened and increased in the love of friendship between husband and wife. And the attractiveness of woman that inclines the husband to her wish is in the mystery of womanhood beautified by high integrity, delicate modesty, tender courtesies, simplicity, and kindness. By being completely herself she has great power to guide him in justice and patience and repentance and to hold him against illicit love. And who can calculate the vast influence of a mother over her children? She is fully the queen to husband and children by helping him to be fully the king of the home.

"This subjection, however, does not deny or take away the liberty which fully belongs to the woman both in view of her dignity as a human person, and in view of her most noble office

[7] Gruenberg, *op. cit.,* pp. 20-21.

as wife and mother and companion; nor does it bid her obey her husband's every request if not in harmony with right reason or with the dignity due to the wife; nor, in fine, does it imply that the wife should be put on a level with those persons who in law are called minors, to whom it is not customary to allow free exercise of their rights on account of their lack of mature judgment, or of their ignorance of human affairs. But it forbids that exaggerated liberty which cares not for the good of the family; it forbids that in this body which is the family, the heart be separated from the head to the great detriment of the whole body and the proximate danger of ruin. For if the man is the head, the woman is the heart, and as he occupies the chief place in ruling, so she may and ought to claim for herself the chief place in love."[8]

The father is naturally the first model both for his sons and daughters. The boys need him as a hero; they need his manly courtesy towards mother to show them a balanced respect for women. The girls need him to model the goodness of men.

Natural helps to further man's leadership in the home should be turned to their most effective, even though limited, use. We should not ignore certain implications of the great suburban movement. It does something at least to keep the father the master of his own domain. The tendency to use the many available tools for "do-it-yourself" making and repairing will help to give him the attention of wide-eyed children and proud wife. Whatever its present drawbacks, television at least keeps the family at home together and can be one more occasion for the

[8] Pius XI, "Christian Marriage in Our Day," *loc. cit.,* Vol. II, p. 134. Cf. *Sum. Theol.,* I, q. 92, a. 3. Motherhood is a full-time job and a trying job during the growing years of the children. But today's mothers live longer and more securely and have many opportunities for a full interesting life after the children have grown up. Open to them are all the various courses in adult education, social work, writing, teaching, counselling, etc.

father to use important authority in selecting suitable programs.

But this very suburban movement also requires of him a greater spiritual and social leadership. The family, uprooted from its former parish and school and community, has to be integrated into a new parish community and into new neighborhood activities. Old spiritual ties have been broken and new ones must be formed. Often the family will be farther from church and he will have to see to it that there is no lessening of church visits or Sacraments received.

The family has been called traditionally the little Church, the little Mystical Body with Christ the Head of the family as He is the Head of the Church. Christ is Prophet, Priest and King, i.e., Teacher, Sanctifier and Ruler, in the family, as He is in the Church. He does not need to be invited into the home; He is already there. And He is represented visibly by the father. As the Pope is the visible head of the Church so in his own way the father is the visible head of the family. Seeing the Pope, you see Christ in the Church. Seeing the father, you see Christ in the family. When the father commands his children, it is Christ commanding. When he teaches, it is Christ teaching. What he does in the exercise of his lay priesthood to help his wife and children grow in holiness is the work of Christ making them holy.

"Since the husband represents Christ, and since the wife represents the Church, let there always be, both in him who commands and in her who obeys, a heaven-born love guiding both in their respective duties. For 'the husband is the head of the wife; as Christ is the head of the Church. . . . Therefore, as the Church is subject to Christ, so also let wives be to their husbands in all things.'"[9]

When it is a deep conviction of the father, and of his fam-

---

[9] Eph. 5:23, 24. Leo XIII, "Christian Marriage," *Social Wellsprings,* Milwaukee, Bruce, 1940, Vol. I, p. 30.

ily, that he is Christ's visible representative then he will be respected and obeyed. He will not forget that Christ redeemed the world by first becoming a carpenter and family provider for His Mother and then waded through a sea of earthy human weakness and contradictions until He ended in crucifixion.

Thereafter sacrifice took on a new meaning. Souls have always cost dearly; they never come cheaply. Christian fatherhood may at times amount to a crucifixion. But the father of a family must be the head who helps Christ purchase both his own soul and the souls of each member of his family. So the Mass, ever present Sacrifice of Calvary, becomes the center of his exercise of sanctifying power. He frequently leads his family into church, into the confessional and up to the altar rail. He leads them to visits to the Blessed Sacrament and to times of adoration, to the making of retreats and days of recollection. He leads them in personal attention to the poor. He leads the family rosary and other home prayers. He will be the first to teach his children to love, respect and pray to their guardian angels and with wife and children he will pray to the guardian angel of the unborn child for a safe delivery. At bedtime he blesses his kneeling wife and children. It is to him that diocesan and parish appeals are directed for the deepening of Christian family life. For he is Christ to them and Christ has shared with him the exercise of sanctifying priesthood, just as Christ the King has shared with him His governing power.

But the father has still more to do because he is more than even ruler and sanctifier. Religious instruction starts long before school days. Mother will have a great part in it because she will have the children with her all day long. But she will wisely leave much to the father. He will at least have the children repeat what they have learned so that they will feel that their responsibility is to him as the head of the family. The father will also read spiritual books to his family, starting with the Bible. He will lead them in preparing the Sunday missal. He will teach them to build a family shrine around which they will center their family prayers, and a family crib for Christmas. He will take each child back to the baptismal font to explain how the child's soul-life began there. In adolescence he will give counsel on choice of vocation and teach the mystery of natural life to the boys.

No one will be repelled or overwhelmed by so intimate an association of the divinely sacred with the familiar and homely if he simply accepts and deeply believes in the Incarnation and in how thoroughly Jesus transformed all things and all human relations. It is the very vocation of a married couple to settle down in a home and to make that home a center of stability for the whole family, a center of family worship that is secondary only to the sanctuary, and a school for training their children to be holy Christians and loyal citizens. For them their home is a place of sanctification, even though at times it may be as messy and trying as Calvary was.

Husband and wife are meant to be sanctified also through the satisfactions and compensations of married life. They are to be sanctified through all their duties, including the duty of love and mating. And the solitude and sense of aloneness with God that is part of growing sanctity must be a solitude within a society and common life wherein they find God. The very lack of physical solitude is its own discipline; but visits to church, retreats and days of recollection can provide times of undivided prayer. In any case, there can be no selfish egoism about married life because the family society is essentially fruitful, issuing in new human persons who demand the full time and the full abilities of both parents. Through this human love and its fruits husband and wife are to be sanctified.

All this power to command, to sanctify and to teach was given a special drive and direction the altar when husband

and wife were the ministers of grace to each other, each being Christ's instrument in giving the other increased divine life and special sacramental graces to live their life together. Marriage is a social sacrament that is meant partly for personal sanctification and partly for the good of the Christian community. After giving the sacrament of matrimony, husband and wife know that henceforth they will communicate grace to each other in proportion to personal holiness in the one giving and in the one receiving. Respecting the indwelling Trinity in each other, their embrace becomes an embrace of the Trinity, enshrined in magnificent dignity. Their children, reborn children of God, become tabernacles of the Trinity. Conscious of God in their midst, they will soften tempers more readily and heal disputes more quickly.

God gives married people a lot of help. In baptism He infuses all the supernatural virtues, including the virtue of chastity, which is a part of the virtue of temperance. Married people also have their infused virtue of chastity; and husband and wife exercise it in their sacramentalized duty of mating. Actually, they must be chaste at all times, not only in their respect for themselves and for one another but also in their respect for other people. Mating is normally the duty of their state and an application of sacramental grace. When they are faithful to this duty in order to raise children for God's honor and glory they are also exercising the supernatural virtue of religion. Moreover, since it is a debt that they owe one another in justice, it is an exercise of the infused supernatural virtue of justice. For those in the state of grace, each act of these supernatural virtues of chastity, religion and justice is meritorious of further grace and of eternal life. That is why there are married saints.

"Love is proved by deeds. This outward expression of love in the home demands not only mutual help but must go further; it must have as its primary purpose that man and wife help each other day by day in forming and perfecting themselves in the interior life, so that through their partnership in life they may advance more and more in virtue, and above all that they may grow in true love toward God and their neighbor, on which indeed 'depend the whole Law and the Prophets' (Matt. 22:40). For all men of every condition, in whatever honorable walk of life they may be, can and ought to imitate that most perfect example of holiness placed before man by God, namely Christ Our Lord, and by God's grace to arrive at the summit of perfection, as is proved by the example set us of many saints."[10]

Many families are proving that such balance of the divine and human in family life is more than a dream. They have caught the vision and taken the God-given means to make it work. The vision and the means are for everybody; they are the way to a full Christian life. On this point as on others the words of Pius XII merit our true internal religious assent: "It is wronging men and women of our times to deem them incapable of continuous heroism. Today, for many reasons—perhaps with the goad of hard necessity or even sometimes in the service of injustice—heroism is exercised to a degree and to an extent which would have been thought impossible in days gone by."[11]

[10] Pius XI, *op. cit.,* p. 133.
[11] Pius XII, *Address to Italian Catholic Union of Midwives,* Oct. 29, 1951, Catholic Mind, 50 (1952) 38.

INDEX

Aaron, 118
Abel, 122
abbots, blessing of, 280
Abhinc Duos Annos, Pius X, Pope, St., 84
Abraham, 87, 88, 89, 91, 122, 205, 260
abstractionism, 231
Acchen, 75 n.
Acts of the Apostles, Luke, St., 1:8, 204; 2:46, 69; 2:47, 69; 9:5, 204; 14:12-16, 86; 17:22, 225
Acts of the Martyrs as conservers of divine tradition, 64
Adam, 58, 67, 89, 130, 160, 161, 210, 223, 224, 276
Adam, Karl, 81
Adams, Henry, 289
"Address to Assisi Congress" (1956), 187
"Address to First International Con-

gress of Catholic Artists" (Sept. 3, 1950), 232, 256
"Address to Italian Catholic Union of Midwives" (Oct. 29, 1951), 300
"Address to the Tenth International Congress of Historical Sciences" (1955), 184, 201
Adoptionists, 74
Advent, 66, 149
spirit destroyed through commercialism, 66
Africa, 129
age of anxiety, 29, 82
Ain-Karem, 259
Alcuin, 75 n.
Alexander VII, Pope, 80
Alexandria, 72
School of, 174
allegory
as analogy of attribution, 32

Allers, Rudolf, 28
Ambrose, St., 105
Amalec, 90
Amen, 111
Amen, (Feb. 1, 1954), 219
American Bishop's Pastoral Letter, (Nov. 1950), 235
Ana de Jesus, Venerable, 156
Anglo-Saxons, 75
Anna, 259
analogy, 31
   definition, 32
   of attribution, 32
   as basis of allegorical symbolism, 32
   of proportion, 32
   in meaning of Scripture, 173
analogues
   distinction between emblems and symbols, 32
angels, 34
angelism, 39
   definition of, 39
   symbols as antidote to, 39
Anger, Joseph, 51
Antioch, 72
Apocalypse, 69, 82
   8:3, 122; 12:7-12, 183; 21:1, 277
   celestial worship in, 69
Apologet, (cap. XVII, M.L.I., 377 A), 210
Apostolic Constitutions, 214, 215
Apostolic tradition, 64
Arianism, 27, 73, 76, 115
   denial of, 115
Aristotle, 36, 344
Art
   appreciation of, 236-239
   art for art's sake, 228
   autonomy of, 242
   causes of, 240-245, 251
   Chinese, 226, 249
   classicism and, 227

   Christian, 233
   Christian faith, inspiration of, 246
   Christian living and, 225
   Christian philosophy of, 223-225
   Christian worship as, 65
   communication in, 231-232
   definition of, 242
   early Christian, 226
   Egyptian, 226
   enjoyment in, 245-246
   "good of the thing made," 247
   Greek, 225-226, 248
   Holy Family as, 239
   humanism and, 227
   and the home, 234-235
   idealism in, 231
   imagination in, 241-242
   imitation in, 244, 245
   limitations of, 253
   judgment of, 253, 255
   Mission Art in 1950 Vatican Exhibit, 232
   mission of, 250
   modern, 233-234
   morality of, 242
   nature in art of early Middle Ages, 228
   Oriental, 226 n.
   originality in, 250-252
   periods of artistic development, 232-233
   philosophy of, 222, 252
   profit as motive of, 246
   realism in, 230-231
   reason in, 242
   Renaissance and, 227-228
   sacramental character of, 52
   symbolism in art of early Middle Ages, 228
   technique of, 243
   the useful in, 252
   virtue of, 225

artist, 221
  definition of, 222
  freedom of, 248
  virtues of, 247, 249-250
Art and Scholasticism, Maritain, J.,
  224, 226, 247, 253
asceticism, 146
Associated Press, (March 14, 1951),
  292
Asperges, 108
Athens, 225
Augustine, St., 30, 52, 54, 56, 130,
  164, 166, 167, 201, 237
  "Christian Instruction," 237
  Confessions, IX, 6, 252
  De Civitate Dei, XX, 10, 52
  De Doctrina Christiana, 4:8, 215
  Hom. X, 3. on I. John, 56
  In Ps. 142, 168, 164
  In Ps. 85, 164, 167
  Sermo 267, "In Die Pentecostes,"
    166
  Tract in Joan., 99
Augustine, St., (Benedictine), 75

Babylonian captivity, 89
Bacchus, 227
Baptism, 46, 50, 51, 52, 97, 100,
  101, 185, 207
  baptismal font, 298
  character of, 136
  and formation of lay apostolate,
    212
  gives share in Christ's priesthood,
    109, 139
  incorporates us into Christ, 107
  meaning of, 267
  Pius XII on, 52
  sacrament of, 135
  St. Augustine on, 52
  St. Jerome on, 52
  St. Leo on, 51-52
Barnabas, 86

Barcelona
  Mass offered in, 67
Beatific Vision, 47
  and habitual grace, 47
Beatitudes, 62, 136
beauty
  appreciation of, 236-239
  definition of, 241
  four causes of, in art, 240-245
Benedicite, 159
Benedict, St.,
  Rule of, 147
  recitation of psalms in Rule of,
    147
  "lectio divina" and meditative
    reading in Rule of, 147
Benediction of the Blessed Sacra-
  ment, 53
Benedictions, 78, 278, 281
Berengarius, 74
Bernadette, Martindale, Cyril, 246
Berulle, Cardinal, 80
Bethany, 263
Bethlehem, 56
Bible, 174, 298
  Westminster Atlas of, 128
  Dictionary of, 128
Blaise, St.,
  blessing of, 278
Blessed Virgin Mary
  Annunciation of, 259
  at Mass, 268
  bearing the Redeemer, 206
  Byzantine Madonna, 246
  consecration to, 263
  co-redemptrix, 261
  Holy Communion and, 270
  Immaculate Conception, 258
  part of laity in promulgation of
    definition of Immaculate Con-
    ception, 13
  Lady of Letters, 259
  Lady of Perpetual Help, 263

Legion of Mary, 53
living presence of, 258
mediatrix of all graces, 161
Mother of Messiah, 261
Mother of Savior, 90
mystery of Christ and, 215
offering Mass with, 270, 272
Old Testament types of, 272
on Calvary, 106, 266-268
pictures of, 246
Queen of Apostles and Missionaries, 206
Queen of Prophets, 259
St. Luke's Madonna, 246
universal mediation of
visitation of, 259
work of, centered in Mass, 264
Blessing at Mass, 127
Boniface, St., 75
Boston Pilot, (June 16, 1956), 289,
291
Bouyer, Louis, 102, 103, 195, 227
Braque, 231
bread
offering at Mass, 66
"breaking bread," 69
at the first Mass, 70
Breviary, 6, 178
reform of, 79
Bugnini, Annibale, 8, 73, 81, 82, 83,
100

Cabrol, Fernand, 5
Callan, Charles J., 89
Calvary, 42, 56, 67, 100, 101, 106,
107, 119, 120, 121, 216, 257, 258,
266, 267, 268, 269, 270, 271, 272,
278, 297
Mary on, 106
"Campion's Strategy Today," 65
Cana, 262, 263
Cana Movement, 53
Cana Conference, 288

Canaan, 87
kings of, 260
wedding at, 261
Canon of the Mass, 74, 99, 117, 123
Canon Law
Canon 1144, 278
Third Book of, 7
Canonization, 61
Canticle of Canticles, 156, 157
Carey, Graham, 235, 236, 240
Castile, 205
Catholic Digest, June 1956, p. 18;
pp. 20-21, 289, 294
Catholic Encyclopedia, 1:363, 246
Caulfield, Dr. Thomas, 82
Cavanaugh, Dr. John R., 288, 289,
291, 292
Ceremonial of Bishops, 6
Cezanne, Paul, 231
Chaldeans, 89
Charlemagne, 75, 77
Christ
Christians made one body with,
107
in eucharist, 101
in Church, 95, 96, 171
as efficient cause of liturgy, 16,
206
as forming Christ in Christians,
132
human nature of, 50
hypostatic union in, 202
Kingship of, 218
as mediator, 37, 68, 80, 98, 106,
193
mission of, 98
prayer of, 91-95
praying in us, 60, 163
presence in members of Mystical
Body, 95
priesthood of, 51, 98, 99
Resurrection of, 66, 96
as revealed in visible world, 131

ritual gestures of, 93
teaching mission of, 213
Truth in Person of, 34
as victim in Mass, 53
as Word, 102, 166
world family in, 204
wounds of, 42
Christian, The
Christ living in, 200
Christian archeology, 5, 15
as conserving divine tradition, 64
monuments of, 64
research in, 85
Christian being: the basis of worship, 42-61
Christian education
product of, 188-189
"Christian Education of Youth,"
Pius XI, Pope, 189
Christian Instruction, St. Augustine, 237
Christian life
definition, 90
present aspect of, 90-91
"Christian Marriage in our Day,"
Pius XI, Pope, 295, 300
Christian optimism, 60
Christian victory
its measure intensive and everlasting, 60
Christian Worship, Duchesne, L., 184
Christendom
triple division of, 205
Christianity, 59, 65, 118, 129, 130, 200, 207, 208, 215, 280
approach to sacramental nature of, 128-132
early aloofness to material things, 70
early Christian worship, 70
essence of, 200
sacrificial relation, 102

Christmas, 90, 149, 298
Christmas celebration, 65
symbols, 66
Church
as active in its members, 185
adaptation to native cultures, 209-211
aim of, 184
and Christ, 96, 99, 102-103, 171, 185
first Christian Church, 70
as completion of Christ, 203
as conserver of Apostolic Tradition, 64
as efficient cause of liturgy, 16
as living organism, 65
as missionary, 41
prolongs Christ's priestly mission, 98
real action of, 95
reverence of approach to mission world, 209
revolt against authority of, 43
teaching mission of, 209, 213
visible Church
as continuation of Christ's humanity, 131-132
and its worship, 64
Eastern Orthodox Church, 129
The Church and the Gospels, Huby, J., 251
The Church: A Divine Mystery, Hasserveldt, R., 210
Church Laws, 63
Clementine Instruction for Forty-Hours Devotion, 7
collect, 110-111
Collected Works, Vonier, A., 120
Colossians, St. Paul's Epistle to, 1:24, 43; 3:3-4, 185
Columbia University Press, 30
and formation of lay apostolate, 212

precise and distinctive effect of, 137
sacrament of, 137
Commemoration of dead, 123
Commemoration of living, 118
Commentarium in Psalmos, Prol., St. Thomas, 241
Communion, 80, 126, 214
outside Mass, 143
procession, 116
Compline, 53
"Conceptions of Divine Love," St. Teresa of Avila, 153
Confessions, IX, 6, St. Augustine, 252
Confirmation, 51
Confiteor, 108, 260
Consecration, of Mass, 99, 120
Contemplation, 36, 37, 97, 150
active contemplation, 152
free gift of God, 158
how it achieves its perfection, 38
liturgy and, 154-158
passive, 37, 152-153
prayer of union, 153
preparation for contemplative life, 143
Corinthians, 167
St. Paul's Epistles to
I Cor. 1:13, 167; 3:23, 37, 48; 10:1-5, 88; 10:21, 126; 10:17, 126, 163; 11:26, 98, 107, 126, 139; 11:17, 139; 11:28, 145; 12:25, 58
II Cor. 2:14, 59; 4:10, 266; 5:17, 46
Corpus Christi
Office of, 143
cosmology, 31
Creation
all to be redeemed, 209
finite extension in time of life of love and praise in Trinity, 160

as glorifying God, 160
of individual man, 44
of animate and inanimate creatures, 160
of man, 160
reason for creation of particular person, 45
variety immultiplicity, 44
Creative Intuition in Art and Poetry, Maritain, J., 226
Credo, see Creed
Creed
Nicene, 75 n., 112-113
at Mass, 147
cross, 200, 278, 280
centrality of, 102
scandal of, 28, 263-264, 266, 267, 268
crucifix, 280
Councils, 13
cubism, 234

Daniel
3, 159; 3:57-87, 4; 7:10, 117
canticle of, 254, 159
Danielou, P., 210
Darwin, 27
da Vinci, Leonardo, 227
Day of Judgment, 184
death, 47, 170
conquered by Christ, 59
De Civitate Dei, XX, 10, St. Augustine, 52
De Divinis Nominibus, VI, St. Augustine, 241
De Doctrina Christiana, 4:8, St. Augustine, 215
De Lubac, Henri, 203, 207
De Montfort, Blessed Louis, 263
De praescriptione, 37, Tertullian, 99
Deuteronomy 12:2, 88

Dewey, John, 28
Deweyism, 232
Dictionary of Dogmatic Theology, Parente, Pietro, 52
Didache, The, IX-X, 213, 214
Dictionnaire d' Archeologie Chretienne et de Liturgie, Cabrol, LeClerq, Morrou, 5
Divino Afflante Spiritu, Pius XII, Pope, (par. 32-33), 175
doctrine
  and forms of worship, 212
  liturgy as teaching, 213
Doctrine of the Mystical Body of Christ, The, Anger, 51
drama
  in early Church, 76
Duchesne, L., 124
Dunsinane, 286
Du principe de l'art et de sa destiation sociale, quoted by Proudhon, 244

Easter, 65,149
  symbols of, 66
  Vigil of, 267
Ecclesiastes, 3:22, 252
Ecclesiastic Traditions
  Pope St. Gregory VII on, 62
Edison, Thomas, 34
Egypt, 88, 89, 267
Elizabeth, mother of St. John Baptist, 259, 268
Elizabeth of Hungary, St., 205
emblems, 32
emotional attitudes on the liturgy, 1-3
England, 66
"enlightenment," 43, 80
Ephesians
  St. Paul's Epistle to
    1:4, 58; 1:23, 203; 2:4-7, 61; 2:15, 18, 164; 2:18, 165; 2:22,

209; 3:18-19, 193; 4:1-6, 220; 4:3-6, 113; 4:13, 191; 4:15, 192; 5:18-19, 176; 5:23, 24, 296
Ephrem, St., 73
Epicurus, 250
Episcopalians
  vernacular chant of, 129
Epiphany, 149
Epistle, 112
Epistles of St. Paul, Callan, 89
Esther, 258
Ethics, 31
Eucharist, 36, 51, 68, 71
  its continuity with covenants of Moses, Noe, and Melchisedech, 98
  dynamic aspects of, 101
  manner of Christ's presence in, 139-140
  meaning of word, 269
  sacrament of, 138, 195, 101
  as sacrifice, 195, 101
"Evangelii Praecones," Pius XII, Pope, 204, 205, 208, 211, 247
Evangelists, 251
Eve, 223, 224, 283
evil, 60, 182
existentialists, 129
Exodus, Book of, 23, 68, 85
exorcisms, 278
Extreme Unction
  Sacrament of, 141-143
Ezechiel, 68

faith, 34, 47, 96, 97
  certainty of, 54
  as inspiration of art, 246
  professions of, 64
Family
  Christian family movement, 53, 288
  dangers to husband-wife relation-

ship, 292-293

diminished male leadership in, 288-290

husband-wife cooperative spirit, 294-295

as "little Mystical Body," 296-297

as "little Church," 296

man's leadership in home, 295-296

"momism" and its causes, 290-291

religious instructions in, 297

worship in, 296-297

Family Life Convention in Boston, (March 1956), 288

Fathers of the Church, 64, 184, 155, 205

writings of, 64

liturgy and contemplation in, 155

Ferdinand, St., 205

Field Afar, Walsh, James E., Bishop, 275, 286

Final Judgment, 63

formalism, 40

symbolism in, 40

Fortescue, A., 70, 71

Fra Angelico, 241

Francis de Sales, St., 10, 276

Francis of Assisi, St., 158

Franciscans, 78

free will, 160

Freud, 27

friendship, 33

Fruits of Contemplation, Osende, 185

Functionalism, 230

Futurism, 231

Gabriel, archangel, 259

Galatians

St. Paul's Epistle to, 4:5, 48; 5:17, 477

Galilee, 95

Garrigou-Lagrange, 313

Gaskell, Charles Milnes, 289

Gasson, in Arnold and Gasson, *The Human Person,* 188

Gelasian Sacramentary, 75

Genesis 85, 282

1:28, 29; 1:31, 274; 2:15, 224, 283; 2:18, 224; 3:6, 224; 3:15, 258; 9:8-12, 86; 14:18-20, 87

Georgics, 250

German Sung-Mass, 80

Germany, 66

Gethsemani, 51, 91, 93, 260, 263

Giguerre, 199

Gihr, N., 166

glory

seed of, in our hearts, 47

Gloria in excelsis, 109-110, 260

Gnostics, 73

God

beatific vision of, 29

as Being,

belief in, 29

dependence on, 145, 277

experience of, 217

God's plan for individual, 37

as holy, 35

and Israelites, 88, 89, 90

as love, 35

love of, 56-57

mystery of, 33

Names of, 32, 33

nature of, 32

proofs for existence of, 31

relation to, 18

theology of, 205

as unchangeable, 35

union with, 146

virtue of art predicated peculiarly of, 225

will of, 29

worship of, 18

Golgotha, 271
Good Friday, 66, 101, 102
Gospel, 112, 163, 193, 203, 207, 210, 251, 260
  essence of (in Mass), 99
  mystery of, 99
  procession, 76, 100
  of St. John, 127
Gospels
  John, St., 33, 35, 43, 46, 47, 48, 49, 50, 51, 58, 59, 60, 64, 92, 94, 95, 99, 103, 104, 110, 119, 126, 127, 160, 161, 164, 182, 183, 203, 204, 225, 227, 261, 262, 268, 270
  Luke, St., 11, 23, 36, 54, 59, 81, 92, 93, 98, 117, 122, 259, 261, 266, 272
  Mark, St., 93, 94, 209, 260
  Matthew, St., 50, 63, 70, 91, 93, 94, 95, 163, 204
Gothicism, 231
"Governance of Rulers," Thomas Aquinas, St., 43
grace
  good of, 46
  habitual and beatific vision, 47
  as mark of members of Christ, 51
  perfects nature, 46
  as share in divine life, 50
Gradual, 112
Graf Zeppelin
  Mass aboard the, 67
Greeks, 94, 225
Gregory of Nyssa, St., 184
  In Cantica Canticorum, Hom. V., P.G., 44:876, 184
  Vita Moysi, P.G., 44:405, 184
Gregory the Great, Pope, Saint, 75
Gregory VII, Pope, St., 62
Gregorian Chant, 15, 226
Gruenberg, Sidonie M., 283, 289, 294

Guardini, Romano, 199, 200, 282
Gueranger, Prosper, 81

Hasseveldt, R., 210
Hayes, Carlton, 227
heaven, 43, 46, 51
Hebrews,
  St. Paul's Epistle to,
    1:7, 87; 4:12, 174; 7:1-3, 87; 7: 24-25, 99, 111; 7:25, 191; 10:12, 14, 17, p. 269
Hebrew poetry, 269
Hegel, 73, 205
Heifetz, Jascha, 237
hell, 60
Herve, J. M., 162
Herwegen, Dom, 250
Highet, Gilbert, 30
Hippolytes, 72
  liturgy of, 72
  eucharist of, 74
history
  central point of, 95
  human, 89
    God's viewpoint on, 89
    divisions of, 89
    of our salvation, 206
History of the Primitive Church, Lebreton-Zeiller, 72
historical books, 206
Hofinger, J., 215
Holmes, Chief Justice, 28
Holy Father
  as vicar of Christ, 212, 222
Holy Ghost, The, Leen, Edward, 50
Holy Orders, 16, 17, 51, 212
  character of, 138
  prime purpose of, 138
  sacrament of, 137
Holy Sacrifice of the Mass, The, Gihr, N., 166
Holy See, 13
Holy Spirit, 38, 64, 72, 73, 80, 94,

95, 96, 97, 111, 112, 115, 127,
156, 160, 166 n., 174
breathes where He will, 156
gifts of, 38, 162
  function of, 48
new conquest by, 61
office of, 97
operating in and through liturgy,
  94
prayers to, in Offertory of Mass,
  115
sent by Christ, 70
soul of Mystical Body, 55, 94
symbols of, 33
unifying operation of, 165
holy water, 280
Holy Week
adaptations, 82
Holy Week Ordinal, 66, 210
Hom. X., 3 on I John., St. Augustine, 56
hope, 47
Houselander, C., 167
Huby, 251
The Human Person, Gasson, Arnold and Gasson, 188
humanism, 43
  and art, 227
  atheistic, 205
  Christian, 276
  definition, 227
Hymns to the Church, von LeFort,
  Gertrud, 84
hyperbole, 240 n.
hypostatic union, 202

idealism
  in art, 231
  kinds of, 231
idolatry, 40, 86
  symbolism and, 40
Ignatius, St., 153
impressionism, 230

In Cantica Canticorum, Hom. V.,
  P.G., 44:876, Gregory, St., of
  Nyssa, 184
Indians
  art of North American, 236
  art of South American, 236
indulgences
  attached to sacraments, 279
Incarnation, 97, 152, 161, 182, 184,
  205, 258, 298
  purpose of, 105, 202
Incarnate Word
  religious community of, 80
In Psalmis 142, St. Augustine,164,
  168
In Psalmis 85, St. Augustine, 164,
  167
*Instruction on the Restored Order
  of Holy Week,* (Nov. 16, 1955),
  S. Congregation of Rites, 177
Introit
  singing of, 109
Ireland, 66
Isaac, 88, 205
Isaias, 267, 276
  1:18, 108; 6:3, 117
Israel, 260, 262
Israelites, 88
  in Babylonian captivity, 89
  God and, 88, 89, 90
Italy, 66

Jacob, 205
Jansensism, 80
Japan
  Christians in, 128
Jarrett, Bede, 228, 241, 242, 248
Jeremias 1:6, 241
Jerome, St., 52
Jerusalem, 70, 72, 260
John, St.,
  Gospel of,
    1:1-5, 43; 1:13, 46; 1:29, 59;

1:37, 99; 2:2, 119; 2:3, 261; 2:5, 262; 3:19, 183; 4:8, 160; 5:22, 104; 5:28-29, 59; 6:54, 126; 6:69, 35; 8:12, 33; 10:7-11, 33; 10:10, 161; 10:17-18, 267; 10:41,94; 11:52, 164; 12:26, 50; 12:26-28, 94; 12:32, 225; 13:34, 126; 14:6, 33; 14:10, 103; 14: 12,203; 14:13, 203; 14:12-13, 50; 14:23, 16-17, 47; 14: 26, 64; 15:1, 33; 15:5, 204; 15:5-6, 51, 15:7, 60; 15:9, 50; 15:14-15, 48; 15:26, 95; 16:13, 95; 16:23, 95; 16:23-24, 111; 16:33, 58; 17:1, 9, 10, 15, 17, 92; 17:4, 110; 17:8, 103; 17:9-17, 49; 17: 11, 21-22, 92; 17:17, 49; 17: 18-19, 49; 17:22-23, 103, 164; 17:21, 23, 57; 17:24, 48; 19:37, 220; 20:22, 23, 95

Apocalypse of, 69, 82
8:3, 122; 12:7-12, 183; 21:1, 277
John the Baptist, St., 99, 214, 262
John of the Cross, St., 153
Journet, Charles, 21, 64, 68, 208
Joseph, St., 234, 257
Joseph, St., of Cupertino, 153
Judea, 259
Judith, 258
Jungman, J., 9, 21, 70, 71, 72, 75, 77, 78, 122, 125
Jurgensmeier, 57

Kingdom of God, 60
Kings, Book of
  I Kings, 15, 90
  III Kings 90
Kiss of peace, 66, 71
Klee, 231

Labor Day, 22
Last Supper, 49, 63, 93, 106
  Prayer at, 49

all other rites derive from, 70
Latourette, Kenneth Scott, 129
lay-apostolate, 54, 55
  call for Christian leaders, 185-186
  common priesthood of Mystical Body, 55
  co-victims with Christ, 53
  in emergency administration of sacraments, 53
  groups in, 53
  meaning of term, 52
  qualities of Christian leaders, 188
  royal priesthood of laity, 55
  sacraments in formation of, 212
  sharers in Christ's work, 52-54
  and science, 29
  vocation to, 29-30
  as work of Church and Christ, 203, 207
Lay Formation
  understanding Holy Week, 5, 11
Lazarus, 93
Lebreton-Zeiller, *History of Primitive Church,* 72
Le Corbusier, 230
LeClerq, 5
Leen, Edward, 50
LeFort, Gertrud von, 84
Legion of Mary, 53
Lent, 149
Leo, Saint, 51-52, 55
Leo III, Pope, 75 n.
Leo XIII, 268
  "Christian Marriage," 296
Levi, tribe of, 87
Leviticus, Book of, 68
  26:21, 119
Liber Usualis, 6
Life of St. Teresa Written by Herself, 156, 157
Liturgy
  changes in liturgy of early Church, 76-77

Christological elements in, 74
confusions in, 79
as conserver of divine tradition, 64, 213
definition of, 15
as discipline, 146
final, efficient causes of, 15-16, 17
educative function of, 192-197
Gallican adaptations of, 76
its interest in special problems, 187
means of prolonging Christ's mission, 219
model for teaching, 215
not a substitute for psychotherapy, 186
participation in, 77
and prayer, 148-157
restorations in, 82-84
Roman, 75
root of union with God, 155
Slavic rite of, 77
St. Teresa of Avila and, 155-157
ultimate aim of, 158, 219
unification of, 77
variations in liturgy of Mass, 78
vernacular in, 219
universal mediation of Mary, 213
Liturgical Arts, Herwegen, (Fall, 1931), 250
Liturgical Books, official list of, 6
Litany, 39
liturgical life
duty to live it, 3
Logic, 31
The Lord, Guardini, Romano, 199, 200
Louis of France, St., 205
Louvain, 129
love, 33, 47
love of God, 56-57
Lucretius, 250

St. Luke
Gospel of,
1:45, 259; 1:49, 54; 2:48, 26; 5:39, 11; 8:28, 59; 9:23, 266; 10:21, 93; 10:23-24, 81; 22:19, 23, 98, 117, 122; 22:32, 92; 23: 24, 272
Acts of, 69, 86, 204, 225
1:8, 204; 2:46, 69; 2:47, 69; 9: 5, 204; 14:12-16, 86; 17:22, 225
Lumen Vitae, Vol. X., no. 2-3., Hofinger, J., 215
Lystra, 86

Macabees, Mother of, 258
McCauliff, George, 249
Magnificat, 152, 251, 259-260, 268, 269
as setting dominant note of all Christian worship, 260
Maher, 187
Manet, Edouard, 230
Manichaeism, 73, 74
recrudescence of, 182
Man's Unconquerable Mind, Highet, Gilbert, 30
Manuale Theologiae Dogmaticae, Herve, J. M., 162
Marcel Gabriel, 243
Maritain, J.,
Art and Scholasticism, 224, 225, 226, 247, 253
Creative Intuition in Art and Poetry, 226 n.
The Range of Reason, 182, 193, 198, 200
Mark, St.,
Gospel of,
7:34, 93; 14:26, 94; 15:34, 260; 16:15, 209
Martindale, Cyril, Bernadette, 246
martyrs, 96, 211

tombs of, 67
martyrdom, 61
Martyrology, 6
Mary, Sister Mary of the Compassion, 229
Mary, sister of Moses, 258
Marx, 205
Mass, 32, 36, 52, 99, 108-127, 175, 215
and Calvary, 271
as Christian culture, 68
development of early Christian Mass, 79
ends of, 269
first Mass, 70
fore-Mass, 69
as heart of worship, 105
institution of, 106
laity offer Christ in Mass, 52
Low Masses, 78
mysteries of Christ in Mass, 100
occupation, 22
of Church Year, 215
our supreme response to God, 36
participation in, 53
places offered, 67
private, 78
Proper of, 100
Requiem, 78, 109
of Saint John, 271
as sacrifice, 79
as social prayer, 117
of Sundays and Feasts, 216
sung-prayer at, 66
Votive, 78
The Mass: A Study of the Roman Liturgy, Fortescue, A., 70, 71
The Mass of the Roman Rite, Jungman, J., 70, 71, 72
materialism, 31, 232
of totalitarian state, 43
Matrimony
consecration of love in, 198

Sacrament of, 139-140, 144, 198
sanctification in, 298-300
Matthew, St., 50, 63, 70, 91, 93, 94, 95, 163, 204
Gospel of,
5:23-24, 163; 6:5, 70; 6:9-13, 94; 6:58, 91; 11:29, 50; 18:19, 94; 18:20, 94, 95; 26:26, 27, 93; 28:19, 95; 28:20, 204
The Meaning of Monastic Life, Bouyer, L., 195
Mediator Dei, Encyclical of Pius XII, Pope
(par. 3), 99
(par. 19), 209
(par. 20), 15, 207
(par. 24), 19
(par. 25), 19
(par. 26), 20
(par. 29), 17, 19
(par. 31), 145
(par. 33), 23
(par. 36), 145
(par. 37), 20
(par. 39), 15
(par. 40), 213
(par. 48), 213
(par. 88), 52
(par. 100), 194
(par. 144), 167
(par. 152), 100, 158
(par. 165), 168
(par. 173-175), 14, 64
(par. 195-196), 234
(par. 198), 5
medieval thinkers, 31
Mediterranean world, 226
Melchisedech, 87, 122
as prefigure of Christ, 87
covenant of, 98
cult of, 98
Memoriale Rituum, 6
Menti Nostrae, Encyclical of Pius

XII, Pope
(par. 44), 176, 265
(par. 73), 56, 265
(par. 87), 15
(par. 96), 220
(par. 118), 232
mental prayer
meditation, 146
methods of mental prayer found
in liturgy, 148
Mersch, E., 57
Messias, 89
metaphor, 32, 172
language of love, 172, 173
in texts of liturgy, 173
metaphysics, 31
Mexico, 66
Michelangelo, 227, 244, 253
Middle Ages, 27, 32, 78, 198, 205,
237
miracles, beginning of, 262
Missal, 6, 80
hand-missal, 80
Latin rite, 79
Missale Romanum, Offertory
Prayer of, 161
Roman Missal, 298
reform of Missal, 79
French translation (1661) condemned, 80
missions
object of missionary activity, 203
role of laity in, 208
ultimate goal of, 203-204
monasteries, 78
Monet, Claude, 230
Morality and the Mystical Body,
Mersch, E., 58
Moses, 118, 205, 258
covenant of, 91
Mosaic law, 175
tabernacle worship of, 88
Mother of the Savior, The, Gar-

rigou-Lagrange, 213
Motu Proprio (n. 2.), Pius X, Pope,
St., 248, 251
Morrou, 5
music, see Sacred music
folk songs and dances, 236
mystery, 27, 31
awareness of, 31
fullness of, 35
of Gospel, 99
insight into, 184
in nature, 34
of our destiny, 37
sense of, 27
Mysteries of Christianity, Scheeben,
M., 130, 133, 135
mystic, 40
necessity of symbols in expression
of, 40
mysticism, 154-158
accidentals of, 154
definition of, 154
free gift of God, 158
and liturgy, 154-155
night of senses, 153
night of spirit, 153
Mystical Body, 14, 68
Christians incorporated into, 51
co-offerers and co-victims with
Christ, 58
co-workers with Christ in, 49
doctrine of, 33
Encyclical on, 265
guided by Holy Spirit, 72
as living organism, 132
members of, 17
as members of living Christ, 48,
95
Mystical Christ at worship in,
217
Passion of, 42, 55
priest as representative of Christ
and members at worship, 17

one-ness of members, 56-57
as supernatural organism, 48
Mystici Corporis, Encyclical of Pius
XII, Pope, 265
(par. 44), 176, 265
(par. 73), 56, 265
(par. 87), 15
(par. 96), 220
The Mystical Body of Christ, Jurgensmeier, 56

Nagasaki, 128
Christians of, 211
nature
subjecting of, 29
naturalism, 80, 82, 83, 230
Nazareth, 56, 234, 259, 267
negro
folk singing of, 236
neo-Adlerians, 29
neo-Freudians, 29
Nestorius, 74
new-capitalism, 43
New Covenant, 68
sealed with Christ's blood, 121
Newman, John Henry, Cardinal,
12-14, 129
on *"consensus fidelium,"* 12-15
New Testament, 68, 85, 106, 112,
150, 164, 175
New York, 237
New York Ttimes Book Review
(April 8, 1956, p. 2), Adams,
Henry, 289
Nicene dogma, 13
Nietzsche, 205
Noe, 85, 91
covenant of God with, 98
"Notes on Modern Art," *Today,*
(Dec., 1949, p. 20), 229
Nuttin, J., 181, 183

obscurantism, 34
Offertory, 47

Offertory prayer, 52, 161, 113-115
procession, 66, 116
Old Testament, 68, 85, 112, 150,
164, 175, 195, 258, 260
in Christian worship, 85
sacramental aspect of its worship,
68-69
"omnis exeunt in mysterium," 31
"On Consulting the Faithful in
Matters of Doctrine," Newman,
John Henry, Cardinal, 129
"On Reconstructing the Social Order," Pius XI, Pope, 229
"On Sacred Music," Pius XII, Pope,
208, 221, 222, 248
(par. 22), 221
(par. 28), 222
(par. 30-32), 248
(par. 38), 208
optimism, Christian
as only true wisdom, 182
Orate Fratres (April, 1951), 246
Orient, 128
Oriental rites
origin of, 73
Osende, *Fruits of Contemplation,*
185

Pacific Ocean
Mass offered on, 67
pagans, 182
Palestine, 51, 89, 203, 260
parables
sower and seed, 62
wheat and weeds, 62
mustard seed, 63
yeast-leaven, 63
Paradise, 58, 223
lost Paradise, 58, 283
Parente, Pietro, *Dictionary of Dogmatic Theology,* 134, 136, 137,
213
Parsch, Pius, 176

Passion of Christ, 32
Passiontide, 149
Passover, 69, 98
  Old Testament meal of, 106
  lamp of, 270
"Pastoral of the American Bishops (1947), 27
"pastorem et fidelium conspiratio," 13
Pater Noster, 71, 124, 147
Patterns, Carey, Graham, 235, 236
Paul, Saint, 58, 85, 86, 167, 176, 189, 209, 269, 225
  Epistle to Corinthians I, 37, 48, 58, 88, 98, 107, 126, 139, 145, 163, 167
  Epistle to Corinthians II, 46, 59, 266
  Epistle to Colossians, 43, 185
  Epistle to Ephesians, 58, 61, 113, 164, 165, 191, 192, 193, 203, 209, 220, 296
  Epistle to Galatians, 48, 277
  Epistle to Hebrews, 87, 99, 111, 174, 191, 269
  Epistle to Philippians, 103, 189, 200, 256
  I Epistle to Timothy, 254
  II Epistle to Timothy, 201
  Epistle to Titus, 141
Peers, Alison, 156
Pelagians, 74
Penance
  sacrament of, 140-141
Pentecost, Feast of, 149
Pepin, King, 75, 77
perfection,
  ethical, 50
Perrone, Father, 12
persecution, 73
person
  as center of natural cause of worship, 17

as child of God, 46
creation of individual person, 44-46
dignity of, 182, 196
efficient cause of, 187
final cause of, 187
formal cause of, 187
God's knowledge of, 45
God's love for, 45
material cause of, 187
as "new creature," 46
notion of, 187
reason for creation of particular person,
as "sharing God-life," 46
spiritual rebirth of, 46
uniqueness of, 45
personality
  conflicts and their causes, 180-183
  conflicts as purification of, 197-198
  conflicts in development of, 197-198
  development through worship, 188
  essentials of personality development, 184
  meaning of, 188
  necessity of integration of, 183
  positive emotions in, 197
  definition of, 187
  psychosomatic disturbances in, 181
Peter, St.,
  Epistle of,
    I, 2: 9, 118; 2:24, 59, 118; 3:18, 107
Pharaoh, 260
Philip, St., Apostle, 94, 225
Philip Neri, St., 153
Philippi, 189
Philippians
  St. Paul's Epistle to,

1:20, 200;2:8-9, 103; 3:7-8, 189; 3:12, 200; 4:8, 189; 48-9, 256
philosophy, 25, 31, 63
  its approach to mystery, 31
Picasso, Pablo, 231
Pius V, Pope,
  reforms in breviary and missal, 79
Pius IX, Pope,
  on testimony of laity in contemplation of definition of Immaculate Conception, 13
Pius X, Pope, St., 81, 247, 268
  Abhinc Duos Annos, 84
  Motu Proprio, 248, 251
Pius XI, Pope, 218, 228
  "Christian Education of Youth," 189
  "Christian Marriage in our Day," 295, 300
  Quas Primas, 23, 218
  "Reconstructing the Social Order," 229
Pius XII, Pope, 56, 62, 64, 81, 144, 145, 167, 174, 175, 186, 189, 203, 205, 206, 207, 209, 210, 211, 213, 221, 232, 233, 248, 256, 264, 265, 300
  "Address to Assisi Congress," (1956), 187
  "Address to First International Congress of Catholic Artists," (Sept. 3, 1950), 232, 256
  "Address to Italian Catholic Union of Midwives," (Oct. 29, 1951), 300
  Divino Afflante Spiritu, 175
  Evangelii Praecones, 204, 205, 208, 211, 247
  Mediator Dei, 5, 14, 15, 17, 19, 20, 23, 52, 64, 99, 100, 145, 158, 167, 168, 198, 207, 209, 211, 213, 232, 233, 234
  Menti Nostrae, 118
  Mystici Corporis, 15, 56, 176, 220, 265
  "On Sacred Music," 221, 222, 208, 248
  Summi Pontificatus, 207, 210
  "To the Tenth International Congress of Historical Sciences," (1955), 184, 201
Plato, 36, 70, 244
A Political and Cultural History of Modern Europe, Hayes, Carlton, 227
Pontifical, 6
Popular Devotions, 7-15, 64
Prayer
  affective, 149, 150
  attention in, 39
  no conflict between public and private prayer, 145
  contemplative, 151-158
  corporate, 92-95
  corporate prayer in early Church, 70
  discursive, 148
  forms of, 148
  function of repetition of, 39
  function of ritual and symbol in, 40
  liturgy and mental prayer, 147
  man's basic need for, 145
  mental, 146
  quality of official prayer, 22
  qualities of, 91
  sincerity in, 40
Preface, 116
  of Christmas Mass, 23
  of Requiem Mass, 47
priesthood, 100
  basic power of, 52
  of Melchisedech, 87
  participations of Christ's priesthood, 51

prayer for, 55
priest as ambassador of Redeemer, 213
priest as mediator between God and man, 52, 212
priest as representative of community before God, 213
respect for, 55
St. Augustine on, 52
St. Jerome on, 52
St. Leo I on, 51-52
vocations to, 55
priesthood of Christ, 51
participations in, 55
Proper of Mass, 100
prophets, 5, 205, 206
Protestantism, 27, 74, 78
Lutheran minister and vernacular in liturgy, 219
Lutheran school system, 129
missionaries, 128
Reformation, 43
Proudhom, as quoted by *Du principe de l'art et de sa destination sociale,* 244
Proverbs
3:17, 252; 4:19, 200
Psalms, 69, 92, 104, 105, 167, 173, 175, 196, 206, 259, 267, 276
15:9, 24; 18, 175; 21, 93, 101; 21:28, 214; 25, 115; 31, 93; 33, 90; 35:10, 193; 36:4, 263; 41, 90; 62, 90; 102:17, 260; 109:4, 103; 111:9, 260; 113:12, 16, 19, 189; 131:90, 90
Psalms
as prayer, 149
as prayer of Christ and Mary, 152, 168
psychiatry, 29
Psychoanalysis and Personality, Nuttin, J., 181, 183
Psychology, Maher, M., 187

pyschology, 31, 37
of men at worship, 39
psychotherapy
liturgy no substitute for, 186
purgatory, 47

Quas Primas, 23, 218
Quinonez, Cardinal, 81

Range of Reason, The, Maritain, J., 182, 193, 198, 200
rationalism, 80
realism, 34, 60
in art, 230-231
only true realism, 60, 182, 277
as shaping worship, 65
Real Presence, 27
denial of, 101
emphasis on, 79
Redeemer, 202, 205
Redemption, 67
mission of, 205
of man and things, 276
Red Mass, 22
Red Sea, 260
Reformation, 43, 205
Religion
of covenant of God with Noe, 85
corruptions in primitive, 86
derivation of Christian rite from Christ's priesthood, 51
Renaissance, 27, 43, 241
art of, 227, 228
artists of, 243
decadence of, 233
heresies of, 244-246
intellectual world of, 227
Madonnas of, 246
secularism of, 244
Renascence, McCauliff, George, 249
Resurrection, Feast of, 197
revelation, 85
reverence, 209

lack of, 28

Ribera, *Vida de Santa Teresa de Jesus,* 156

rites
derivation of Christian rite, 51
Eastern Orthodox, 129
Oriental origin of, 73
Roman, 75
Slavic, 77

Ritual, 6

ritual, 36, 40
as instrument of worship, 36
mosaic, 85

ritualism, 39

Romans
St. Paul's Epistle to,
1:20, 86; 1:23, 86; 5:2, 114; 5:5, 165; 6:3; 6:5, 266; 7:19-23, 265, 7:23, 275; 8:7, 275; 8:15, 17, 176; 8:16-17, 115; 8:18, 8:19, 21, 276; 8:21, 209; 8:22-23, 223; 8:26, 166; 8:32, 190; 11:33, 44;12:1-2, 116; 13:1, 54

Romanticism, 231

Roman Pontifical, 6

Roman Sacramentary, 75

Rome, 83, 187

rosary, 80

Rouault, George, 241

Rubrics, 4

Sacraments, 135-143, 162, 167, 206
as dependent instrumental causes of sanctifying grace, 135
efficacy of, 97
first and immediate effect of, 132
instruments of sanctification, 206
matter and form of, 97, 99
as means of prolonging Christ's mission, 99
as acts of Christ in his Church, 135

as causes of worship, 17

sacramental character, 133, 134
of Baptism, 52
essence of, 51
imprint of, 51
purpose of, 51

sacramentals, 128, 162, 274
basis of understanding of, 276-277
classes of, 278
dispositions for receiving effects of, 279
do not supplant Mass and sacraments, 279
examples of, 280-282
for families, 280-281
fruits of, 279
in occupational life, 282-284
as instruments of grace, 275
link with Christian asceticism, 277
link with worship, 279-280
meaning of, 278
not necessary for salvation, 279
not superstition, 278-279
as school of theology, 287
use of, 284-287

Sacred Books, translations of, 252

S. Congregation of Rites, "Instruction on the New Holy Week Liturgy," (Nov. 16, 1955, par. 23), 210, 177

Sacred music
in apostolate 208
as community worship, 146, 254-255
in Early Church, 76, 77
German Sung-Mass, 76, 77
joy in, 255
and laws of art, 221
qualities of, 248
service of, 254
universality of, 251

Sacred Scriptures, 174
Sacred Signs, Guardini, Romano, 282
Sacramentaries, ancient, 78
sacrifice, 20-21
    of cross, 98, 99
    of Isaac, 88
    of Melchisedech, 87
    of New Testament, 21
    of Old Testament, 21
    translation to external element in worship, 20
saint
    description of, 186
    the saints and corporate worship, 155
Saint Peter's Basilica, 22, 187
Salem, 87
Salome, 270
Salvation of the Nations, The, Danielou, P., 210
Samuel, 259
sanctity
    definition of, 186
    formed by life centered in worship, 200
    in secular life, 200
    normal development of Christian person, 188, 189
    work of Christian personality, 201
Satan, 42, 43, 149, 182, 261
    vanquished by Christ, 59
Saul, 89, 90, 204
Savior, promised to Abraham, 89
Scheeben, M., 130, 133, 135
Schweitzer, Albert, 129
science, 29, 30, 34
    layman's vocation and, 29
Scripture, Sacred, 33, 64, 173, 174, 251, 285
    accommodated sense of, 173

literal and spiritual sense of, 173-174
Second Sunday of Advent, Secret, 157
Secret, 116
secularist, 182
seminary training
    rubrics, 4
    Mediator Dei, (par. 198), 5
"sensus" and *"consensus fidelium"* Newman, J. H. on, 12-15
Septuagesima Sunday, Collect of, 190
Sermo 267, "In die Pentecostes," 166, Augustine, St., 166
Sermo IV, Leo I, Pope, St., 51-52
Sermon on Mount, 62, 91
Sheed, Frank, *Society and Sanity,* 25
"Short Breviary of the Laity," 53
Sign of Cross, 277, 279-280
Simeon, 267
simile, 32
sin, 47
    original, 47
    original and personal, 183
social problems, field of, 205
Social Theories of the Middle Ages, Jarrett Bede, 228, 241, 242, 248
Social Value of Public Worship, Giguerre, 199
society
    of totalitarian state, 43
solitude, 91
Solomon, 90
Song of Songs, see *Canticle of Canticles*
Spain
    Mass offered in, 67
Splendor of the Church, The, De Lubac, Henri, 203, 207
Spirit of Catholicism, The, Adam, Karl, 81

spiritual formation, 199
  according to St. Teresa of Avila, 192
  by life centered in worship, 200
  importance of, 199
  integration of, 187
  teaching of, 187
  through active participation, 199
Spiritual Life, The, Tanquerey, A., 47
Stations of Cross, 216
Steinmetz, Albert, 34
suffering
  in Mystical Body, 55, 60
Summa Contra Gentiles, 33, 144
  Bk. I., ch. 29-34, 33
  Bk. IV., ch. 73, 142
Summa Theologica, 16, 18, 38, 46, 47, 50, 51, 68, 95, 123, 131, 133, 160, 244, 247, 249, 252, 295
  I, q. 6, a. 1 ad 2, 160
  I, q. 12, a. 1; q. 60, a. 5, 244
  I, q. 92, a. 3, 295
  I-II, q. 57, a. 3 ad 2, 249
  I-II, q. 42, a. 3, 247
  I-II, q. 43, a. 3, 247
  I-II, q. 113, a. 9; q. 113, a. 9 ad 2, 46, 50
  II-II, q. 24, a. 3, 47
  II-II, q. 34, a. 1 ad 3, 244
  II-II, q. 35, a. 4 ad 2, 252
  II-II, q. 81, a. 7, 18
  II-II, q. 82, a. 1 ad 1, 18
  II-II, q. 83, a. 3 ad 1, 18
  II-II, q. 92, a. 2, 198
  III, q. 48, a. 6, 95
  III, q. 56, a. 1 ad 3, 95
  III, q. 61, a. 4 ad 1, 68
  III, q. 63, a. 3, 51
  III, q. 64, a. 3, 16
  III, q. 63, a. 3, 133
  III, q. 48, a. 6; q. 73, a. 5 ad 2, 131

  III, q. 83, a. 4 ad 3, 123
Summi Pontificatus, Pius XII, Pope, 207, 210, 219
symbols, 32, 40, 172, 173
  as antidote to angelism, 31
  Christian, 36
  as distinct from emblems, 32, 38
  as embodying man's natural theology of worship, 37
  and formalism, 40
  function in approach to God, 38
  as instrument of worship, 36,
  and idolatry, 40
  as language of love, 172, 173
  in liturgical texts, 173
  necessity in speech of mystic, 40
  need of, 37
  of Holy Spirit, 33
  purpose of, 37
  of Trinity, 33
  as typifying known and unknown God, 38
synagogue, 69, 73

Tanquerey, A., 47
Temple, 68, 69, 267
Teresa of Avila, St., 153, 155, 156, 158, 192
  Tertullian, 37, 99, 210
theodicy, 31
theology, 32, 37, 167
  how achieves its perfection, 38
  moral, 63
  queen of sciences, 32
Theology of the Mystical Body, The, Mersch, E., 134, 185, 203
Therese of the Child Jesus (Little Flower), 158
This War is the Passion, Houselander, C., 167
Thoughts and Things, Carey, Graham, 236

Timothy
  St. Paul's Epistle to,
  I Epistle, 4:4, 254
  II Epistle 1:7, 201
Titus
  St. Paul's Epistle to
  2:14, 141
totalitarian state
  dogmatic materialism of, 43
Toscanini, 243
Toynbee, 73
Tract in Joan., Augustine, St., 99
tradition, 63, 167
  adherence to, 80-81
  definition of, 63
  kinds of, 63
  means by which conserved, 64
transcendentals, 31, 236
  appreciation of, in art, 236
Trent, Council of, 78, 79, 216
  Session XXII, Denz. 949, 216
  reforms of, 78
Trinity, 18, 43, 95, 109, 160
  adoption into family of, 48, 55,
    58, 59, 162, 268
  as taught through worship, 189-
    192
  divine life is Christ-life, 49, 50
  glory of, 98
  in Baptism,97
  indwelling of, 18, 22, 47, 48,
    170, 171, 184
  in last blessing at Mass, 127
  no creativeness apart from, 43
  participation in life of, 159-160,
    162, 50
  prayer to in Offertory of Mass,
    116
  sacraments administered in name
    of, 95
  Second Person of, 44
  symbols of, 33

truth, 62, 34
  appreciation of, in art, 238
  of form, 241
  intuition of, 241-242
  in person of Christ, 34

ultra-scientism, 28
Underhill, Evelyn, 65, 72, 102, 172
Ur, 89

Van Steenberghen, F., 129
Vatican, 232
  1950 Holy Year Exhibit, 332, 336
  pavilion of modern art, 234
vernacular, 79
  caution against, 80
  in liturgy, 11, 219
Vespers, 53
Vida de Santa Teresa de Jesus,
  Ribera, 156
Virgil, 250
virtues
  infused, and gifts, 48, 162
  theological, and moral, 48, 145
Vita Moysi, P. G., 84: 405; Gregory
  of Nyssa, St., 184
vocation, 37
  as creatures, 159
  of individual Christian, 144
  purpose of, 50
Vonier, A., 120

Wagner, 250
Walsh, James, E., Bishop, 275, 286
What is Christian Art, Carey, Graham, 240
White, Helen, C., "Campion's Strategy Today," 65
White Mass, 22
wine
  at the first Mass, 70
  offering at Mass, 66
Worship, Underhill, Evelyn, 65, 72

worship
  adaptive character of, 74
  ancestry of, 68
  and use of reason, 25-41
  appreciation of beauty and power of, 163
  as antidote to naturalism, 147
  as an art, 65
  asceticism of, 147
  basis in Christ as exemplar, 91
  centers in persons, 67
  centrality of cross in, 102
  changes in, 76-81
  characteristics of, 72
  Christian's duty in, 98
  Christ worshipping in us, 90
  Christological element in early, 74
  constituents of, 90
  definition, 18
  as divine tradition, 63
  doctrine and forms of, 212
  effects of, 20
  essence of, 97, 98
  experience of the whole Christ, 187
  external element in, 20-22
  fruit of, 176-179
  function of, 64
  and governing mission of Church, 211-212
  history of, 68-83
  intellectual content of, 189
  interior and exterior, 24, 36

  key problems of, 65
  life-principles of, 18-19
  as living tradition, 62-84
  meritorious and exemplary causes of, 19
  obstacles to, 27
  in Old Testament, 68-69, 98
  as our vocation, 37
  participation in, 74, 80
  personal preparation for, 175
  as prime source of sanctity, 209
  purification of, 88
  purpose of, 176
  recent changes in, 219
  relations to man, 21
  relation to mental prayer, 147
  repetition of ritual and prayer in, 39
  sense of community exercised in, 197
  and teaching mission of Church, 213-220
  types in Early Church, 70-76
  unification of, 77
  unifying operation of Holy Spirit in, 165

Yale University, 129
YCS, 53
YCW, 53

Zeiller, in Lebreton-Zeiller, *History of the Primitive Church*, 72